The *Smallville* Chronicles

Critical Essays on the Television Series

Edited by Lincoln Geraghty

The Scarecrow Press, Inc.
Lanham • Toronto • Plymouth, UK
2011

Published by Scarecrow Press, Inc.
A wholly owned subsidiary of The Rowman & Littlefield Publishing Group, Inc.
4501 Forbes Boulevard, Suite 200, Lanham, Maryland 20706
http://www.scarecrowpress.com

Estover Road, Plymouth PL6 7PY, United Kingdom

British Library Cataloguing in Publication Information Available

Library of Congress Cataloging-in-Publication Data

The Smallville chronicles : critical essays on the television series / edited by Lincoln Geraghty.
p. cm.
Includes bibliographical references and index.
ISBN 978-0-8108-8130-3 (cloth : alk. paper) — ISBN 978-0-8108-8131-0 (ebook)
1. Smallville (Television program). I. Geraghty, Lincoln, 1977–.
PN1992.77.S626S43 2011
791.45—dc22 2011017638

∞™ The paper used in this publication meets the minimum requirements of American National Standard for Information Sciences—Permanence of Paper for Printed Library Materials, ANSI/NISO Z39.48-1992.

Printed in the United States of America

CONTENTS

Acknowledgments v
Introduction: Investigating *Smallville* vii
Lincoln Geraghty

PART ONE
TEXTS AND CONTEXTS 1

CHAPTER ONE From Comic Book to *Bildungsroman:* *Smallville*, Narrative, and the Education of a Young Hero 3
Stan Beeler

CHAPTER TWO Televisual Transformations: Myth and Social Issues in *Smallville* 25
Karin Beeler

CHAPTER THREE The Kryptonite Closet: Silence and Queer Secrecy in *Smallville* 45
Jes Battis

CHAPTER FOUR No Flights, No Tights: *Smallville* and the Roles of Special Effects in Television 65
Rayna Denison

PART TWO
AUDIENCES AND METATEXTS 87

CHAPTER FIVE *Smallville:* Superhero Mythos and Intellectual Property Regimes 89
Ian Gordon

CHAPTER SIX Vids, Vlogs, and Blogs: The Participatory Culture of *Smallville's* Digital Fan 109
Juli Stone Pitzer

CHAPTER SEVEN "I've a Feeling We're Not in Kansas Anymore": Examining *Smallville's* Canadian Cult Geography. 129
Lincoln Geraghty

CHAPTER EIGHT Sacrifice or Salvation? *Smallville's* Heroic Survival amid Changing Television Trends 153
Michael S. Duffy

Index 173
About the Contributors 183
About the Editor 187

ACKNOWLEDGMENTS

I would like to thank my editor, Stephen Ryan, for his immense patience while I completed this project. It seemed putting this volume together was a task fit only for Superman, but thanks to Stephen and all the contributors it finally came off. I had valuable assistance from staff at the Kobal Collection in locating and purchasing images for this book; to them I offer my gratitude. Funding for those images came from the Centre for Cultural and Creative Research at the University of Portsmouth, so my thanks must also go to the committee for awarding me the money. I must also thank my colleague Van Norris in the School of Creative Arts, Film and Media at Portsmouth who devoted his time and energy to taking pictures planned for the front cover of the book (some of which are included inside). His enthusiasm for composing shots and playing with Superman props knows no bounds! Finally, to my partner Rebecca, thank you for buying me all those *Smallville* DVD box sets for Christmas and birthdays—you helped make the research fun!

INTRODUCTION
Investigating *Smallville*
Lincoln Geraghty

Smallville's first of ten seasons aired on the WB (Warner Bros.) Network in October 2001. Subtitled *Superman the Early Years* in UK promotional material for Channel 4, the series took the traditional Superman story and turned it into an American teen action drama about Clark Kent's life at high school before he donned the famous blue tights and red cape. Instead of seeing Superman take on supercriminals in Metropolis, the audience got to see how he first developed his powers and learned to cope with girls, school, and teenage angst. Without his fancy costume, *Smallville* showed Superman as a vulnerable and innocent teenager. The series was just as much a teen melodrama as a science fiction or fantasy action serial. Although largely overlooked by critics—many Superman fans saw it as too far a departure from the comic book canon—its similarities to previous teen television like *Dawson's Creek* (1998–2003) endeared the Superman story to a whole new generation of viewers. The setting, style, narrative, and cast of fresh-faced actors suggested that the Superman story was not only ready for a televisual makeover but also still relevant for a post-9/11 American audience. In a sense, the regression back from the big city (Metropolis) to small-town life (Smallville) attests to the major impact 9/11 had on the American psyche.

The reinvention of America's most famous superhero was a cathartic act, representative of television's return to innocence in times of political and social uncertainty. Placing the series in the wider of contexts of America's postmillennial malaise and the changing television industry, this collection investigates the multiple narratives of the *Smallville* universe. Issues relating to gender, sexuality, identity, myth, history, and politics are explored in connection with how the series uses the Superman story and the concept of genre television to comment on contemporary social issues. As a teen television series, *Smallville* also boasts a large cult fan following whose knowledge of and devotion to the series is exemplified by fans' use of new media technologies. Chapters in this volume not only analyze the TV text and its televisual and cultural contexts but also investigate the complex relationship its audience has with the characters and narrative through blogging, fan fiction, traveling to filming locations, and creating websites.

Superman: From Comic Book to American Icon

In a book about *Smallville*, one cannot ignore the great weight of history represented in the Superman mythos. Despite its contemporary nature as teen melodrama, *Smallville* is a story about Superman, his upbringing, and how he became the superhero we know today. Thus, all that Superman embodies reflects upon and brings meaning to the character of Clark Kent in *Smallville*. As a teen superhero, Clark grapples with the very same problems and internal angst that troubled the original Clark Kent in the comic books, early radio plays, television series, and film adaptations. Because he is a superhero from Krypton living in disguise as a human reporter from Smallville, Superman personifies the moral and ideological tensions at the heart of America—he represents all that America strives to be and all that America knows it is not. While I do not wish to cover the enormous history of the Superman mythos in this introduction, it is important to recognize the significance of myth and the superhero in American culture and locate the figure of Superman within it. For John Shelton Lawrence and Robert Jewett, the popularity of television series like *Smallville*, film series like *Star Wars*, and comic book superheroes "indicates that Americans have not moved beyond mythical consciousness."[1] Indeed, the myth of the superhero is rooted in what they call the American Monomyth, described as "a tale of redemption."[2] The classical monomyth concerned the rite of passage and initiation of a lone hero who undertook great voyages and adventures, for example, the Greek heroes Hercules and Odysseus. The American version combines the lone hero motif with an inherent urge to do good and be redeemed, to bring about the salvation of those less fortunate; the most obvious example of this would be the messianic figure of Jesus Christ. Both the initiation myth and the salvation myth form the unique American Monomyth, and at the heart of them both is the underlying sense of freedom. In the case of Hercules and Odysseus, freedom was personified by the pursuit to attain manhood through heroic acts of adventure; freedom for Jesus meant freedom from sin for those he had sacrificed his life to save; and for Superman freedom was represented in notions of democracy and protecting the American way of life. Jewett and Lawrence stress that the American Monomyth "secularizes the Judeo-Christian redemption dramas that have arisen on American soil."[3] Therefore, the superhero is both a messianic figure and an icon of American idealism.

As in all superhero narratives where the superhero and supervillain exist to do battle, this idealism is constantly under threat from outside forces. America perceives itself to be the moral and political authority in the world, and thus Superman is a protector and policeman—saving people from those who do harm but also protecting America from criminals and alien forces that would seek to tear down what America stands for. At the height of Superman's popularity in the comics, he stood as an example to readers that America was good and worthy of being protected: "The superhero by his very existence asserts American utopianism . . . a highly potent cultural myth."[4] As a role model, Superman represented "the qualities of individualism and the collective identity of WASP America,"[5] and through individual effort the collective enterprise that is America could be realized. More than that, Superman was an ideal in himself. The audience projected their real identity onto Superman[6] and thus embodied the ideological message that to be a good American one had to strive to follow the American Monomyth: save yourself to save the country.[7] Historically, Danny Fingeroth sees the superhero myth as "more than a function of happenstance." For him, "The creation of a legion of special beings, self-appointed to protect the weak, innocent, and victimized at a time when fascism was dominating" Europe stems from creators Jerry Siegel and Joe Shuster who envisioned Superman as a godlike man who would heed the call of those who suffered persecution.[8] Sure enough, superheroes can be many things to many people, and that is why Superman has managed to survive for over seventy years in the cultural memory of his fans. *Smallville* simply takes the myth and the man and recycles him for a new generation:

> Like most important signs, the superhero supports a varied and contradictory battery of readings. He is both exotic and the agent of order which brings the exotic to book. His costume marks him out as a proponent of change and exoticism, yet he surprises us by his adherence to an almost archaic code of personal honour.[9]

Siegel and Shuster founded Superman in an era that needed heroes, during the Depression, New Deal, and the start of the Second World War, but in tying him to "the American Way," his character came to stand for "an ideological construct that among other things unites two seemingly disparate values—individualism and consumerism—with democracy and labels it American."[10] Thus nostalgia for Superman, Superman as nostalgia for a mythic past, causes subsequent adaptations to reflect upon the character of Superman/Clark Kent and what he means at a particular time. Multiple readings depend on previous readings, and therefore previous personifications of Superman impact what we see in *Smallville*.

The first major television adaptation of the Superman story starred George Reeves who donned the red cape for the TV movie *Superman and the Mole Men* (1951) and the series *Adventures of Superman* (1952–1958). According to Bruce Scivally, "though fit and athletic," Reeves did not "naturally possess Superman's physique" or Kirk Alyn's more toned body (Alyn played Superman in 1940s cinema serials), yet he was handsome, and his charisma made him popular with a family audience.[11] As an icon of American masculinity during the 1950s, Superman reassured the family unit that traditional gender roles were still in place. While masculinity was coming under attack by the conformist principles of Cold War America, it was given a boost through the rugged looks and personality of Reeves' Superman. Elaine Tyler May argues that attempts were made to contain the communist threat by returning to the family values of a pre–World War Two America where men went to work and women stayed at home. However, with the disruption that the war brought, husbands were displaced from both the home and the workplace by their wives; this led to a sense of masculinity in crisis as the traditional male breadwinning role became increasingly obsolete.[12] At that time, such masculinity was valorized as part of the nation's communist containment strategy, indicating that "the decade's focus on rigid gender roles, respect for authority, patriotism, and hygiene was part of a larger fear that [America] might unravel from within."[13] However, unlike the male protagonists of popular books such

George Reeves as Superman in The Adventures of Superman *(1952–1958). Credit: Motion Picture TV Inc. and the Kobal Collection.*

as Sloan Wilson's *The Man in the Gray Flannel Suit* (1955) and William Whyte's *The Organization Man* (1956) who are caught in a suburban nightmare, unable to escape the encroaching conformity symbolized by the white picket fences and mundane daily routine of work and family responsibility, Superman (and thus Reeves) of the fifties represented the possibility that the honest American male could still make a difference. We can see vestiges of this version of American masculinity in the setting of Smallville, small-town America writ large, and how it is depicted in *Smallville*. Clark's father, Jonathan Kent (played by John Schneider), is a responsible husband and a role model for Clark. He lives to work hard, maintain his farm, and provide for his family. His honesty is integral to the series as he tries to protect Clark from the influences of Lex Luthor and his corrupt father, Lionel.

As the embodiment of American masculinity, Superman was the flip side to Clark Kent's more understated, even effeminate, human persona. Still, both represented a certain sense of self-improvement. In trying to woo Lois Lane, Clark Kent relied on personality and intelligence to impress—the physicality of Superman was only employed to perform his superhero role. Turning from "mild-mannered reporter" to muscle-bound superhero mirrored the transformation many American men attempted during the 1930s and 1940s by adopting healthy lifestyles and taking up bodybuilding. As a "fantasy image, Superman gave promise to every other obsequious American office worker: Beyond those glasses and that mild-mannered demeanor beat the heart of a hero."[14] Perhaps this dichotomy is best seen in Christopher Reeve's portrayal of Clark Kent/Superman in the *Superman* films starting in 1978. More of an intellectual who had to build up his body to perform the role, Reeve was an educated man who represented a more youthful Superman. He followed in the method actor tradition and literally became the Man of Steel by eating more, weight lifting, and taking advice from Darth Vader himself, Dave Prowse.[15] The films moved Kent's relationship with Lois Lane front and center, and in trying to impress his work colleague he was often conflicted in performing his other role as superhero. This tension can be seen in Tom Welling's portrayal of Clark Kent in *Smallville* where trying to fit in at high school and be closer to Lana Lang is hampered by his inherent need to rush off and save someone in danger. There is clear continuity between Reeve's Superman and *Smallville*, not least because Christopher Reeve appeared

Christopher Reeve as Superman in Superman III *(1983). Credit: Warner Bros., DC Comics, and the Kobal Collection.*

on the show playing the role of Dr. Swann in the episode "Legacy" (2004). Also, like *Smallville*, the *Superman* films represented a change in national direction. Whereas *Smallville* spoke to a nation looking for reassurance in the myth of superhero post the trauma of 9/11, as argued earlier, *Superman* tuned the nation into a celebration of American values and ideals the year after the Bicentennial. After the loss in Vietnam, the political scandal of Watergate, and Nixon's impeachment, "the values that were celebrated were the ones that Superman had always represented—truth, justice and the American Way."[16]

Clark Kent: A Superhero for the Teenage Generation

Upon the announcement in 1999 that the flagship television series *Buffy the Vampire Slayer* (WB, 1997–2001; UPN, 2001–2003) was leaving the American network WB for rival United Paramount Network (UPN), the president of the WB began looking for another action/adventure show to take its place. In 2000, Alfred Gough and Miles Millar were asked to create a show about a teenage Clark Kent. Reluctant to re-create the *Superboy* (1988–1992) series, Gough and Millar decided to create something fresh that would attract the young audience of the new millennium. Peter Coogan describes the fascination for superhero and comic book narratives making their way to the big and small screen around this time as a "renaissance," showing that "the superhero is a popular character type, an interesting protagonist and a useful metaphor."[17] Moreover, while the superhero as archetype was being refashioned for the twenty-first century, the way we consumed heroes, read them, watched them, and interacted with them changed too. The superhero became a cross-media phenomenon where a single character or group could be spread out across a range of media forms—one universe, even multiple intersecting universes, accessible through graphic novels, comic books, on the Web, on TV, in films, and in video games.[18] The superhero as convergent media archetype offered Hollywood studios ample opportunity to revive old heroes such as Batman and Superman and launch new ones such as those seen in *Heroes* (2006–2010), spinning their stories and characters across different media at the same time. With the Superman mythos to draw upon, the world of *Smallville* offered the WB Network plenty of room to build new stories, revitalize old characters, and introduce new ones to an audience primed by the superhero renaissance.

The central character in *Smallville* is of course Clark Kent, but Clark Kent as a young man before he assumes the mantel of world savior. In this, Tom Welling's portrayal of Clark is imbued with a sense of vulnerability as he learns to cope with puberty at high school at the same time as he learns to control his superpowers and discovers his alien heritage. Welling came on board because he saw a serious side to playing the young Clark and a connection to the vast history that informed the character. Although the series was a teen-focused drama, with the fantastical elements emphasizing unavoidable problems incurred along the narrative journey from adolescence to adulthood, Welling saw a reverence and seriousness to the adaptation that would inevitably carry it through to being one of the longest-running science fiction series on television.[19] What is more, Gough and Millar installed such an important moral center to the series that despite its youthful leanings, *Smallville* was very clearly an adult show that questioned the notion of humanity, our concepts of right and wrong, and some of the values at the core of the Superman persona. Rather than concentrating on the superhero, *Smallville* focuses on the person, the man Clark Kent (albeit an alien from Krypton who looks human), whom M. Keith Booker sees "as the primary identity of its main character." For him this is no coincidence since Gough and Millar wrote the script for *Spider-Man 2* (2004), which, through Peter Parker, emphasized the human qualities of the superhero who has to learn to control his powers before he can take on a disguise to do his work.[20]

Smallville's cast of characters act as signifiers for those American values that Superman represents. Clark is an honest boy who wants to do well by his loving adoptive parents, Jonathan and Martha. Lana is the wholesome female love interest who sets an almost unattainable goal for Clark to pursue. In trying to start and then maintain a relationship with her, Clark is forced to constantly reevaluate his morals—does he fulfill his destiny to become Superman for the sake of the world, or does he abandon his parents and his duty to live a happy life with Lana? This dualism underlines many of the early episodes of the series, particularly when Clark is challenged at school to be the perfect son while also keeping a big secret from Lana. But the series is full of moral dualisms, and its moral universe has "distinct boundaries between good and evil" that are consistently tested through the central relationship between Clark and Lex Luthor. For Robert McManus and Grace Waitman, "These boundaries

Tom Welling as Clark Kent in Smallville *(2001–2011). Credit: Warner Bros. TV and the Kobal Collection.*

are metonymically created through the show's primary protagonist and antagonist. . . . Clark Kent represents 'truth, justice,' and 'other stuff,' as he says [in "Drone" (2002)]; whereas Lex Luthor represents lies, selfishness, and ultimate evil."[21] But Lex does not start out that way; *Smallville* is as much about the descent of him as a character as it is about Clark ascending to become Superman. Clark is raised to be a good person, a basis for his superhero persona, but Lex is raised by his father Lionel to be a ruthless businessman. At times the two young men mirror each other; they both see goodness in people and respond to each other's friendship. Indeed, much can be read into their relationship in terms of an underlying homoeroticism as has been discussed in previous scholarship and in chapter 3 by Jes Battis in this volume.[22] Yet the archenemy relationship in superhero narratives must, in a sense, always be there in order for the goodness and moral worth of the superhero to shine through. It is a comment on the nature of the hero. In *Smallville*, "Lex Luthor stands for the moral shortcuts that Clark Kent must resist to avoid becoming the tyrant as his father Jor-El seemingly wants."[23]

As a teen melodrama, scholars have analyzed the generic nature of the new Clark Kent character. Miranda Banks sees him in *Smallville* as an example of the new and improved teen hero who is able to empathize with his fellow schoolmates and in his endeavor to be with Lana is open to listening to, supporting, and following her lead. Like so many teen dramas at the time of *Smallville*'s inception, such as *Dawson's Creek* and *Roswell* (1999–2002), both on the WB Network, the young male protagonists were taking on new gender roles that would position them as equals to their female counterparts, not superior to them. Dawson, Max from *Roswell*, and Clark were new role models on television that spoke to a generation of viewers going through similar problems in their own lives and looking for ways to cope with them on a daily basis. These young men "are effortlessly in touch with their feminine sides, and much more likely to tend to the emotional needs of the women around them than act out with anger or violence."[24]

As part of the WB Network brand, teen television was aimed at a knowing audience. *Smallville*, *Dawson's Creek*, *Roswell*, and *Buffy* paid homage to their TV forebears as well as their mythic heritage, as in the case of Superman. As I mentioned above in reference to the superhero renaissance, this was because the teen audience was becoming increasingly aware of other media texts through the convergence of media entertainment such as film, TV, video games, and the Internet. According to Valerie Wee, the WB Network created series that spoke to teens but also spoke about other popular media texts through intertextuality and popular culture references: "The WB recognized the 1990's teen audience's heightened media and cultural literacy; theirs was a pop-culture awareness built upon an obsession with popular entertainment in its myriad forms."[25] In *Smallville*'s Chloe Sullivan (played by Allison Mack), we can see this conceptualization of the digital teen through her ability to use the Web to help Clark investigate the latest meteor freak at school or search for clues to Lex's latest scheme by hacking into government and Luthorcorp files. As with many of its series, the WB Network used *Smallville* to create a brand that was attractive to young audiences. In part, this brand was based on the characterization of Clark Kent as a teen superhero, learning to be Superman as we know him and drawing upon the ideologies, myths, and values of the American icon. But also, this brand was based on the viewing practices of the audiences and the ways in which they consumed and understood the media. It was a "pre-sold product with a distinct and committed fan base" where Warner Bros. "was able to profit from multiple revenue streams, from the show's licensing fees to the network, the returns on advertising rates, and subsequent earnings from ancillary media releases and tie-ins." According to Valerie Wee, *Smallville* has "synergistic potential."[26] As a series, *Smallville* tells us much about the nature of contemporary media production and marketing. In the following section, I want to briefly outline some of the contexts in which we might understand the development of what has been termed American quality television and how *Smallville* can be seen as an example of a mainstream cult television series.

Smallville: Teen Science Fiction Fantasy and American Cult Television

In his study of "moments of television," Derek Kompare sees television at this moment as "a cultural artifact, a capitalist product, a content distribution platform, a technology of citizenship, a human activity, and an object of scholarly study."[27] Indeed, as a TV text, *Smallville* is all of those and will be discussed in these terms in the critical chapters that make up the contents of this book. Above all, Kompare sees television as "meaningful," in that when understanding its impact we must take into account its production, the institutions that produce it, and the contexts in which people watch it.[28] For sure, much of what I have discussed in this introduction provides the institutional and cultural contexts through which we can begin to comprehend *Smallville* as a television series; but also, in the chapters that follow, each author takes it upon him- or herself to focus on certain key elements that create meaning and are therefore in need of further study. Implied in all chapters, however, is this sense that *Smallville* is a quality television drama, characterized in the WB Network's attempts to make programming to attract a niche audience, in its high production values and use of special effects to create a certain style, and in its attention to more complex and interwoven narratives that encourage a sense of long-term commitment to watching and rewatching. While quality television is a cross-genre term that can apply equally to police and medical dramas as it does to science fiction and horror, in the latter two we can see the potential for what Catherine Johnson calls the development of "quality/cult" television that is rooted in the history of quality television but uses intertextuality and the features of the serial format to extend a television series' potential to attract and maintain a cult fan base.[29] *Smallville* is thus a quality series but also a cult TV series because of its huge and active fan following and its use of intertextuality that feeds that audience.

Hybridity and intertextuality are common features of contemporary television programming. Jason Mittell believes that "cases of mixture often foreground generic conventions even more than 'core' examples of a genre, as often unstated generic assumptions rise to the surface through textual juxtapositions, production decisions, and reception controversies."[30] Indeed, the medium of television "brings intertextuality to us" through its televisual flow of multiple texts: from the actual programs to the commercial breaks. As different texts jostle to get the viewers' attention, multiplied by the increase in digital and satellite channels, the boundaries between texts and their interpretations remain open and incomplete—leaving room for exploitation, reinflection, and parodic subversion.[31] The aesthetics of cult television series reference and pay intertextual homage to previous series; so, in *Smallville*, the Superman myth is not only overtly indicated in the use of characters from the comic book canon or through

Clark Kent himself but is implied in the more subtle "color palette" used in every episode: the red, blue, and gold hues used in his costume.[32] Likewise, in its use of innovative production methods and generic styles, cult television experiments with form to attract new viewers and offer greater textual pleasure to fans.[33] For example, the use of the hard-boiled detective narrative seen in *Smallville*'s "Noir" (2007) or the all-singing musical episode, "Once More, With Feeling" (2001), in *Buffy the Vampire Slayer*.

Textual pleasure is integral to the cult television series and, as will be explored in part 2 of this volume, is important to those *Smallville* fans who engage with the narrative text and the many extratextual practices that define being a fan. For Matt Hills, cult television is attractive to fans because it offers fans the space in which to question the fictional and nonfictional elements of the narrative, to explore the multilayered universe in which it is set, and to follow an extended story over time as it develops. Cult series are usually made up of a "perpetuated hermeneutic" (central mystery) set in a "hyperdiegesis" (unfinished world) stretched over an "endlessly deferred narrative."[34] Therefore, fans are imbued with a sense of ownership and power as they interact with and travel across the range of episodes that make up a series and travel across and between different cult series through convergent media. Applying the work of Angela Ndalianis on the contemporary television series, I would then call *Smallville*, extending Hills' notion of the "hyperdiegesis," a "neobaroque" series, whereby the narrative draws "the audience into potentially infinite or, at least, multiple directions that rhythmically recall what Focillon labels the 'system of the series,' or the 'system of the labyrinth.'"[35] Offering interwoven plots, characters, backstories, spin-off potential in the Justice League storyline, and previously unseen footage (through the cross-media form of the DVD extras which fill in backstory to bigger plot elements seen in the series), *Smallville* fits with contemporary television's tendency to not only rely on the weekly episode but to build narrative suspense and fan loyalty through the multiplication of formats offered by media convergence (TV, Internet, comics, DVD). The textual universe, the "hyperdiegesis," is extended and complemented by the extratextual world of the network's marketing strategies, fan activity, and even the physicality of the series' production in locations around the city of Vancouver, Canada: "Cross-media narrativisation are, in some instances, becoming important disseminators of story information within the franchise as it disperses its form not only across the series of its own medium, but across multiple media."[36]

Contents

This book is split into two parts. Part 1, "Texts and Contexts," discusses *Smallville* as a superhero text, analyzing the intertextual references to the Superman canon in the contexts of its production as a teen television series set in small-town Kansas (albeit made in Vancouver on Canada's west coast). It focuses on the social, political, and cultural contexts of the series, acknowledging readings of race, class, and gender, and also examines the contemporary nature of U.S. television in terms of technology and special effects use. The second part, "Audiences and Metatexts," looks beyond the fictional text and concentrates on the metatext of *Smallville*'s participatory fan culture and the substantial legal issues connected to the contested comic book icon, Superman. In this it examines the multiple fan-created websites and blogs, their resistance to the dominant reading of the series imposed by its creators and those who own the franchise, and the legal battles between parties who have a vested interest in profiting from Superman and *Smallville*, and it discusses the implications of filming a U.S.-funded show in Canada for interpreting it as a cross-border and geographically displaced television text.

In chapter 1, Stan Beeler argues that *Smallville* is an example of how subsequent iterations of a narrative in new media can have a lasting effect upon its structure. Although comic books are an exemplary medium for both the initial development and long-term maintenance of a mythos, they cannot compete with television for the sheer weight of narrative development. The series, unlike the film versions of the narrative, has presented its audience with the slow growth of character. Over the last ten years, we have seen Clark mature both physically and as a fictional protagonist. This form of narrative is known as a *Bildungsroman*, and Beeler applies this to the teen series of Clark Kent's journey from farm boy to superhero. Tom Welling's Clark Kent is divorced from the iron-jawed heroes of the filmic and comic book versions of the mythology because the narrative focus of the series is substantially different from both film and comic book versions. Contesting critics such as Jane Feuer who argues that the protagonists in television drama in the 1980s never really develop across a series, Beeler posits that the long-running serial narrative of contemporary television is particularly suited to character development that fosters audience sympathy in a way that transcends the earlier strategy of simple recognition of static characters in fixed relationships. In *Smallville*, Clark Kent is a character coming to grips with the advantages and limitations of maturation as a gifted individual. Moreover, over the length of its run, the cast of *Smallville* has paralleled the aging and concomitant maturation of its core audience. As Kent's powers appear and his control over them develops, he and his companions proceed through the normal emotional and physical development of young North Americans. Friendships, career aspirations, and romances blossom or die while the series mirrors the lives—albeit in metaphorical splendor—of the young people who watch it.

Karin Beeler follows on from this analysis of the contemporary superhero's journey from teen to adult to discuss, in chapter 2, the mythic nature of the *Smallville* series as a re-creation of the Superman story, one of the most prominent hero-savior narratives in American culture. She argues that the myth of the savior is only one of the many mythic elements of this series. *Smallville* draws on numerous mythic and apocalyptic images dependent on metamorphosis and combines these images with a host of social issues that affect modern American youth. Savior figures, agricultural gods, vampires, sirens, and various examples of the monstrous are incorporated into the show to create a televisual experience that reinforces the symbolic dimension of young characters who struggle with what it means to be "different." Since myths reflect social attitudes, it is not surprising that the mythic elements in *Smallville* also serve as a way of highlighting social issues relevant to North American youth. For Beeler, the series foregrounds the social and psychological issues of youth that highlight the culture of the body. For example, issues such as eating disorders, obsessions with beauty, and disability, as well as stories about sexual desire and the unusual possession of loved ones, figure prominently in the series. In a telefantasy context, the metamorphoses of modern-day youth in *Smallville* echo the familiar stories of transformation evident in ancient myth while also providing some unique modern twists facilitated by contemporary special effects. Beeler reminds us that television replicates itself through strategies of intertextuality or intervisuality, perpetuating slightly altered versions of familiar images that its viewers would already have consumed in other contexts. *Smallville* makes use of this practice by embedding references to myths of change found in other television shows and films. For Beeler, this allows the series to remake myths for a young generation who live in the rapidly changing world of the twenty-first century.

Chapter 3, a reprint of Jes Battis's article from 2008, explores the network of queer secrets and closets within *Smallville*, as well as the relationship between Clark Kent and Lex Luthor. For Battis, the relationship between Clark and Lex is one that is rich with possibilities (both erotic and ideological). His focus lies in the erotic potential emerging from this relationship, with Clark's eroticism rooted in pastoral traditions, and Lex's eroticism emerging from urbanity. This chapter discusses the spectrum of fascinating ways in which the Clark/Lex relationship has been rewritten by *Smallville*, transformed from the traditional antagonistic pairing between hero and villain that *Superman* comic lovers recognize, to a far more ambiguous friendship between two highly secretive and vulnerable men. As Battis points out, the series is all about keeping secrets, Clark's identity as Superman, hiding his superpowers and his love for Lana Lang, but it is also a series about intimate bonds between friends. At times throughout the narrative the two come into conflict with each other, and it is within these overlapping boundaries that Battis finds the real heart of the series. As many science fiction and telefantasy series allude to, *Smallville* suggests that emotional bonds between characters reflect certain tendencies and tensions in our own lives, and, unsurprisingly, these tensions, situated in the difficult teenage world of high school, are made all the more obvious. Clark's feelings for Lana and his friendship with Lex put him in the middle of a triangle that offers comfort but also pain—as we soon learn when Lex betrays him and Lana eventually has to leave Smallville. It is perhaps no secret that since *Smallville* is such an open text there are plenty of alternate readings one can take from the narrative, and the Clark/Lex pairing is but one of a number in which producers and fans revel.

Chapter 4 sees Rayna Denison taking issue with Gough and Millar's condensed credo for the series: no tights, no flights. She argues that this no tights (no superhero costume) and no flights (a reduction in "super" abilities) ethos positioned the *Smallville* series away from the Superman franchise's history and mythology and defined the show as one that took

Clark Kent, rather than Superman, to be the core identity of the central character. This decision allowed the show's makers to approach the spectacle of the Superman franchise in a new way, slowly building up Clark Kent's repertoire of superabilities in line with the tight turnaround times for episodic production. This chapter examines the discourses around the adaptation of the "super" elements of the Superman franchise in *Smallville* and investigates the roles of special effects technologies in the creation of the Clark Kent/Superman character. Within the show itself, there are constant moves to alternately foreground different kinds of specific effects, sometimes physical effects like stunts, sometimes visual effects, sometimes combinations, and composited or even in-camera effects shots. This, along with the development and refinement of the show's special and visual effects, enables a consistent production of spectacular imagery. However, as with the case of flight, that imagery can be grounded in emotional or psychological spectacles and character development, as much as in moments of display or "wonder." In critiquing special effects usage, Denison also focuses on the importance of production techniques and schedules to the production of spectacle and considers the ways in which spectacle functions in the different media of the Superman franchise and the wider contexts of science fiction television. For example, the frequent use of CGI establishing shots, composited cityscapes, and CGI-enhanced landscapes found in *Smallville* all concur with claims that visual effects production is becoming increasingly common, and is going increasingly unnoticed, within television production.

Moving away from the textual to the contextual, chapter 5 by Ian Gordon offers a survey of the complicated legal issues at the heart of defining who owns the Superman brand and canon and how this affects those with a vested interest in producing *Smallville*. The series has so far made some $300 million for the Time Warner corporation, which is currently engaged in a lengthy and complex legal battle with the heirs of Jerry Siegel and Joe Shuster, the creators of Superman and Superboy, about the ownership of the characters. Among the various things at stake is a share of the profits from various media incarnations and licensed products of those characters. One aspect of the case and claims to a share of profits turns on whether Superboy is a derivative character of Superman and in turn whether *Smallville* is an adaptation of Superboy. These two terms "derivative work" and "adaptation" have defined legal meanings. With this in mind, Gordon examines the issues in adapting a comic book superhero for a youthful television audience, particularly given *Smallville* producers' "no tights, no flights" stance (as outlined in Denison's chapter). Gordon highlights the various ways the producers connect the show to the Superman mythos without ever mentioning the word Superman and questions whether *Smallville* is an adaptation of Superboy or Superman in legal terms at all. The debates at the heart of the legal battle signal just how important the Superman mythos is, no matter in which incarnation, to the millions of fans who watch the films, view the television series, and read the comics. As part 2 emphasizes, fans of *Smallville* feel that they have just as much of a vested interest in the text as the creators or studios that vie for ownership rights. Fandom is about a sense of ownership, so the implications of a court ruling that might threaten the legacy and legality of *Smallville* are huge to the community that made the series popular in the first place.

As outlined in chapter 2, through the modernization of the Superman story, *Smallville* tackled the contemporary issues of coming of age, equality, relationships, politics, economics, and social structures. Yet, in addition to changes to the traditional comic book storyline, the *Smallville* franchise sought to capitalize on the new digital generation, "generation D," in order to create a global audience and fan base of both males and females. It is this fan base that gets interrogated in chapter 6. Juli Stone Pitzer explores the relationship between the *Smallville* franchise and its new-millennium audience. She argues that the digital revolution has enabled new marketing strategies for the series and its ancillary markets. With the seemingly unlimited accessibility generation D has at its fingertips, from smart phones to TiVo, this digital audience has found new ways to consume and produce fan media. These new fans are not limited to collecting *Smallville* merchandise and attending events like Comic-Con. Instead, generation D is increasingly producing online fan sites, vidders (fan videos), blogs, vlogs (video blogs), and participating in forums enabling global fan base formation. Pitzer analyzes the ways in which new and old media have converged in the creation of a new digital fan that can participate as consumer and producer of new media texts thus modifying the relationship between the *Smallville* television franchise and its audience. As so often is the case now, cult fandom has gone mainstream, and practices once performed by the most die-hard fan are now common across media audiences. This reflects the pervasive nature of media technologies today, the way we access media texts from the past and present, but it also reflects how the Hollywood media industries are keen to engage in those very same practices to try and attract fans to a text. Fan loyalty is both created and desired by television studios, and *Smallville*'s fandom highlights the multiple ways in which producers and fans are engaged in a tug-of-war of competing practices and conflicting interpretations. All of which, however, makes *Smallville* a meaningful example of how media texts and metatexts converge to allow fans access to a pleasurable cross-media universe.

Chapter 7 discusses the notions of cult television and fan tourism, where I argue that *Smallville* is a Canadian TV text (despite its being made by a Hollywood-based studio) because being filmed in Vancouver means its fictional locations have become real sites of pilgrimage for its many devoted fans—both in North America and abroad. As with other science fiction series shot in Vancouver, including *The X-Files* and *Battlestar Galactica*, fans of *Smallville* participate in creating an online record or travelogue of where important locations and scenes have been shot, adding their own personal commentary and reflections on their visit. Those towns and locations actually used in the series (Cloverdale, British Columbia, for example) also contribute to this online discourse by advertising themselves as the "Home of *Smallville*," organizing special tours and yearly events. Investigating the cult geography of Vancouver, British Columbia, as Smallville, Kansas, reveals important changes in genre programming, whereby American TV series are becoming increasingly international in production and reception, and allows us to interrogate the ever-changing nature of global television fandom where boundaries of economic and cultural capital are becoming blurred through the use of new media technologies, and concepts of place and space are evolving as a result of fan interaction. I argue that we must recognize the various affective mechanisms for fan interaction, both between the text and fan and between the fan and the virtual environment. Bloggers who write about their experience in Cloverdale, visiting the *Smallville* filming locations, are associating themselves with the real town and, by extension, drawing connections with the fictional town of the series—yet both hold equal meaning for them. Furthermore, through the paratextual practice of blogging, a third space is visited when fans click into the website to leave their comments. Thus, all three spaces of *Smallville* fandom allow for interaction across and beyond the series, giving fans more opportunities to extend the narrative of the series into their real lives, virtual lives, and the life of the text.

For Michael S. Duffy, season eight of *Smallville* was a new beginning for the show, narratively, thematically, and creatively, both on screen and behind the scenes. At the end of its seventh year, the series lost both its original creators and show runners, Al Gough and Miles Millar (who left to pursue full-time work writing and producing feature films), and one of its central stars, Michael Rosenbaum, who had played Superman nemesis Lex Luthor to critical acclaim for the past seven years. To fill the gap, *Smallville*'s new producers introduced Tess Mercer and Davis Bloome, two new nemeses who were both more complicated than they first appeared. More interestingly, though, the show seemed to find new breathing room in both the absence of its long-time villain and its new creative production team; more than ever, *Smallville* seemed ready to acknowledge its own history and its vast and diverse—and often critical—fan base (many of whom are not intimately familiar with "traditional" Superman comic book lore), and in doing so, it achieved high-level moments of self-reflexivity. While moving forward significantly, the characters also pointedly reflected on past events and seasons while the producers planted interesting twists within the show's narrative, signature visual effects moments, and iconography. Thus chapter 8 focuses on season eight of *Smallville* and how since then the series continued to renew and reinvigorate itself, despite network transformations, creative upheavals, cast shake-ups, and even character ownership/rights entanglements, remaining one of the most stable, reliable genre hours on television for audiences worldwide. As the actors and characters have "grown up" throughout the series (as discussed in chapter 1), so also has the global television market matured into something very different, and much more complicated, than it was in 2001. For Duffy, *Smallville*, Clark Kent, and the hero he will eventually become are interesting metaphors for the transforming television industry, just as the show continues to convey Superman's core values and his longevity, strength, and lasting sense of purpose throughout history. As the world changes, it seems Superman will always be there for us in one incarnation or another, but *Smallville* as a production has successfully endured trials equal to those of its central hero, and like him, the show continues to surprise its observers with its consistently creative combination of classic mythology and contemporary narrative storytelling.

Notes

1. John Shelton Lawrence and Robert Jewett, *The Myth of the American Superhero* (Grand Rapids, MI: Eerdmans, 2002), 6.
2. Robert Jewett and John Shelton Lawrence, *The American Monomyth* (Garden City, NY: Anchor Press, 1977), xx.
3. Jewett and Lawrence, *The American Monomyth.*
4. Richard Reynolds, *Super Heroes: A Modern Mythology* (Jackson: University Press of Mississippi, 1992), 83.
5. Reynolds, *Super Heroes*, 82.
6. Jewett and Lawrence, *The American Monomyth*, 60.
7. The tagline for the first season of *Heroes* (2006–2010) riffs off this idea quite nicely: "Save the Cheerleader, Save the World."
8. Danny Fingeroth, *Disguised as Clark Kent: Jews, Comics, and the Creation of the Superhero* (New York: Continuum, 2007), 17.
9. Reynolds, *Super Heroes*, 83.
10. Ian Gordon, "Nostalgia, Myth, and Ideology: Visions of Superman at the End of the 'American Century,'" in *Comics and Ideology*, ed. Matthew P. McAllister, Edward H. Sewell Jr., and Ian Gordon (New York: Peter Lang, 2001), 178.
11. Bruce Scivally, *Superman on Film, Television, Radio and Broadway* (Jefferson, NC: McFarland, 2008), 47.
12. Elaine Tyler May, *Homeward Bound: American Families in the Cold War Era* (New York: Basic Books, 1999).
13. Mary Caputi, *A Kinder, Gentler America: Melancholia and the Mythical 1950s* (Minneapolis: University of Minnesota Press, 2005), 142.
14. Michael S. Kimmel, *Manhood in America: A Cultural History* (New York: Oxford University Press, 2006), 140.
15. Scivally, *Superman on Film*, 82.
16. Scivally, *Superman on Film*, 76.
17. Peter Coogan, *Superhero: The Secret Origin of a Genre* (Austin, TX: Monkey Brain Books, 2006), 23.
18. Angela Ndalianis, "Comic Book Superheroes: An Introduction," in *The Contemporary Comic Book Superhero*, ed. Angela Ndalianis (New York: Routledge), 4.
19. Jake Rossen, *Superman vs. Hollywood: How Fiendish Producers, Devious Directors, and Warring Writers Grounded an American Icon* (Chicago: Chicago Review Press, 2008), 254.

20. M. Keith Booker, *"May Contain Graphic Material": Comic Books, Graphic Novels, and Film* (Westport, CT: Praeger, 2007), 112.

21. Robert M. McManus and Grace R. Waitman, "*Smallville* as a Rhetorical Means of Moral Value Education," in *The Amazing Transforming Superhero! Essays on the Revision of Characters in Comic Books, Film and Television,* ed. Terrence R. Wandtke (Jefferson, NC: McFarland, 2007), 177.

22. See also Glyn Davis, "'Saying It Out Loud': Revealing Televisions' Queer Teens," in *Teen TV: Genre, Consumption and Identity*, ed. Glyn Davis and Kay Dickinson (London: BFI Publishing, 2004), 127–140.

23. Coogan, *Superhero*, 98.

24. Miranda J. Banks, "A Boy for All Planets: *Roswell, Smallville* and the Teen Male Melodrama," in *Teen TV: Genre, Consumption and Identity*, ed. Glyn Davis and Kay Dickinson (London: BFI Publishing, 2004), 26.

25. Valerie Wee, "Teen Television and the WB Television Network," in *Teen Television: Essays on Programming and Fandom*, ed. Sharon Marie Ross and Louisa Ellen Stein (Jefferson, NC: McFarland, 2008), 52.

26. Valerie Wee, *Teen Media: Hollywood and the Youth Market in the Digital Age* (Jefferson, NC: McFarland, 2010), 154.

27. Derek Kompare, "More 'Moments of Television': Online Cult Television Authorship," in *Flow TV: Television in the Age of Media Convergence*, ed. Michael Kackman, Marnie Binfield, Matthew Thomas Payne, Allison Perlman, and Bryan Sebok (New York: Routledge, 2011), 95.

28. Kompare, "More 'Moments of Television,'" 97.

29. Catherine Johnson, "Quality/Cult Television: *The X-Files* and Television History," in *The Contemporary Television Series*, ed. Michael Hammond and Lucy Mazdon (Edinburgh: Edinburgh University Press, 2005), 60–61. For further discussion on the concept of quality television, see also Mark Jancovich and James Lyons, eds., *Quality Popular Television: Cult TV, the Industry and Fans* (London: BFI Publishing, 2003); Janet McCabe and Kim Akass, eds., *Quality TV: Contemporary American Television and Beyond* (London: I. B. Tauris, 2010).

30. Jason Mittell, *Genre and Television: From Cop Shows to Cartoons in American Culture* (New York: Routledge, 2004), xii–xiii.

31. Jonathan Gray, *Watching with The Simpsons: Television, Parody, and Intertextuality* (New York: Routledge, 2006), 78–79.

32. Rhonda V. Wilcox, "The Aesthetics of Cult Television," in *The Cult TV Book*, ed. Stacey Abbott (London: I. B. Tauris, 2010), 36.

33. Stacey Abbott, "Innovative TV," in *The Cult TV Book*, ed. Stacey Abbott (London: I. B. Tauris, 2010), 95.

34. Matt Hills, *Fan Cultures* (London: Routledge, 2002), 131.

35. Angela Ndalianis, "Television and the Neo-Baroque," in *The Contemporary Television Series*, ed. Michael Hammond and Lucy Mazdon (Edinburgh: Edinburgh University Press, 2005), 87.

36. Ndalianis, "Television and the Neo-Baroque," 99.

Part One
TEXTS AND CONTEXTS

Through the lens of a superhero. Picture courtesy of Van Norris.

CHAPTER ONE

FROM COMIC BOOK TO *BILDUNGSROMAN*: *SMALLVILLE*, NARRATIVE, AND THE EDUCATION OF A YOUNG HERO

Stan Beeler

The Superman story is remarkable in its persistence as a nonreligious myth in modern Western civilization.[1] Other contemporary mythic narratives have had brief periods of popularity followed by relative obscurity, but Superman has been quite popular—albeit in a niche market—for almost all of its seventy years of existence. The television series *Smallville*, which is based upon the teenage years of the Superman figure, is a shining example of the remarkable flexibility of form that has enabled the Superman story to last for such a long time. One of the most interesting aspects of this current incarnation is the transition of the basic narrative thrust of the character from adolescent power fantasy to a more nuanced study tracing the development of a gifted young man over the course of ten years. This form, when expressed as a novel, is known as a *Bildungsroman*. Comic books and television series have often been—with justification—accused of flat and static characterization, yet it is my contention that *Smallville* is one of a new breed of series that have broken out of the narrow confines of simple repetition. Despite the fact that the series has not completely eschewed the wish-fulfilling aspects of the heroic male figure at the center of this tale, the nascent Superman of *Smallville* is far more concerned with developing his human life as Clark Kent than any of the other—both earlier and concurrent—versions of this myth. Clark and his core group of friends and enemies go through a process of maturation that is closely linked to the physical changes in the actors who represent them on the small screen. This change in focus from repetitive adventures to a series of epiphanies is the result of a number of complex factors that include the development of the series as an adaptation as well as the changes in audience demographics. For this reason, the television series *Smallville* would be impossible to analyze in isolation from the tradition of Superman narratives that have engaged the North American consciousness over the last seventy or so years.

Smallville—when seen from the perspective of adaptation theory—is indeed innovative in its application of the mythological structure of the tale to the parameters of contemporary serialized television. It is perhaps most interesting to note that *Smallville* has had to make internal narrative accommodations in its narrative structure. That is, there have been changes in the structure of the storytelling of the series that have been made necessary by the series' long life. Although *Smallville* was originally developed for a teen audience, the cast has aged ten years over the course of its broadcast life. The fact that the target audience has also slowly drifted away from the original parameters for which it was created could have killed *Smallville*. However, the series creators have managed to develop the diegetic progression of the series in tandem with the passage of time in the real world as reflected by the appearance of the actors. *Smallville* is an adaptation that has managed to apply the raw material of a comic book myth that was designed for a short period in the life of its primarily adolescent male audience to a slowly shifting modern demographic slice. *Smallville* has maintained its audience through the application of narrative structures that follow the long-term development of both male and female characters.[2]

Smallville the Adaptation

The Superman mythos, first created by Jerry Siegel and Joe Shuster, began its existence in the medium of a syndicated newspaper strip but really came into its own when it moved from this short format to longer comic book publications. The comic book format collected and expanded upon the newspaper narratives and thus started the tradition of Superman as a serialized narrative. This step forward into a new medium is the first sign of the incredibly adaptive nature of the charismatic figure of Clark Kent/Superman and provides the scholar with a paradigmatic example of a type of modern myth that can be transformed in an almost infinite manner while maintaining its narrative kernel. All iterations of the Superman story reassure its successive audiences that the Man of Steel is a viable and contemporary figure. Linda Hutcheon defines adaptation as:

> - An acknowledged transposition of recognizable other work or works
> - A creative and an interpretive act of appropriation/salvaging
> - An extended intertextual engagement with the adapted work
>
> . . . With adaptations we seem to desire the repetition as much as the change.[3]

When a decision is made to develop an adaptation rather than a wholly new work, there are a number of factors that are involved. In many cases the economic considerations are of paramount importance, and in the case of an expensive proposition like a television series, the fact that the Superman mythos has a long history of engaging audiences in all of its numerous media expressions is an important factor in the decision to go ahead with the production. When an adaptation has been selected, then the creators have a number of related factors to deal with. Since adaptations depend upon the audience's desire for the repetition of a familiar item in a new format, there must be a conscious effort to maintain a certain degree of fidelity to the original as well as the selection of a sufficient number of innovations to keep the audience from simply yawning and changing the channel. In the case of the Superman mythos, it is quite difficult to determine what defining elements must be included. Over seventy years of adaptation have resulted in a baroque network of variations upon the basic comic book creation that have impinged upon the collective awareness of a chronologically disparate audience. *Smallville*'s development in the early part of the twenty-first century means that its targeted teen audience would be more aware of the recent Superman films and the TV series *Lois & Clark: The New Adventures of Superman* (1993–1997) than the comics, radio, or even older television series.

Although there have been nonvisual adaptations of the Superman mythos, for the main part, most variants upon the theme have incorporated a highly recognizable set of visual markers as well as the usual primary characters and significant plot elements. Some of the most common textual elements are:

1. Superman arrives on Earth as a child from another planet in a meteor shower.
2. He grows up in Smallville and is given the name of Clark Kent by adoptive parents.
3. He has an archenemy named Lex Luthor.
4. His power is derived from Earth's sun.
5. He is hurt or changed by meteor rocks from his home planet.
6. His friends and enemies often have the initials L.L.
7. He has a childhood sweetheart named Lana Lang and an adult romantic interest named Lois Lane.
8. Clark Kent works as a newspaper reporter for the *Daily Planet* in a city with the generic name Metropolis.

The visual elements that show up in most adaptations of the Superman mythos are:

1. Superman is a square-jawed black-haired hero who wears a costume, but no mask.
2. When not in costume, his sole disguise is a pair of black-framed glasses and a business suit.
3. Kryptonite is for the most part green and glowing, although there are other colors which also glow.
4. The *Daily Planet* has a distinctive ornament on the roof.
5. The Superman logo is part of the costume and the myth.
6. Superman can fly.

The two lists of common elements of Superman adaptations are by no means exhaustive, nor are they always present in the original comics or adaptations. Nevertheless, when one of these elements is missing or significantly modified during the process of adaptation, the audience notices. When a new character or plot variation is added, there is a distinctive backlash from cult fans who have been acclimatized to the mythos in an earlier format. However, Superman has such a long-lasting mythic existence that has so many iterations across such a broad spectrum of media that cult fans who are attached to the "purity" of the story are not all that numerous. For this reason, no matter what the medium or name—Superman, Superboy, Supergirl, or indeed *Lois & Clark* or *Smallville*—texts that use a sufficient number of these elements satisfy Hutcheon's primary criteria for adaptation—repetition of the familiar combined with novel variations.

The creators of *Smallville* have not seen fit to significantly alter the basic narrative premises of the Superman story. They have added a few characters, most significantly Chloe Sullivan (Allison Mack), the un-girlfriend, and the important negative parental figure of Lionel Luthor (John Glover). As we shall see later in this chapter, the more significant alterations are not in the basic facts of the tale, but in the way the story unfolds. On the other hand, although all of the basic plot elements of this list are seen in *Smallville*, many of the key visual aspects of the myth have been significantly altered.

To accommodate the contemporary notions of male beauty and the cynical attitudes of contemporary teenagers, most of the alterations have been in the physical variations as applied to Clark Kent. Welling is not the angular hero of the comics, films, or earlier television series; he has more sensitive features and a full-lipped, sensuous mouth, yet he remains definitely masculine. He no longer wears glasses when in Clark Kent guise, and in fact he never wears the traditional blue and red skin-tight costume. When he does wear blue and red, it is the rural chic of denim and plaid, which leads to the name the "Red-Blue Blur." For the first few seasons of the series, Clark has no secret identity; he simply has more abilities than most of the teenagers around him. He maintains the secret of his powers through stealth and speed, eliding the common contemporary audience complaint that his friends must be blind to be fooled by a pair of glasses.

The fact that *Smallville*'s Clark Kent cannot fly is an important variation of the visual paradigm of the series. Although it would not be difficult for a modern special effects team to provide a convincing version of flight for Welling's character, it is a significant advertising point that this Superman story is not a silly tale of flying men. Like the removal of the disguising glasses, this is another nod in the direction of a more sophisticated—and perhaps more female—contemporary audience.

The Target Demographic

Smallville's general audience—a group that we may conclude is not particularly invested in one of the earlier, or indeed parallel, versions of the Superman story—anticipates a new spin on the familiar elements of the mythos and is often pleasantly surprised when one or more of these elements is altered, omitted, or augmented. As mentioned above, a number of the hallmarks of the series have been transmuted to satisfy both the change in medium and the shift in target demographic. Miranda J. Banks comments upon the apparent paradox of a series that focuses upon a male protagonist and yet is clearly designed to please a female audience: "This gendered designation does not necessarily imply that the target viewership is male. Yet with the inclusion of the science-fiction aspect . . . producers are seemingly trying to widen the male audience for what otherwise would be a more female-oriented teen melodrama."[4] Since the creators of the series appear to have a two-point strategy in mind to attract both young male and female viewers, *Smallville* devotes much of its attention to the women in Clark Kent's life. Therefore, many of the episodes have plots that are centered on the politics of relationships and the difficulty of finding and maintaining a social position in a high school environment from a substantively female point of view. On the other hand, the traditional young male Superman audience is provided with a number of plot lines that deal with father-son tensions, the desire to be comfortable in the aggressively conformist environment of the North American high school, football, and plenty of scantily clad attractive females in sexually suggestive situations.

One of the most important aspects of contemporary television's demographic target is the venue in which it is presented. Since the fracturing of the television market through the introduction of a vast number of specialty cable channels, audiences are more prone to selecting their viewing material by channel than by time slot. This means that networks are very selective about the type of television that is appropriate for their particular audience share. Dawn Ostroff, president of entertainment for *Smallville*'s home network, CW, describes her demographic imperatives as follows:

> I think the CW is more boy-friendly than most people think. There are some really dynamic women at the core of those shows that will hopefully be interesting to men. . . . Our target audience is 18–34 women. There was white space out there where this is a demographic that was at least being spoken to from an advertisers' point of view and the competitive landscape. [*sic*] And women love to watch action-adventure franchise shows.[5]

Unlike most of the incarnations of the Superman mythos, the series focus in *Smallville* is upon concerns that are of interest to both young men and women—hence its value to a network like CW, which is interested in expanding its audience share to the high-spending male demographic. In the spring of 2010, a CW press release commented upon the economic reasons for the renewal of *Smallville* for its tenth season:

> Smallville recently moved to Friday nights, currently ranking as the network's #1 series in its time period among [wo]men 18–34 and men 18–49. Smallville has also improved CW's overall ratings in its Friday 8:00–9:00 pm time period by 67% among adults 18–34, 200% in men 18–34, 75% in adults 18–49, 183% in men 18–49 and 74% in total viewers (3.12 million).[6]

Moreover, although it is not covered in this statistical breakdown, we cannot ignore the fact that *Smallville* is attractive to one of the core audience sectors of cult fandom, high-spending gay male viewers. In fact, gay male viewers might be a significant proportion of the increased male audience. Glyn Davis, among other commentators on the series, points this out: "It would seem that the writers of the show are aware of their queer audience: The friendship between Clark and Lex is a fairly obviously homoeroticised one."[7] Most observers of the series have noted that in the early years Lex's fascination with Clark is a primary motivating factor for many of the plot structures. However, it is also obvious that this relationship is in no way static. In the first few seasons, Lex's friendly overtures toward Clark provide a convenient deus ex machina where money and the influence he provides often smooth the way for Clark and his entourage of high school students. As the relationship develops, Lex becomes something of a spurned lover who attempts his revenge through physical and emotional means. This culminates in season six when Lana is manipulated into marrying Lex. Although Lana is also manipulated and hurt, Clark is the obvious target of Lex's intervention. This is made absolutely clear in season eight's "Requiem" (2009) when Lana and Clarke are permanently separated by a bomb that Lex has designed to make Lana absorb enough kryptonite to kill Clark. Lex's attempts to develop a bond with Clark take on an ironic cast in "Scion" (2011) when Clark discovers that Lex has created a clone of himself using a mixture of his own and Clark's DNA. Lois frames this succinctly with the question, "Are you trying to tell me that Conner is the genetic love-child of Clark Kent and Lex Luthor?" The movement away from one lover to the next is a normal part of maturation in a North American environment, and the science fiction elements that support this rite of passage only serve to make the emotional development of *Smallville*'s cast more realistic to its audience, whatever their gender or sexual orientation.[8]

Smallville as an Extended Narrative Form

Since the 1990s, hour-long prime-time television drama has shown a definite tendency toward the narrative complexity inherent in serial drama. *Smallville*, although relatively episodic in its initial two seasons, has embraced the technique of the season-long story arc and, as the series has lasted past the normal five- to seven-year run, has developed narrative strategies to permit the cast to modify their roles to fit the appearance of young men and women who have matured past their teen years into their twenties.

These narrative strategies have made *Smallville* an example of a technique that allows subsequent iterations of a narrative in new media to have a dramatic effect upon its structural emphasis. As Richard Berger indicates, each adaptation of the Siegel and Shuster character Superman "can alter the status and authority of pre-existing versions of a text."[9] Although comic books are an exemplary medium for both the initial development and long-term maintenance of a mythos, they cannot compete with television for the sheer weight of narrative development. *Smallville*, now in its tenth season of airtime, is arguably the most persistent—if not the most popular—incarnation of the Superman character, and Tom Welling one of the most recognizable faces to play the role. By the end of the tenth season, avid fans will have had about 158 full hours of screen time to enjoy Welling's particular young adult brand of superhero. This massive amount of narrative development time has enabled the writers of the series, unlike the film versions of the narrative, to present its audience with the slow growth of its primary characters. Over the last ten years, we have seen a young man and his close friends mature both physically and as fictional protagonists. Welling's Clark Kent is divorced from the relatively static presence of the iron-jawed heroes of filmic and comic book versions of the mythology because the narrative focus of the series is substantially different from both film and comic book versions. Although Jane Feuer convincingly argues that the protagonists in television drama in the 1980s never really develop,[10] it is my contention that the long-running serial narrative of contemporary television is particularly suited to a specific type of character development that fosters audience sympathy in a way that transcends earlier televisual narrative strategies that relied upon simple recognition of static characters in fixed relationships. Over the course of ten years, both characters and audience mature, and this shared process of maturation develops a bond between fictional entities and their observers that is unique in the history of narrative fiction.

This is not to say that long-running serials like *Smallville* completely forgo the narrative strategy of repetition. In fact, many critical theorists who have studied the nature of contemporary serialized art forms suggest that judicious use of repetition is at the heart of its attraction to a contemporary audience. In *The Limits of Interpretation*, Umberto Eco suggests that we must reevaluate traditional notions of repetition because modern art has eschewed Romantic ideals of creativity. Eco believes that contemporary art moves beyond the Romantic distinction between crafts/industry and art. This is especially true when we consider the intricate relationship between industry, craft, and creativity that is essential to the production of film and television. To the Romantic, true art forces its audience to reconsider the spiritual world, while crafts and industrial production simply modify physical elements of existence. Eco notes that the Romantic segregation of art from craft and industry is a relatively new distinction, and the contemporary integration of craft, industry, and art is similar to paradigms present in baroque culture. Eco points out that industrial art forms of mass media were initially rejected because of an aesthetic preference based upon Romantic ideals:

> This excess of pleasurability and repetition, this lack of innovation, were felt to be a commercial trick (the product had to meet the expectations of its audience), not the provocative proposal of a new, and difficult to accept world vision. The products of media were equated with the products of industry insofar as they were produced in series, and the "serial" production was considered alien to the artistic invention.[11]

The similarity of contemporary serial television and baroque art is clearly represented in Angela Ndalianis' "Television and the Neo-Baroque." In it she points out that neobaroque art (modern television) moves away from the series format into the linked narrative structures of the serial.[12]

Although the long-running comic book narrative structure has certain similarities to that of a ten-year-long television series, there are certain inherent differences necessitated by the use of human actors to represent the archetypal characters. For example, in another text Eco delineates the paradoxical narrative expectations of the highly serialized comic book Superman:

> [H]e must be an archetype, the totality of certain collective aspirations, and therefore, he must necessarily become immobilized in an emblematic and fixed nature which renders him easily recognizable (this is what happens to Superman); but since he is marketed in the sphere of a "romantic" production for a public that consumes "romances," he must be subjected to a development which is typical, as we have seen, of novelistic characters.[13]

Eco is contrasting the static nature of the traditional hero from mythology or religion "whose image had immutable characteristic and an irreversible destiny" with the protagonist of contemporary dramas with whom we identify because we share the unpredictable nature of the world around us.[14] He sees this focus on a continuously unfolding plot as the reason for serial narrative structures. Superman is a special case of a narrative creation because he partakes in both the immutable nature of the heroic myth, and the transitory nature of human life:

> But Superman is myth on condition of being a creature immersed in everyday life, in the present, apparently tied to our own conditions of life and death even if endowed with superior faculties. . . . He possesses the characteristics of timeless myth, but is accepted only because his activities take place in our human and everyday world of time.[15]

Eco believes that the serial drama of Superman comics unfolds by deliberately forgetting the continuity of the story: "Where what has happened before and what has happened after appears extremely hazy."[16] It is my contention that the comic book narrative structure described by Eco used to be similar to the structure of episodic television drama. However, contemporary long-running dramatic serial television is much closer to the evolving world of a novel. The narratives last for an immense amount of real time; Tom Welling has been visiting our living rooms in the guise of Superman for about ten years of real human experience. Although the comic book character has lasted a considerably longer stretch of time, the characters in a comic are not anchored in the physical reality of actors who, like their audiences, grow older. This immanent manifestation of the physical character means that it would be impossible to maintain the fiction of unending high school life for a television character. Welling's Clark Kent must mature or he would devolve into a clownish caricature, a man playing a boy's role in an unconvincing attempt to preserve his youth. Of course it is only the rare occurrence in which a television series lasts beyond the two to five years that is the norm for the medium, so the necessity of evolving characters is not all that common.[17] Nevertheless, it does occur, and the medium has made a number of adjustments to accommodate this new category of long-lived serial drama.[18]

One of the methods that narrative television has employed to maintain a convincing relationship with its audience is a reciprocal application of information concerning the passage of time within the diegetic universe created for a series as well as the "real world" that surrounds it. This is, perhaps, at its most effective when series creators use the audience's instinctive knowledge of music to invoke a subliminal understanding of the intended time frame of a scene or episode. The ever-changing landscape of contemporary popular music is a powerful link that binds the fictional world of *Smallville* to the passage of time in the real world around it. The diegetic and nondiegetic music that accompanies the series has shifted to keep in time with the evolving tastes of the target demographic. In fact, audiences will often develop a nostalgic bond with the series as they relive memories of experiences in their own lives triggered by the music embedded in the narrative and present on the DVDs. As the following statement from the *Smallville* fan site Kryptonsite indicates, the music of *Smallville* is an important component of the series' attraction:

> Ever since the Smallville pilot in 2001 featured the music of bands like Lifehouse and Coldplay, playing the popular music of the times has always been a Smallville tradition. There have been two Smallville soundtrack albums commercially released. The first, The Talon Mix, contains music from the show's first two seasons; the second, The Metropolis Mix, contains mostly music from Seasons Four and Five.[19]

The music is keyed closely to the diegetic time frame of the episodes. For example, in episode "Zero," which was broadcast in March 2002, there are a series of flashbacks to events in a Metropolis club (Zero). The first flashback is introduced with a banner indicating that these events happened three years earlier. When Lex (Michael Rosenbaum) enters the club, the music playing is the Lo-Fidelity AllStars/Pigeonhed hit "Battleflag," which was on the Billboard dance charts in 1999. Lex has arranged the club visit so that a female friend, Amanda Rothman (Jud Tylor), will catch her fiancé, Jude Royce (Corin Nemec), having an affair. Lex's strategy is successful, and Amanda throws her engagement ring in Jude's face. As the outraged man attacks Lex with a knife, the music switches to Faithless' "God Is a DJ," another song that was popular in clubs in 1999. The phrase from the lyrics "God Is a DJ" gains narrative significance as it coincides exactly with Jude's death. The series creators have exactly matched the diegetic music of the flashback to the venue (a dance club) and the time frame (about three years before the broadcast date) with an eye for accuracy that would be appreciated by their music-sensitive young adult audience. The scenes represented as current time are of summer rather than March in Kansas, so the audience would automatically place the flashback as 1999 rather than 2000. The UK club-music genre of the two songs is substantially different from most of the series' musical selections. This is the auditory equivalent of matching military uniforms to time frame in a historical drama, and it clearly demonstrates the linkage between the diegetic life of the characters and the real-world existence of the audience. The song is used as a historical referent as well as a plot element throughout the episode.

Smallville and the Cult Fan

Sensitivity to the audience's taste in contemporary music is not the only way in which the creators of *Smallville* develop a dynamic relationship with the young men and women who watch the show. Contemporary television drama has readily incorporated a narrative feedback channel provided by the Internet that allows series creators to have a dialectic relationship with their audience. As the complex narratives of contemporary television drama develop past the airing of their initial conceptualization, audience members are moved to express their opinions of the series in a much more subtle fashion than the "brute force" analysis provided by Nielsen ratings.[20] The producers of contemporary television have a wealth of information at their disposal. Through the use of Internet feedback channels, they have access not only to who is watching, but also why they are watching. This information can lead to, perhaps even more significantly, what would inspire the audience to watch even more. Of course, attention to this extra information is not without its own perils. The constructive (or not-so-constructive) criticism of a long-running TV series that is freely available on authorized and unauthorized series websites tends to be the product of the highly specialized group of viewers who are often known under the sobriquet "cult fans." The cult fan, by definition, is someone who is not only willing to invest time in the passive enjoyment of a television series, but also happy to go the extra mile and actively engage in ancillary activities such as writing detailed commentaries on episodes or season-long plot arcs. Moreover, the cult fan may decide to write and publish online fan fiction, which can be a clear indication of the elements of a series that pique the interest of at least one segment of the audience. Cult fans are willing to devote an excessive amount of time with both the diegetic and nondiegetic aspects of a series and are extremely pleased when they discover elements of the narrative that are designed to reward their more-than-casual knowledge of the series. For example, in the episode entitled "Nicodemus" (2002), Waylon Jennings' song "Good Ol' Boys" is playing as diegetic music in Jonathan Kent's half-ton truck. The self-referential significance of this is that the song was the theme music for *The Dukes of Hazzard* (1979–1985). John Schneider, the actor who plays Jonathan Kent in *Smallville*, was costar of the *Dukes of Hazzard.* The cult fan, unlike the casual observer, would be well aware of the actor's resume and derive pleasure from this small aside to those "in the know."

This special fan group is, of course, not only attracted by the extradiegetic details like references to the careers of actors. In fact, the diegetic completeness of a series like *Smallville* is the primary element that attracts the highly involved cult audience. As Sarah Gwenllian-Jones indicates, the cult series experience is created by cooperation between the fan and the medium:

> Immersive engagement with the fictional world depends upon uniting what is conveyed by the text with the reader's own experiences and knowledge, facilitating a sense of vicarious presence in the imaginary environment. . . . Immersive experience is an alchemical effect of text and imagination, a species of willed hallucination that transports the reader into another realm. It is not a passive experience; the reader must play an active part in creating and sustaining its integrity, drawing on memory as well as imagination to reinforce its perceptual substance.[21]

The cult fan uses aspects of his or her background knowledge of the real world—for example the popular music of the ten years of *Smallville*'s run—to fill in gaps in the artificial diegetic world of the series. The active engagement of cult fans means that the slowly evolving diegetic world of *Smallville* is much more engaging than series that have no cult involvement. Cult fans really care about the dual entities composed of actor and fictional character and are therefore quite willing to see their inevitable progression through time. The cult fan does not mourn the aging of Tom Welling as long as it leads to a more mature, yet even more attractive, Clark Kent—a young man who can still be considered an appropriate romantic interest for the maturing fan on both an emotional and physical level.

Unfortunately for the economic "science" of television production, the plethora of information provided by cult fans is often not directly applicable to all television series. This particular type of "active audience" may not be the targeted demographic for a series. Although the cult audience is not the only sort of audience that has distinct opinions and interpretations of television, they are the most visible, as they tend to "publish" their opinions.[22] While no corporate entity can afford to disdain any market segment in the postcable fragmented audience environment, it is also true that cult TV fans are not necessarily the kind of audience that attracts advertisers for certain types of items. The cult audience may be willing to spend a high proportion of their income on media and media-related items, but they may not be the people who will buy high-ticket items like luxury cars or furniture. Thus, the detailed feedback that is provided to the creators of a series may only be of use to develop a series targeted at a cult audience. *Smallville* is, happily, a series that is broadcast on a network that is dedicated to a younger, primarily female audience and is therefore attractive to advertisers who may well fit with the purchasing profile of the female cult fan.

Smallville and Emotional Maturity

Because of its narrative adaptation to ten seasons of broadcast history, *Smallville* is a series that has come to predicate its plot upon the development of character. Indeed, the series applies the modern technique of ensemble casting and plotting in order to provide a relatively diverse audience base with characters that are personally engaging. This means that each of the circle of friends who surround Clark have been represented in loving detail as they move along a path of personal development. In a traditional series with limited character development (like a soap opera), we may find a character occasionally reversing role from protagonist to antagonist, but the notion of a character maturing into a new function in a series is quite rare. Of course, *Smallville* is from time to time also guilty of simply reversing character functions to provide variation, but the slow development of a new role through character development is an interesting addition to the repertoire of television plot structures and is worth discussing in some detail.[23]

Considering the subject material of the series, it is not surprising that Clark Kent is one of the characters that has been afforded the luxury of gradually maturing. Clark Kent is a character coming to grips with both the advantages and limitations of maturation as a gifted and—as mentioned above—highly attractive individual. His relationship with his friends, lovers, guardians, and of course his enemies reflects this position as a central figure in the social structure of a small American town.

Moreover, over the course of its ten-year run, the cast of *Smallville* has paralleled the aging and concomitant maturation of its core audience, which is primarily composed of young people with similar backgrounds. (Although, I would wager that there are very few superpowered aliens in the core demographic.) As Clark Kent's powers appear and his control over them develops, he and his companions proceed through the normal emotional and physical development of young North Americans. Friendships, career aspirations, and romances blossom or die while the series mirrors the lives—albeit in metaphorical splendor—of the young people who love the series and have followed it since its inception. The characters that inhabit the archetypal hometown, Smallville, are like friends from the audience's own places of origin—be it small town or urban center. The politics of high school in North America are similar no matter what the physical location. We watch their lives develop, their friendships, their loves, their careers, and their marriages begin, end, and rekindle. Old friends move away or die, and new friends are welcomed into the circle that is centered upon the life of Clark Kent. Audience engagement with the narrative is boosted because the ensemble cast provides them with a full spectrum of characters with whom they may identify. Clark stands in for many a young man who gradually becomes the center of attention because of his looks and talents, even though he may not want or appreciate the interest of those around him. In keeping with the "coming-of-age" theme of the series, the early years of the show represent Clark as a young man with unfulfilled potential. His parents see that he is destined for greater things, but in the context of high school, he is not really a figure of public acclaim. His "light-under-a-bushel" persona is also represented through the age-old story of unrequited love. Clark's infatuation with Lana is constantly frustrated by factors that are beyond his control, and despite his hidden powers he cannot win the love of his life. In fact, it is most often the things that make him special and therefore potentially more attractive—were he to reveal himself—that intervene when he tries to develop his relationship with Lana. Yet the series would not have lasted for so long if the initial position of Clark's secret versus his love for Lana had remained static. Although the series creators manage to maintain the tension for a long time, eventually Lana finds out Clark's secret, and the inevitable tragic breakup follows. Before this happens, there are a number of episodes that—through the science fiction magic of alternate time lines—allow viewers the temporary pleasure of a great revelation that is soon erased. In "Reckoning" (2006), Clark reveals his powers to Lana and proposes to her. This leads to a tragic car accident in which Lana is killed and Clark must plead with his Kryptonian father, Jor-El (Terence Stamp), for a "do over." It is not until the sixth-season episode entitled "Promise" (2007) that Lana finally discovers Clark's powers and manages to keep the knowledge in the primary diegetic time line of the series. Tragically, this discovery coincides with Lionel blackmailing Lana into marrying Lex.

The unrevealed secret life of Clark Kent is paralleled by the sexual tension between the couple. Lana is a typical young woman coming to grips with her social popularity and the difficulties of commitment. The series allows aspects of female maturation to be presented in detail through her relationship with Clark. It takes until season five, in the episode entitled "Mortal" (2005) before Clark and Lana physically consummate their relationship. Clark has lost his powers through the intervention of Jor-El, and when the powers are restored, Clark is afraid to make love to Lana lest he damage her. This reluctance to maintain a normal physical relationship on Clark's part culminates in an argument in "Fanatic" (2006), and the relationship begins another nonphysical phase that lasts until Lana gains superpowers two seasons later in "Wrath" (2007). Although it is a common conception that a television series can maintain its audience's interest only as long as the sexual tension between primary characters is not resolved, Clark and Lana's brief interludes of cohabitation did not spell the end of the series. In fact, it would seem that this relationship is a paradigm for twenty-first-century feminism. Their physical relationship is untenable unless there is equality between the partners, and the series creators will not allow the relationship to blossom unless Lana is equal to Clark.[24] This is a clear example of the narrative innovations of *Smallville* when compared to the practices of earlier versions of the series. In this series, Clark and Lana's relationship can develop beyond its initial tension, and it does until its final and tragic end in "Requiem" (2009), when Lana, now more or less equal to Clark in powers, can no longer be with him because of the kryptonite she has absorbed.

Chloe, in the initial episodes of the series, is the mirror image of Clark in an emotional sense; she desires a man who does not seem to care for her, and her unrequited love causes a host of personal problems. As the series develops, she reconciles herself with her role as Clark's friend rather than his lover and goes on to develop her own powers and natural talents. In "Fortune" (2011), Chloe and Clark are briefly convinced that they have married each other while under the influence of a bottle of magical champagne. After the illusion is dispelled, they agree that their lives are much better now that they are just friends. Chloe's emotional development is in some ways as problematic as Clark's. After the group has left high school, she develops a relationship with Jimmy Olsen that culminates in marriage and then separation. When she is able to form another relationship, it is with Oliver Queen (Green Arrow), and she struggles to maintain emotional distance.

In the initial few seasons of the series, the rudimentary social positions of unrequited love and schoolyard crushes are characteristic of a melodrama and do not seem to alter, but as the series progresses, all of the characters follow the course of human development and transcend—for better or for worse—the initial template of their existence. *Smallville* often uses the metaphor of superpowers to represent the emotional and physical maturation of its characters. For example, in "Heat" (2002), the meteor-powered seductress biology teacher Desiree Atkins (Krista Allen) elicits a sexual response in Clark that manifests itself as uncontrolled heat vision. This sexual metaphor is continued in the series from time to time for humorous effect, driving home the core message that coming of age is difficult for all adolescents—be they human or superpowered alien.

One of the best examples of the development of the *Smallville* characters beyond their adolescent emotional positions is found in the ninth season. In "Escape" (2010), Clark and Lois accidentally meet Chloe and Oliver on a weekend getaway at a Scottish-themed bed-and-breakfast resort. The episode is structured like a traditional romantic farce with the two couples' sexual history playing a prominent role in the unfolding of the plot. Chloe is possessed by a banshee spirit who wishes to seduce men then kill them. She arrives in the shower with Clark, and—of course—Lois arrives at the most inappropriate moment. The spirit then possesses Lois, and she attempts to seduce Oliver. This episode is not part of the major plot arc of the surrounding episodes which deal with the interactions between the conflicting goals of the Kandorians/Zod and Amanda Waller/Checkmate. However, in the greater narrative development of the series, it presents a clear emotional breakthrough. Ndalianis mentions that the episode "Hush" (1999) from the series *Buffy the Vampire Slayer* (1997–2003) serves a similar function. Although its plot is not directly related to the episodes before and after it, "Hush" is the culmination of the affair between Buffy and Riley.[25] The relationships between Chloe and Oliver and Clark and Lois have reached a stage that represents the sexual maturity of men and women of the same ages as the actors. The confusions and mixing of partners through supernatural means is not as important as the fact that Clark and Lois and Chloe and Oliver are able to go away for a weekend together without fear of parents or social stigma. This would be unimaginable for the teenagers who were the focus of the series in the first five seasons. In the context of the series as a whole, this is the first episode that has Clark in a normal, adult sexual relationship with a woman. In fact, when Chloe asks if Clark has overcome his fear of damaging normal human partners during sex, he says that his training with Jor-El has afforded him the control necessary to perform the act. This episode is the culmination of the narrative device of adolescent sexual repression that has been running through the series since its inception. Indeed, all of the various incarnations of the Superman story since its beginnings in the 1930s have more or less represented the Man of Steel as celibate. (This, of course, does not include the standard science fiction deviations from the primary time line.) *Smallville* is, perhaps, the only adaptation of the mythos that explicitly thematizes the sexuality of the hero, although all of them present Superman in a platonic love relationship with Lana or Lois.

Conclusion

Smallville is an important example of the process of adaptation, not only because it takes material from a long tradition in a host of media formats, but because it represents a specific innovation in serial television. While many contemporary series have developed in the direction of a serialized format, these developments have not been so closely related to the paradigm provided by the *Bildungsroman*. Like its novelistic precursors, *Smallville* focuses on the moral and psychological growth of its protagonist. However, unlike the first example of the genre, Goethe's *Wilhelm Meisters Lehrjahre* (1795–1796), the series presents a group of protagonists, both male and female, through the sometimes painful process of maturation. The *Bildungsroman* has traditionally presented the development of a single individual. *Smallville*, like most contemporary television, is an ensemble production, and it would have been impossible to present Clark Kent's progress to adulthood without paralleling the process with his companions.

The initial seasons of the series used material developed for an audience that was primarily composed of adolescent heterosexual males and altered it so that it could be enjoyed by young women and a significant number of gay men. This was done by means of altering some of the basic visual and narrative components of the underlying mythic structure, adding a focus on romantic relationships, and altering the appearance of the central figure of Clark Kent so that he would appeal to an audience interested in Clark rather than Superman. Because these adaptations were so successful, the series ran much longer than is normal for a dramatic television series, and the actors and audience moved beyond the initial limitations of a teenager's life. Instead of abandoning the show, the creators and the network opted to adapt the series so that it could represent the long-term development of friendships and romances that were founded in the youth of the characters. I believe that this is significantly different from the strategy used by that other long-term serial narrative form, the soap opera, for several reasons. The first is that the soap opera does not really attempt to move along with the development of its audience. Soaps assume a more-or-less static emotional age for their audience, although they cover a very broad spectrum of physical ages. The second is that *Smallville* is designed to appeal to an audience that is much more active than the soap audience. The cult fans that follow the series are willing to share their likes and dislikes in a thorough deliberate elaboration upon the broadcast canon of the series. *Smallville* may be a sign of the new kind of narrative strategy for youth television. It is a series that has chosen to grow with its audience.

Notes

1. One might argue that the vampire myth is its only equal.

2. Information concerning the development of the Superman myth is drawn from a number of sources including the following: Aaron Taylor, "'He's Gotta Be Strong, and He's Gotta Be Fast, and He's Gotta Be Larger Than Life': Investigating the Engendered Superhero Body," *Journal of Popular Culture* 40, no. 2 (April 2007): 344–360; Phillip Thurtle and Robert Mitchell, "The Acme Novelty

Library: Comic Books, Repetition, and the Return of the New," *Configurations* 15, no. 3 (2007): 267–297; Matt Yockey, "Somewhere in Time: Utopia and the Return of Superman," *Velvet Light Trap: A Critical Journal of Film & Television* 61 (Spring 2008): 26–37.

3. Linda Hutcheon, *A Theory of Adaptation* (New York: Routledge, 2006), 8–9.

4. Miranda J. Banks, "A Boy for All Planets: Roswell, Smallville and the Teen Male Melodrama," in *Teen TV: Genre, Consumption and Identity*, ed. Glyn Davis and Kay Dickinson (London: British Film Institute, 2004), 20.

5. James Hibberd, "Q&A: CW's Ostroff Talks Pilots, 'Vampire Diaries' and More," *The Hollywood Reporter*, 2010, http://www.hollywoodreporter.com/blogs/live-feed/qa-cws-ostroff-talks-pilots-53226 (accessed 4 March 2010).

6. "Smallville to Return for a Tenth Season on the CW," *The CW*, 2010, http://blog.cwtv.com/2010/03/04/smallville-to-return-for-a-tenth-season-on-the-cw/ (accessed 31 March 2011).

7. Glyn Davis, "'Saying It Out Loud': Revealing Television's Queer Teens," in *Teen TV: Genre, Consumption and Identity*, ed. Glyn Davis and Kay Dickinson (London: British Film Institute, 2004), 136.

8. Peter Billingham, "Can Kinky Sex Be Politically Correct? *Queer as Folk* and the Geo-Ideological Inscription of Gay Sexuality," in *Popular Television Drama: Critical Perspectives*, ed. Jonathan Bignell and Stephen Lacey (Manchester: Manchester University Press, 2005), 122. *Smallville* is not the only show that attracts both a young female heterosexual audience as well as a gay male audience. Peter Billingham notes of the Russell T. Davies series about gay life in Manchester, *Queer as Folk* (1999–2000): ". . . audience research revealed that the series's largest single demographic group was young women between the ages of eighteen and thirty."

9. Richard Berger, "'Are There Any More at Home Like You?': Rewiring Superman," *Journal of Adaptation in Film & Performance* 1, no. 2 (2008): 87.

10. Jane Feuer, *Seeing Through the Eighties: Television and Reaganism* (London: British Film Institute, 1996), 128. As Feuer notes, "More often they [serial narrative characters] perpetuate the narrative by continuing to make the same mistakes."

11. Umberto Eco, *The Limits of Interpretation* (Bloomington: Indiana University Press, 1994), 84.

12. Angela Ndalianis, "Television and the Neo-Baroque," in *The Contemporary Television Series*, ed. Michael Hammond and Lucy Mazdon (Edinburgh: Edinburgh University Press, 2005), 83–101.

13. Umberto Eco and Natalie Chilton, "Review: The Myth of Superman," *Diacritics* 2, no. 1 (Spring 1972): 15.

14. Eco and Chilton, "Review: The Myth of Superman," 15.

15. Eco and Chilton, "Review: The Myth of Superman," 16.

16. Eco and Chilton, "Review: The Myth of Superman," 17.

17. We might consider the situation of the actors in the original *Star Trek* (1966–1969) television series and their reappearance in the *Star Trek* films as similar. For the first few films, the actors' physical changes were not intrusive, but after a while, the action/adventure theme of the series demanded that a new cast take their place in subsequent films.

18. At this point I should note that although the subject of this discussion has numerous similarities with that other long-running narrative television format, the soap opera, there are sufficient differences in its audience, narrative structure, and cinematography that I will exclude it from this chapter.

19. "The Music of *Smallville*," *Kryptonsite*, 2011, http://www.kryptonsite.com/smallvillemusic.htm (accessed 31 March 2011).

20. Nielsen ratings indicate approval or disapproval simply through audience share rather than nuanced commentary on "quality" provided by discursive Internet commentary.

21. Sara Gwenllian-Jones, "Virtual Reality and Cult Television," in *Cult Television*, ed. Sara Gwenllian-Jones and Roberta E. Pearson (Minneapolis: University of Minnesota Press, 2004), 84.

22. Dorothy Hobson, "From *Crossroads* to *Wife Swap*: Learning from Audiences," *Critical Studies in Television* 1, no. 1 (May 2006): 127. Hobson points out that it is not only the cult audience that actively participates in television. When discussing John Carey's comments on her own work, she states: "He points out that viewers are playing a 'game' with the production when they discuss characters, that they have a creative input, they add their own interpretation and understanding, and involve their own feelings and thoughts about how the situation should be handled. Just as I contended that there are as many different *Crossroads* as viewers, Carey sees the series as 'popular art' with communal participation."

23. Clark's recurring experiences with nongreen variants of kryptonite are the usual mechanism for reversing character traits in *Smallville* and are actually used quite effectively in the season two to season three transition. Clark deliberately uses red kryptonite in a metaphorical play on the theme of teenage substance abuse.

24. Of course there is the fourth-season arc in which Lana gains magical powers through her reincarnation of an ancient sorceress, Isobel. At this time Lana becomes sexually active with her new boyfriend Jason Teague (Jensen Ackles), so one might consider the possibility that Lana's powers are a metaphor for sexual maturity.

25. Ndalianis, "Television and the Neo-Baroque," 96.

CHAPTER TWO

TELEVISUAL TRANSFORMATIONS: MYTH AND SOCIAL ISSUES IN *SMALLVILLE*

Karin Beeler

The long-running television series *Smallville* is a re-creation of the Superman story, one of the most prominent hero-savior narratives in American culture. The myth of the savior (inscribed in the opening title song "Save Me" and in multiple facets of the television show) is a prominent feature of the narrative and visual space of the series, but it is only one of the many mythic elements of this post-9/11 telefantasy. *Smallville* draws on numerous mythic and apocalyptic images dependent on metamorphosis and combines images from myth with a host of social issues that affect modern North American youth. Savior figures, agricultural gods, and various examples of the monstrous are incorporated into the series to create a televisual experience that reinforces the symbolic dimension of young characters who struggle with what it means to be "different." While much of the show's preoccupation with social, sexual, or mythic categories of difference is presented in the context of Clark's teenage experience, this concern with difference still continues to be evident in the show's tenth and final season episode "Scion" (2011), when a more mature Clark discusses the concept with his genetically engineered "son" Conner/Alexander who has half his DNA and half of Lex Luthor's.

Since myths reflect social or cultural attitudes, it is not surprising that the mythic elements in *Smallville* (especially during the first few seasons) also serve as a way of highlighting social issues relevant to the youth audience: obsessions with beauty, teenage infatuation and sexual desire, eating disorders, and the experience of social isolation or family background.

As Eric Rabkin has argued, myths often express fantastic physical transformations as a dramatic expression of a character's psychological state.[1] *Smallville* foregrounds the social and psychological issues of youth that highlight the culture of the body. In a telefantasy context, the metamorphoses of modern-day youth in *Smallville* echo the familiar stories of transformation evident in ancient myth. As Catherine Johnson defines it, telefantasy is a term that describes "a wide range of fantasy, science-fiction and horror television programmes";[2] these are genres that also foreground difference (e.g., social and genetic differences) along with their "significant representations of 'fantastic' events and objects that confound culturally accepted notions of what is believed to be real."[3] Yet *Smallville*'s focus on difference through the use of mythic elements actually bridges the gap between the world of telefantasy and accepted notions of what an audience believes to be real since the language and visual imagery used in the telefantasy contexts easily substitute for "real" social issues.

Mythic elements in *Smallville* also reinforce the series' connection to American films and television shows that make use of similar visual expressions and narratives of transformation. Not surprisingly, the focus on a televisual and filmic past in *Smallville* echoes the impact of a cultural phenomenon such as *Star Trek* which "looked to the past as a means of broadcasting its messages. The use of myth in this storytelling process further entrenches *Star Trek* as history."[4] *Smallville*'s use of familiar telefantasy or fantasy and science fiction film character types and mythic patterns thus creates much of its social relevance for contemporary youth who may also be familiar with the cult phenomena of Superman films or comics. Other spectators of the television series may find that extreme character types or situations in *Smallville* resemble characters or situations from fantasy and horror films (*The Wizard of Oz* [1939]; *Children of the Corn* [1984]) or from a show like *Buffy the Vampire Slayer* (1997–2003), which overlapped with part of *Smallville*'s run. The longevity of the series also plays a significant role in the multiple transformations of characters in *Smallville* and may help explain how the series can develop even as it maintains a self-reflexive, self-contained mythology, one of the key aspects of a television serial.[5] In other words, *Smallville* can evoke within its confines a nostalgia for an older, more stable mythos as it does in the season nine episode "Upgrade" (2010), where the character Zod tells Kal-El/Clark that he has become far too calculating to play the naive farm boy anymore. Season ten's "Scion" also creates a sense of nostalgia for an earlier part of the series when Clark teaches his newly discovered son Conner (who is the genetically engineered son of Lex and Clark) how to control his abilities. This episode echoes Clark's struggle as a teenager[6] to control his superhuman powers in the early part of the series, while also drawing attention to the simultaneous fear of change and desire for change that characters in the series experience. The televisual narrative of the mythic characters in *Smallville* is thus articulated through visual patterns of duplication and mutuality, as is the case in the season nine episode "Conspiracy" (2010), when the villain Zod acquires superpowers because of Clark's blood. These visual patterns include images of transformed bodies and the monstrous—which are conveyed with various cinematographic techniques such as camera angles and special effects—that reinforce key social issues for youth in the twenty-first century.

According to Alan Dundes, myth belongs to the past even though it continues to have an important impact on the present.[7] The stories of myths can also be described as transcending historical specificity. William Bascom says that myths belong to the remote past,[8] but it is clear that mythic characters or narratives in literature, film, or television also reflect the social attitudes and rituals of a specific time. Umberto Eco has indicated that a mythic character "embodies a law, or a universal demand"[9] but also acknowledges that a mythic character like Superman in the comic strip is both "timeless" and "immersed in everyday life."[10] According to Debra Moddelmog,

> myth is a narrative, recurring in various forms, throughout a significant period of cultural history, which has acquired, and continues to invite, a number of diverse meanings as readers seek to identify the psychic, social or sexual unknown that the myth expresses. . . . Yet these analyses do not close up the myth, explaining it to everyone's satisfaction; in fact, they are likely to provoke further interpretations by compelling other readers to enter the dialogue surrounding the myth. Like a snowball rolling down a hill, a myth sustains its mythic nature, in part, by the build-up of commentary that inspires further transformation and interpretation of the myth.[11]

Perhaps the changing dimensions of a myth through the ages are an extension of the theme of transformation as an important narrative and visual device within the myths themselves. Ovid's *Metamorphoses* serves as an illustration of this device in ancient myths where individuals are transformed into animals or plants. *Smallville* picks up on the theme of metamorphosis, even including the concept in the title of season one, episode two, "Metamorphosis" (2001). This is a theme that resonates with the teenage characters during the first few seasons of *Smallville* and with Clark's teenage "son" Conner/Alexander in season ten. These characters are at a crossroads or at a particular stage in their lives that demands some kind of transformation. Eric S. Rabkin has linked the physical transformations of individuals in myth or fantastic literature to their psychological states.[12] In the telefantasy narrative of *Smallville*, mythic figures such as the hero-savior, agricultural "gods," and examples of the monstrous reflect the kinds of transformations that affect young people in a physical and in a psychological sense. The first few seasons of *Smallville* in particular address the kinds of experiences that reinforce "difference" among high school teenagers. This is not surprising because the teenage years are a time of significant changes in a person's body, in their sense of identity, and in their relationships with peers.

One of the key figures linked to transformative possibilities in *Smallville* is the figure of the savior who is a prominent mythic component in the series. This aspect is one of Clark Kent's key characteristics even before he realizes his greater potential as the "Red-Blue Blur" or "the Blur," the name applied to Clark's superfast mode after Jimmy Olsen captures Clark on film. The figure of the savior is also a powerful antecedent in world mythology, and as Lincoln Geraghty points out in his study of *Star Trek*, an expression of the American Monomyth which may involve characters such as the "cowboy or superhero"[13] who have an "inherent urge to do good and be redeemed, to bring about the salvation of those less fortunate."[14] Saviors may also be distinguished by their difference. Clark's difference is visually/mythically represented through the unusual circumstances surrounding his arrival on Earth; he appears to his future adoptive parents, Jonathan and Martha Kent, in a cornfield. His appearance and difference echo the unusual arrivals of other mythic heroes like Moses who is discovered by Pharaoh's daughter in the bulrushes, or like Jesus whose birth has been associated with the setting of a stable. The Kents initially see Clark upside down because their truck has been literally turned upside down due to the near collision with Clark's spaceship which crashed into the cornfield. Clark is thus "delivered" to Earth in an atypical fashion—by means of a spacecraft from Krypton. This future savior grows up on a farm and spends a good deal of time in a barn, which suggests a parallel with Jesus' birth. In a post-9/11 world, one could argue that *Smallville* not only extends a seemingly timeless desire for hero-savior figures, but also reflects the very specific cultural anxiety of Americans concerning the alien other (e.g., terrorism on American soil) and a need to find some way of addressing uncertainty or averting disaster. The myth of Superman attempts to assuage this anxiety in its televisual continuity of the Superman savior figure but also reconfigures the savior myth by situating it in relation to the lives of American teenagers and their encounters with violence and humiliation.

Smallville's pilot episode evokes multiple facets of savior figures, including their role as scapegoat. For example, in the series pilot episode, Clark becomes a complex blend of a scarecrow/Christ figure/dying maize god when he is tied to a cross in a cornfield by Whitney, Lana's boyfriend, who feels threatened by Clark's relationship with Lana. As Tom Douglas mentions in his book *Basic Groupwork*, "Difference is a marker. When things are going wrong and there is no obvious rational cause that can be discovered, irrational behavior tends to take over and blame is allocated to those who are marked in the group by some form of difference."[15] A red *S* is also painted on Clark's chest as an icon of difference and transformation. For the students who painted the *S* on Clark's body, it apparently signifies Smallville and functions simultaneously as their desire to brand Clark with their collective school identity, while also reducing him to an individual target of humiliation that echoes the archetype of the scapegoat.[16] The mythic significance of the *S* also references the shield in the Superman myth, and later in the series the *S* is replaced with the Kryptonian *S*-shaped infinity symbol, thus reinforcing the importance of change in the series. In the first episode, however, the *S* on Clark's body does not just echo a mythic prototype of the sacrificial hero; the *S* also highlights his difference as the victim of Whitney's male anxiety about his relationship with Lana and serves as a symbol of Whitney's need to humiliate Clark. This humiliation is played out in the form of the high school football team's homecoming ritual of taking a "freshman" and stringing him up in a cornfield. The myth of the scapegoat/scarecrow thus acquires a resonance for a younger audience familiar with bullying or other acts of humiliation which may include the kinds of initiation rites or "hazing" found in fraternities or sports teams in the United States.[17] These hazing rituals involve elements of transformation that can involve changing the physical appearance of the victim by marking the individual. This serves as a modern expression of William Holman Hunt's nineteenth-century painting of the scapegoat, which depicts a goat that is "marked" with a visually arresting red fillet around its horns.

While the scarecrow also has a strong agricultural association because of its historical use in farming communities in the United States and in other countries,[18] for teen audiences familiar with other films and television, it may have an even more powerful cultural presence because of its link to humiliation in film (*The Wizard of Oz*) and its association with horror in other visual narratives. In the 1939 version of *The Wizard of Oz* that *Smallville*'s generation of viewers might have seen on television or on DVD, the scarecrow is the man of straw that Dorothy encounters while walking down the Yellow Brick Road. This particular scarecrow is presented as a scapegoat figure when he is set on fire by the Wicked Witch of the West and thus serves as a possible antecedent for Clark and for Jeremy Creek, another Smallville high school student who had previously been humiliated in a similar fashion by the football team. The scarecrow is also a common figure in the horror genre, in part because of its function as a human substitute to scare away crows from the crops, but perhaps because of its link to villainy in the comic book world in the Batman comics[19] and films,[20] where he also functions as an archetype of a Jungian shadow figure.[21] It is this dual dimension of the scarecrow (as victim and villain or "monster") that creates a rich mythic texture in the pilot episode of *Smallville* since the scarecrow is not only embodied through Clark but through the character of Jeremy Creek who seeks revenge upon those responsible for tying him to a stake in a field. The latter initially becomes a victim when he is hit by meteor rocks but is then transformed into a villain or "monster" when he kills the same boys responsible for his suffering. As a human scarecrow, Clark duplicates the earlier image of Jeremy on the cross, which in turn visually duplicates a scarecrow in the cornfield that the young Lex Luthor sees. This pattern of replication functions as a way of reinforcing and transforming the myth of the scapegoat/scarecrow by inspiring "further transformation and interpretation of the myth."[22] This is accomplished visually in the pilot with cinematography that emphasizes the scarecrow motif. A few minutes into the pilot, we see a shot of a crow perched on a post. A rock hits the post and scares away the crow. The agent of this action is presumably the young Lex Luthor who is shown in the next shot. As Lex walks through the cornfield wearing a dark school blazer with the crest of a cross, he hears someone call out, "Help me." He turns, and on the left side of the screen there is a low-angle shot of a faceless scarecrow wearing a red and white flannel shirt. He runs away through the field, falls, and leans against a post. Then he hears someone call out to him. In a separate shot, the camera tilts upward while providing a low-angle shot of Creek, a human scarecrow who has an *S* emblazoned on his chest. Jeremy is also wearing red, and white and brown striped shorts that bear something of a resemblance to the shirt of the earlier scarecrow. Shortly after this sequence, Jeremy and Lex are struck by meteor rocks. This scene with Lex and Jeremy foreshadows a later scene in the pilot when Clark is shown tied to a cross in the cornfield. Like the earlier "scarecrows," he is also shot from a low angle (an angle that often suggests heroism) before Lex frees him. Thus, mythically and visually, he echoes the previous scarecrows through his placement in the sequence of shots that involve Lex's response to another scarecrow experience.[23]

Though he is often reluctant to fulfill his destiny in the early part of the series, Clark assumes the role of mythic savior in multiple ways over the course of ten seasons while still providing a link to contemporary American culture. Joseph Campbell defines the savior aspect of a hero as an essential component: "The main character is a hero or heroine who has found or done something beyond the normal range of achievement and experience. A hero is someone who has given his or her life to something bigger than oneself."[24] He fulfills the role of hero in the physical deeds that he carries out when he uses his superpowers to placate or defeat individuals who would harm others. Many of these individuals are meteor freaks who suggest an element of the monstrous. They also happen to be his peers, but in Clark's case, peer loyalty must be sacrificed because of his commitment to principles that may not be acknowledged by his own age group. This commitment to "something bigger" is not an easy task for a teenager, since studies and parental observations have shown that teenagers often have difficulty looking beyond the self. Despite his superpowers, Clark still exhibits a certain inconsistency that is typical of teenagers and their friendships. One of the key elements of a savior is that he is willing to sacrifice his own needs and even himself to help others. Clark appears to play the role of this kind of hero by convincing himself that he does not reciprocate Lana's feelings for him in part because of his concern for her welfare. He tells Chloe that he worries about Lana's safety if he were to tell her about his true identity. Yet it is important to note that this "sacrifice" of Clark's is not painted without ambiguity. Depending on the perspective, his silence or secrecy surrounding his identity may be viewed as an ultimate form of selfishness or fear of commitment and not as a sign of concern for Lana's welfare. The contemporary viewer is bound to question whether Clark's master narrative of protection or "the engine of secrecy that powers *Smallville*"[25] as a show is actually the one that viewers should endorse. Again and again the series shows how keeping this secret (as well as other secrets) may still endanger the lives of others, thus suggesting that this particular form of sacrifice may not be effective. In addition to providing dramatic intrigue, perhaps the relevance of the code of secrecy in the early seasons of *Smallville* is that it serves as a metaphor for visually depicting the secret lives of teenagers who may share certain kinds of information with some friends, but not with others, as is demonstrated in the first few seasons through the friendship between Clark and Chloe. She knows about his superpowers, while Lana does not, and is therefore in a better position to help Clark.

What may distinguish *Smallville* from earlier iterations of the Superman narratives is just how much saving *Smallville*'s Clark actually requires, and how much screen time is actually allotted to other characters performing the normally exclusive role of savior-hero. While earlier representations of Superman repeatedly address his Achilles' heel (vulnerability around kryptonite), *Smallville*, perhaps because of its serial format,[26] appears to go even further by depicting how other characters visually and narratively perform the role of hero. As a teenager, Clark is regularly presented as the savior who needs help. In the first few seasons, Clark's parents physically and psychologically "save" their son often. They not only move him away from the paralyzing power of kryptonite but also provide parental advice; the latter form of assistance is a standard device in other examples of teen or family television drama, thus reinforcing *Smallville*'s links to realistic social situations. Clark's friends Chloe and Pete also help their friend. These friendships suggest the importance of the group in a high school setting and help promote the idea of the group as hero even though it does not abandon the significance of the single hero as the One. Perhaps this consideration of the heroism of multiple characters is a reflection of the relativism of a postmodern era that supports a shift from centralized systems of power to models that favor decentralization. Rather than creating episodes that rely on the audience's expectation that Superman will step in and provide a predictable rescue (some of his rescues are decidedly anticlimactic), the series often demonstrates how other characters have already stepped in to take his place, albeit temporarily. For example, in the pilot episode, Lex "saves" Clark, who has been strung up like a scarecrow, by taking him down from a wooden post that resembles a "cross"; Clark's fall restores his power since it breaks his "crown of thorns" or Lana's necklace which has a green kryptonite pendant. This scene allows Lex to play the role of hero, a role that he did not assume as a frightened child when he could not help Jeremy Creek. Lex's association with the cornfield suggests a parallel with the Mayan god of maize Hun Hunapu. The latter was depicted as a tonsured god who was decapitated at harvest time.[27] Like the maize gods of mythology who die and are reborn, Lex experiences a kind of death and a subsequent rebirth. When he was struck by meteor rocks, he lost his hair, thus signifying the death of a former self and a transformation into a new Lex. He also experiences a rebirth in the cornfield when he returns to the same cornfield as an adult to save Clark. The image of a resurrected Lex (he was supposedly dead) is again conveyed at the beginning of season ten in the episode aptly called "Lazarus" (2010) when Clark has a vision of the adult Lex wearing a white suit in a cornfield, but in this scene Lex is also presented in the context of the evil that Clark or Kal-El must fight.

Another character who is transformed into a savior figure for a brief period of time is Pete, Clark's best friend from high school. In season seven's "Hero" (2008), Pete returns to Smallville and also acquires special superpowers after eating gum laced with kryptonite. In his words, he finally gets "a taste of what it felt like to be . . . a hero." The transformation is accomplished visually through special effects that show how Pete acquires the power of elasticity. He is able to save Kara (Clark's Kryptonian cousin) from being hurt by a falling speaker at a concert by superextending his arms and moving her out of harm's way. The special power is also captured on a cell phone camera by Jimmy who witnesses this deed at the concert, thus illustrating how *Smallville* includes the socially relevant device of cell phone technology and the now ubiquitous practice of preserving moments with this contemporary device. Clark's response to this new ability is that he wants to find a way to reverse it in an effort to normalize Pete; a version of this conversation could easily be found in a real-life situation when friends who knew one another from a different time and place reunite and have difficulty accepting that their relationship is no longer the same. Pete's response that "things change" applies to this kind of social situation and to the kinds of metamorphoses that are the stuff of myth. After he loses his superpower,[28] Chloe tells Pete that she sees him as a hero because he risked his life to protect her secret—that she is a "meteor freak" with a power. The episode confirms that the definition of savior or hero (as opposed to superhero) does not involve an extreme physical power, but a psychological power: the willingness to save someone else's life.

The role of savior in *Smallville* is assumed by a number of other characters, including Chloe, who saves Clark in a Montreal cathedral in the episode "Quest" (2008) so that he can in turn do the same for others. She also plays a key role in the season ten episode "Collateral" (2011) when she helps move Clark and other heroes (including the Green Arrow) from the virtual reality world back to the "real" world. In the same season's "Lazarus," Lois Lane saves Clark by pulling a blue kryptonite knife out of his body. Even the unlikely figure of Lionel Luther takes his turn at playing hero; Lionel, the archenemy of Jonathan Kent, experiences a shift in character in the series when he claims that his actions are based on an interest in protecting Clark, although Lionel's motives are questionable throughout the series and he eventually returns to his more sinister self. The presence of other "heroes" suggests the relativization of the savior figure in a postmodern, post-9/11 world of contradictions, where it is difficult to conceive of the concept of one person saving humanity from destruction or where the concept of heroism is mutable. Multiple forces are at work in the complex world of the twenty-first century which often resists the idea of a single source of power. Yet despite the number of other heroes that appear in the series, Clark remains as a fairly constant signifier that moves the series along, and when he "disappears," as heroes in myth tend to do (e.g., Odysseus and his seven-year sojourn on Calypso's island), he eventually returns. Even the title of the series (*Smallville*) and the terms "Red-Blue Blur" or "the Blur" seem to suggest a resistance to the iconic power of the Superman name and run the risk of depersonalizing the character of Clark/Kal-El. Yet oddly enough, this depersonalization could be a way of sustaining the mystique traditionally associated with Superman. Unlike earlier series, such as *Lois & Clark: The New Adventures of Superman* (1993–1997), or the *Superman* films, Clark/Kal-El in *Smallville* is not always linked to the human or the superhuman, but to the nonhuman concept of speed ("the Blur"), or in the case of Lois's nickname for Clark, to a place, "Smallville." The series thus tries to navigate between the intimate and the remote, and it is this dramatic and visual shift in the series that is also evident in the reassignment of the hero status to other characters, thus reinforcing the importance of the concept of mythic transformation in *Smallville.*

The show even goes so far as to include characters engaging in a self-conscious discussion of what it means to be a hero within the dialogue of the episodes. In one episode, "Quest," with a Jungian focus, Joseph Campbell is also mentioned:

> *Chloe:* "So, tell me exactly what the article is about."
>
> *Jimmy:* "Well, it's all very Joseph Campbell—hero's journey and all that."

Jimmy then continues with a discussion of symbols, which are also important in the identification of heroes and in the representation of hero envy in relation to Lex: "Apparently Lex is pretty taken with the symbols, too—not surprisingly, since he's wearing one on his chest." Jimmy is here referring to the symbols for savior and traveler that were carved into Lex's chest. His scar evokes the *S* that was painted on Clark in the pilot episode of the series. The marked body can be a key signifier of heroic status: a birthmark or a scar is often one sign of identification that can facilitate recognition of the hero. This certainly applies to the Greek hero Odysseus whose nursemaid identified him when he was disguised,[29] or to a character like Harry Potter, whose battle scar on his face becomes equated with heroism since he survived a battle with the dark force known as Voldemort. In these examples, the scarred body would seem to enable mythic, heroic significance. However, in Lex's case, the symbols appear to function as a kind of mimicry since even when he does assist others, he often has questionable motives for doing so; he is, after all, a key villain in the series who replicates his own monstrosity by creating clones of himself.

The Monstrous and the Social

In *Smallville*, the role of the hero is often intimately linked with the monstrous, the alien, or the concept of the freak. Joseph Campbell has stated that the hero often contains the monster within himself or herself: "the ultimate dragon is within you, it is your ego clamping you down."[30] The mythic hero is also a mythic monster, and more often than not, this monster is representative of the monster within the self and represents a character's struggle with otherness or alienation. While the savior myth is a key component of the series, the mythic image of transformation is illustrated more graphically through the depiction of the monstrous or alien other, which allows the series to reflect on the social issues of youth/ teenage angst and desire, particularly in the first few seasons of *Smallville*. Clark is after all an alien presence, and much of his teenage anxiety revolves around his abilities, which he cannot control. Clark's desirable superhuman abilities (e.g., helping to lift heavy machinery on the Kent farm) shift from enhanced abilities to examples of monstrous difference, excess, and unbridled teenage desire. The images of the monstrous become a metaphor for male adolescence and hormonal fluctuations. As Miles Millar, one of the show's creators, has stated, "super powers are just like puberty. They sort of show up one day, and at first, they're rather scary and he can't always control them."[31] For example, in the episode "Heat" (2002), when Clark's heat vision burns a hole in a movie projection screen during his viewing of a biology film, he is presented as a dangerous, godlike force similar to the gods of Greek mythology who express their lust or power. Fire has associations with Hephaestus, the god of fire, who ejaculated on the earth (the goddess Gaia) after he attempted to rape Athena. The destructive power of eyes is reminiscent of the deadly gaze of a figure like Medusa whose gaze was able to turn people to stone. Clark is understandably terrified by his lack of control. The entire episode may be viewed as a metaphor for sexual urges and the sexual education of Clark. For example, his father, Jonathan Kent, has a man-to-man talk with Clark about how to control these feelings. It is significant that in later seasons during Clark's ongoing relationship with Lana, the only time he does not worry about his superhuman strength and identity in the sexual context is when Lana herself becomes a meteor "freak" in the episode "Wrath" (2007) and is transformed into someone with special powers. Fast-motion photography and special effects are used to show them depart to have sex, and their amorous activity causes earthquakes in the Smallville area. This echoes a mythic relationship between a godlike power and earthquakes (Poseidon was the Greek god of earthquakes) while at the same time suggesting a particularly memorable, "earth-shattering" act of consummation for a young couple. Since the relationship between Clark and Lana has been equalized in this instance, they do not appear monstrous to one another; however, for Chloe, Lana's transformation appears to be an example of the monstrous since it is a disruption of the norm. Chloe appears more comfortable when Clark and Lana's relationship is defined by their *inability* to relate to one another as equals.

Because the series presents the mythic experience as a wider social experience and not just the experience of the hero, other characters (like Lana) also experience the monstrous in their lives, and the images become a means of discussing the hopes and fears of teenagers in general. Representations of the alien or monstrous in the *Smallville* narrative that are the result of a mythic-like transformation include the representation of "meteor freaks"—individuals who have been altered as a result of contact with green kryptonite. Those who acquire special physical abilities also develop changed identities that accompany these physical changes, and these changes are generally an extension of some form of teenage angst and the expression of sexual desire. One of the key episodes to address the topic of transformation in an explicit manner is "Metamorphosis." In this narrative, Greg, a collector of insects, is enamored with Lana. One day he is attacked by his insects that become coated with green kryptonite; as a result, he is transformed into a "spider-man" who has the ability to make webs and whose other senses are heightened. As Eric Rabkin argues in the case of mythic or fantastic metamorphoses, the physical change is just an extension of a psychological trait that has been resident in the individual all along. Greg is a stalker in the physical and in the psychological sense, and his transformation into a spider-man only reinforces this. In the Ovidian tale of Arachne, for example, Arachne's renown in the art of weaving is reiterated in her transformation into a spider, a creature that creates webs that arc works of art.

> Then, going off, she [Minerva] sprinkled her with juice,
> Which leaves of baneful aconite produce.

Touch'd with the pois'nous drug, her flowing hair
Fell to the ground, and left her temples bare;
Her usual features vanish'd from their place,
Her body lessen'd all, but most her face.
Her slender fingers, hanging on each side
With many joynts, the use of legs supply'd:
A spiders bag the rest, from which she gives
A thread, and still by constant weaving lives.[32]

It is worth noting that Arachne's transformation is accomplished through a similar means as Greg's—through contact with a "pois'nous drug." In her case it is aconite; in Greg's it is kryptonite that turns him into a monstrous creature. The spiderlike creature that Greg has become can be viewed as vampiric and thus evokes the many examples from telefantasy and film that present the predatory aspect of teenage boys infatuated with a particular girl. Greg's murder of his own mother is also an extreme act that symbolizes the escalation of parent-teenager conflicts experienced by many families as parents witness the metamorphosis of their children into the child/adult hybrid more commonly referred to as "a teenager." It is worth noting that in their audio commentary for this particular episode, Gough and Millar point out how important it was for the character of Greg (Chad E. Donella) to be "real" or authentic, and they agreed that the actor certainly brought this element to his performance.

An example of monstrous identity in a feminine form is presented in the first-season episode "Craving" (2001). Jodi Melville is a girl who eats kryptonite-laced vegetables and manages to lose weight, but she must feed on the fat of people in order to satisfy her ravenous appetite. The parallel to myth can be found in many examples of world mythology that highlight monstrous, cannibalistic appetite such as the story of the Cyclops, the man-eating creature in Homer's *Odyssey*, or the African tale, "The Eye of the Giant,"[33] about a man who unwittingly consumes his siblings. The pervasive myth of the vampire that inundates contemporary culture (especially through the influence of the telefantasy *Buffy the Vampire Slayer*) also reinforces this concept of excess, perhaps because "appetite" is such a basic part of human experience. Yet Jodi's excessive hunger also resonates in a more contemporary way because it is a reflection of the contemporary social battle many teenagers—the majority of whom (85 to 90 percent) tend to be girls—wage against eating disorders such as anorexia nervosa or bulimia.[34]

The character Greg in "Metamorphosis" and the cannibalistic woman in "Craving" are clearly monstrous figures and not heroes, even though they may aspire to that category of an unattainable image of perfection that one associates with heroic endeavor. Greg may see himself as Lana's Prince Charming, and Jodi aspires to an unattainable ideal of bodily perfection, but their actions are primarily destructive. This distinction between hero and monster is often evident in the early part of *Smallville*'s run, but it is a distinction that is blurred as the series develops. In a sense, this telefantasy series is similar to a television program like *Buffy the Vampire Slayer*, which Catherine Johnson has described as a series that "constructs a narrative structure that allows it to combine repetition and change."[35] A character in *Smallville* whose body suggests the monstrous (like the previous characters in the early part of the series), but who does have some heroic qualities, is John Corben/Metallo. He is introduced in season nine, in the first episode called "Savior" (2009). However, his transformation is not animal or plant based like the meteor mutants Greg and Jodi; he has a different kind of hybrid identity since his transformation involves the union of the organic and the technological in the form of a green kryptonite mechanical heart that is fused with his skin, thus making him a cyborg. According to Donna Haraway, the cyborg is a powerful "myth."[36] The immediate parallel in a human, medical context would probably be a pacemaker (the union of the human and the machine), but John Corben also reflects generation Y's or the millennial generation's use of technology as an extension of their being. And yet the spiderlike appearance of John Corben's kryptonite heart still reminds us of *Smallville*'s past images of transformed human beings, including the buglike character of Greg in "Metamorphosis" who was obsessed with Lana, thus illustrating how *Smallville* creates its own mythic structure that repeats and refashions the monstrous.

The visual prominence of John's heart (its fluorescent green color and the fact that he wears his heart on the outside of his body) emphasizes the domain of desire. John wears his heart on his sleeve, so to speak, and it therefore seems fitting that he makes his romantic feelings for Lois Lane known to her in "Upgrade" (2010). However, the conspicuousness of the kryptonite heart combined with its spiderlike appearance as a visual dominant (in the context of mise-en-scène centrality) also symbolizes a monstrous form of excess and unpredictability that can easily transgress boundaries. It is significant that his monstrous appearance is also linked to Clark's transformation in this episode since the latter is transformed as a result of his encounter with red kryptonite. When Clark makes contact with red kryptonite in "Upgrade," he gives in to irrational impulses. John Corben, who had engaged in battle with Clark on a previous occasion, actually ends up "saving" Clark. He stabs Clark with a shard of green kryptonite, telling him that sometimes people do not know when they need to be saved. He does this in order to counter the effects of red kryptonite in Clark's system. Red kryptonite turns Clark into a kind of monster with violent and amoral impulses. His eyes glow red as the kryptonite enters his bloodstream; the coursing of the kryptonite through his veins visually suggests that he has transformed into a demon.

Not surprisingly, John's intervention in "Upgrade" is much like the kind of intervention that is often necessary for individuals who are addicted to drugs, and so the mythic image of the monster serves as an appropriate metaphor for the dangers of addiction. The two characters are therefore linked through their respective metamorphoses. The monstrous appears to be equated with some kind of villainy, but ironically one monster can actually be used to "kill" another, and thus becomes a savior in the process; this is what happens when John saves Clark: the green kryptonite, which is normally Clark's worst fear, cancels out the negative effects of red kryptonite. By juxtaposing different forms of the monstrous and different kinds of saviors, the series builds on the ancient notion that saviors or "monsters" may take the most unlikely of forms—Clark, the alien boy who fell from the sky, or John Corben, the cyborg with a heart of green. The blending of a savior with the monstrous takes the notion of mythic metamorphosis in a new direction even as this combination retains vestiges of ancient myth. Yet while ancient myths and the series *Smallville* may suggest the desire for heroes to defeat the monster within, *Smallville* also repeatedly articulates the need to transform the self in an age of shifting technological and social boundaries.

In his analysis of the film *Superman Returns* (2006), Matt Yockey argues that "the film uses intertextuality and self-reflexivity in order to express continuity with the past as well as the promise of change" and is consistent with what "Umberto Eco sees as instrumental to the appeal of

Superman texts."[37] It is not surprising, therefore, that a character's metamorphosis in *Smallville* can suggest parallels with contemporary American society while also evoking ancient myth. While the Superman myth in previous "texts" (e.g., comic books, films) is one component of this developing myth, references to non-Superman films (e.g., *The Wizard of Oz)*, television shows, or literature also contribute to the mythic intertextuality and intervisuality in *Smallville.* In the tenth-season episode "Harvest" (2010), Lois is almost killed by a group of villagers who believe that her sacrifice will ensure a plentiful harvest. The link between sacrifice and harvest is a key component of ancient myths, but this episode also draws attention to the show's relationship to other examples of film that incorporate mythic imagery. When Lois tells Clark to speed them "away from these children of the corn," the show not only highlights the importance of the savior and his connection to the cornfield, but also emphasizes how its characters may be just as aware of film (e.g., the original *Children of the Corn* and its sequels) or horror "texts" (e.g., Stephen King's short story "Children of the Corn," 1977) as its viewers, thus cementing the relationship between the reality of the characters and that of *Smallville*'s fans who may be avid viewers of other kinds of telefantasy (e.g., *Buffy the Vampire Slayer*) or genre film. *Smallville* also includes references back to its own narrative universe, thus creating its own unique mythic past through this embedded self-referentiality and images of transformation. When Zod tells Clark in season nine that he is no longer the farm boy from Smallville, this suggests the self-conscious aspect of the series reflecting on itself as an ancient, mythic text while also alluding to Dorothy's line from *The Wizard of Oz*: "We're not in Kansas anymore." The visual techniques of cinematography such as the replication of low-angle shots in the scarecrow/savior sequences in the pilot episode highlight this relationship that incorporates the static and the transformative, the familiar and the unknown. Television series can facilitate this kind of duality of being in the moment yet beyond the moment because of television's interconnectedness with other visual media.

Television programs thus have some elements of self-containment, but they also have a relationship to other television programs. This relationship has been described in the context of the "flow" of television: the positioning and scheduling of programs in relation to other programs. However, because of the transformation of television into a DVD product and into a media phenomenon interlinked with online culture, other kinds of intervisual and intertextual relationships are now possible. The continuity of a television serial like *Smallville* reinforces the duality of stability and change that the serial form appears to facilitate. But, even outside the constraints of *Smallville*'s broadcast television format, in its DVD manifestation and through its online presence, *Smallville* as a television series can generate its own mythos and social network, in addition to any connections it may have to earlier Superman narratives or ancient myths. For example, bonus features on various *Smallville* DVDs include documentaries about the show and a *Smallville* digital comic book; these "extras" extend the mythic universe of the series proper and offer a host of connections for consumers while still containing the scope of these connections. In other words, these DVD features replicate and proliferate the myth of *Smallville*, creating a social environment for its audience that imitates the mythic/social interaction within the series itself. This allows *Smallville* to remake myths for a generation of viewers who live in the rapidly changing world of the twenty-first century, while still acknowledging the mythic past, whether that past takes the form of earlier moments in the series or characters and their stories of difference in world mythology.

Notes

1. Eric S. Rabkin, *Fantastic Worlds* (Oxford: Oxford University Press, 1979), 24.

2. Catherine Johnson, *Telefantasy* (London: British Film Institute, 2005), 2.

3. Johnson, *Telefantasy*, 4.

4. Lincoln Geraghty, *Living with Star Trek: American Culture and the Star Trek Universe* (London: I. B. Tauris, 2007), 56–57.

5. Catherine Johnson discusses the importance of seriality in the telefantasy *Buffy the Vampire Slayer* and notes that "it becomes increasingly difficult to distinguish between the one-off and continuing narrative strands within each episode of *Buffy the Vampire Slayer* as the single episode plot devices become inextricably bound up with the continuing narratives." *Telefantasy*, 116.

6. Shawn Shimpach describes Clark as "a sensitive young man with identity issues" (115) and as a "typical WB teen" (108), thus highlighting *Smallville*'s presentation of "Superman" as an American teenager in the context of what it means to be a teenager in WB television shows. Shawn Shimpach, "Smallville: 'No Flights, No Tights'; Doing Business with Superman," in *Television in Tran-*

sition: The Life and Afterlife of the Narrative Action Hero (Malden, MA: Wiley-Blackwell, 2010).

7. Alan Dundes, *Sacred Narrative: Readings in the Theory of Myth* (Berkeley and Los Angeles: University of California Press, 1984), 6.

8. William Bascom, "The Forms of Folklore: Prose Narratives," in *Sacred Narrative: Readings in the Theory of Myth*, ed. Alan Dundes, 5–29 (Berkeley and Los Angeles: University of California Press, 1984), 9.

9. Umberto Eco and Natalie Chilton, "Review: The Myth of Superman," *Diacritics* 2, no. 1 (Spring 1972): 15.

10. Eco and Chilton, "The Myth of Superman," 16.

11. Debra Moddelmog, *Readers and Mythic Signs: The Oedipus Myth in Twentieth-Century Fiction* (Carbondale: Southern Illinois University, 1993), 4.

12. See Rabkin, *Fantastic Worlds*.

13. Geraghty, *Living with Star Trek*, 58.

14. Geraghty, *Living with Star Trek*, 57.

15. Tom Douglas, *Basic Groupwork* (London and New York: Routledge, 2000), 92. See also Douglas's book *Scapegoats: Transferring Blame* (London and New York: Routledge, 1995) for further discussion of scapegoats in society.

16. The cover of the DVD box set of the first season of *Smallville* depicts the *S* emblazoned on Clark Kent in the cornfield, bound to a post.

17. See Alyson R. Peluso, "Hazing in Sports: The Effects and Legal Ramifications," *The Sport Journal* 9, no. 1 (2006), http://www.thesportjournal.org/article/hazing-sports-effects-and-legal-ramifications (accessed 31 March 2011).

18. Roger Welsch, *Seasons on the Farm: A Celebration of Country Life through the Year* (St. Paul, MN: MBI Publishing, 2007), 88.

19. Julian Darius, *Batman Begins and the Comics* (Raleigh, NC: Lulu Press, 2005), 63–65.

20. In the film *Batman Begins* (2005), four years after the *Smallville* pilot episode, the Scarecrow appears as a villain wearing a frightening mask made of stitched burlap.

21. Lawrence C. Rubin, *Using Superheroes in Counseling and Play Therapy* (New York: Springer Publishing, 2007), 80.

22. Moddelmog, *Readers and Mythic Signs*, 4.

23. Jes Battis provides another socially relevant reading of the scarecrow episode when he states that a queer viewer might be particularly aware of "the murder of Matthew Shepherd, a gay teen who was fatally beaten, tied to a fence, and then left to die in a similarly rural area outside of Laramie, Wyoming. Shepherd's death, in 1998, occurred just three years prior to the debut of *Smallville* in 2001, and although the majority of the show's audience may have conveniently forgotten about the Shepherd case by then, most queer spectators could not possibly

have." Jes Battis, "The Kryptonite Closet: Silence and Queer Secrecy in *Smallville,*" *Jump Cut: A Review of Contemporary Media* 48 (Winter 2006), http://www.ejumpcut.org/archive/jc48.2006/gaySmallville/index.html (accessed 31 March 2011). Reprinted in this volume.

24. Joseph Campbell, *Power of Myth* (New York: Anchor Books, 1991), 151.

25. Battis, "The Kryptonite Closet."

26. There is even a recently published comic book (Super DC Heroes) by Paul Kupperberg called *The Kid Who Saved Superman* (Mankato, MN: Stone Arch Books, 2010).

27. Robert J. Sharer and Loa P. Traxler, *The Ancient Maya World* (Palo Alto, CA: Stanford University Press, 2005), 729.

28. The temporary transformations in *Smallville* appear to be a modern departure from transformation myths found in classical cultures: many transformations in Ovid's *Metamorphoses* are permanent or irreversible. For example, the myth of Narcissus involves the transformation of a man into a flower, and Arachne, a famous weaver, becomes a spider. *Smallville* regularly appears to undermine the ancient mythic significance of the true savior by presenting other saviors. However, by making the superpowers acquired by other heroes only "temporary," as in Pete's case, the series is able to return to Clark's role as the key savior.

29. In his *Poetics* (chapter 16), Aristotle mentions the recognition of Odysseus's scar by the nurse and swineherds as an example of the least artistic kind of recognition since he considers this inferior to the kind of recognition that results from an unraveling of events as in the tragedy *Oedipus Rex.*

30. Campbell, *The Power of Myth*, 184.

31. Cited in Hal Hinson, "Getting to the Heart of a Hero," *New York Times,* 27 January 2002, 10.

32. Ovid, *Metamorphoses*, http://classics.mit.edu/Ovid/metam.6.sixth.html (accessed 31 March 2011).

33. See "The Eye of the Giant," in Rabkin, *Fantastic Worlds*, 53–55.

34. "Bulimia Nervosa," *Womenshealth.gov*, 2009, http://www.womenshealth.gov/faq/bulimia-nervosa.cfm (accessed 31 March 2011).

35. Johnson, *Telefantasy*, 117.

36. Donna Haraway, "A Cyborg Manifesto: Science, Technology, and Socialist-Feminism in the Late Twentieth Century," in *Simians, Cyborgs and Women: The Reinvention of Nature* (New York: Routledge, 1991), 149–181.

37. Matt Yockey, "Somewhere in Time: Utopia and the Return of Superman," *The Velvet Light Trap* 61 (Spring 2008): 26.

CHAPTER THREE

THE KRYPTONITE CLOSET: SILENCE AND QUEER SECRECY IN *SMALLVILLE*

Jes Battis

> "Closetedness" itself is a performance initiated as such by the speech act of a silence—not a particular silence, but a silence that accrues particularity by fits and starts, in relation to the discourse that surrounds and differentially constitutes it.[1]

> Clark: It's just an allegory, Lex. "Talisman" (2004).

Smallville is a show about secrets and silences. Its multiple narrative threads depend upon a vast and thriving network of lies, secrets, deferrals, misrepresentations, backward glances, and half-truths—all of which coalesce, in one way or another, around the character of Clark Kent. Clark's personal secrets become a vitiating force within the show, a force beyond his control, which expands to adversely affect his friends, family, and loved ones. Furthermore, it seems that the more Clark attempts to conceal about himself, the more he puts those people closest to him in routinely life-threatening danger.

Although *Smallville* appears to revolve around one "big" secret—Clark's identity as an alien from the planet Krypton—this actually depends upon a much more complicated discourse of secrets, a web of competing speech acts that transform and distend Clark's own supercloset into an array of silences that actually come to define a whole constellation

This chapter was originally published in *Jump Cut: A Review of Contemporary Media* 48 (Winter 2006), http://www.ejumpcut.org/archive/jc48.2006/gaySmallville/text.html (accessed 5 April 2011).

of identities for him. Kryptonite, as the title of this chapter suggests, is an intimate part of Clark's own state of closetedness—it is the opposite side of his extraterrestrial secret, the secret of his sole weakness that he must obscure at all costs. It is difficult, then, if not impossible, to separate Clark from his secrets, or to determine the invisible lines that divide Clark the teenager from Clark the alien. But the character who most often attempts to invoke this act of separation—who frequently and sometimes violently attempts to rip Clark's secrets out of the private realm—is none other than his closest friend, Lex Luthor.

I intend, in this chapter, to read the relationship between Clark and Lex as one that is rich with possibilities (both erotic and ideological). I am particularly interested in the erotic potential emerging from this relationship, with Clark's eroticism rooted in pastoral traditions, and in Lex's eroticism emerging from urbanity. I am not a historian searching for empirical proof of same-sex desire. By the same token, I agree with Rictor Norton's caveat within queer studies that "the critic of 'homosexual literature' is under no special obligation to be an expert sleuth in detecting erotic innuendo."[2] What I do want is to discuss the spectrum of really fascinating ways in which the Clark/Lex relationship has been rewritten by *Smallville*, transformed from the traditional antagonistic pairing between hero and villain that *Superman* comic lovers recognize,[3] to a far more ambiguous friendship between two highly secretive and vulnerable men.

That *Smallville* is often cited as a "family" show continues to surprise me, given its routine depictions of violence, sexuality, horror elements, murders, drugs, damning family secrets, and attractive, seminaked teen bodies. The whiteness, heterosexuality, and alleged "wholesomeness"[4] of those bodies is what, in all probability, manages to give *Smallville* its reputation as a family-friendly television program. But the show does, in fact, possess what I think can be easily read as much more subversive elements. In fact, it is *Smallville*'s very innocuous nature as a family-oriented, *Dawson's Creek* (1998–2003) like program that gives it an unexpected potential for reversing stereotypes and destabilizing some familiar oppressions on television.

Smallville's setting within a close-knit, rural Kansas town (which is actually Cloverdale, BC, less than an hour from downtown Vancouver) makes it a sort of remediation of pastoral traditions. It is an ideal site for visually renovating what was once a preeminent English literary form (and which remains a unique genre for expressing social anarchy while cloaking that anarchy through careful anachronism and the invocation of golden ages "now passed away"). Several prime-time shows have emerged within the last few years that utilize the nostalgic image of the small town in order to create an ideal site of secrecy and betrayal, including *Dawson's Creek*, as well as more recent offerings such as *One Tree Hill* (2003–Present) and *Everwood* (2002–2006). What all of these shows have in common is their depiction of white, attractive, able-bodied, and heterosexual characters, all ostensibly chaffing at their own small-town ideologies, while more accurately using their disaffection as an excuse to have lots of sex with each other.[5]

What makes *Smallville* different is its unique celebration of the pastoral, its connection of Clark's life as a farm boy with his own superior moral development, and its continuing valorization of his parents' indestructible marriage (as opposed to the various broken-family models from which his friends have emerged). Other shows celebrate only the close-knit friendships that often emerge within small towns, while reinscribing the towns themselves as dens of entertaining emotional dysfunction. In contrast, *Smallville* actually celebrates the physical site of the town as an alternative to the morally suspect realm of Metropolis, which looms less than three hours away (or a few minutes away if, like Clark, you have superspeed).

Clark's character becomes inextricably tied to images of farm life and domestic happiness, sharing traditional bacon-and-eggs breakfasts with his loving family on the Kent farm, just as Lex becomes inescapably associated with the broken promises, crime syndicates, and suspect financial dealings of Metropolis. As comic book characters, these two have always been iconic. But *Smallville* does its best to complicate that iconicity by insisting simultaneously that Clark and Lex can never be wholly "normal," yet they can never be completely allegorical, either. If *Smallville* exists at all, it is because *Lois & Clark: The New Adventures of Superman* (1993–1997) paved the way for it, bringing the Superman myth "down to earth," so to speak, by exploring the fraught romantic relationship between Lois Lane and Clark Kent. The show's placement of "Lois" before "Clark" seemed to augur a surprising and welcome narrative emphasis on Lois Lane, but spectators soon came to realize that this was a show very much about "being" Clark Kent. While *Lois & Clark* explored the tension between living as both Clark Kent and Superman, *Smallville* set out to explore the pre-Superman years instead, the angst-ridden existence of Superman as an adolescent.

Clark's problems on *Smallville* are legion: he is gorgeous, white, athletic, surrounded by loyal friends, the product of a loving and supportive family, the confidante of a young billionaire (Lex), and the love object of two women, Lana Lang and Chloe Sullivan. *Smallville* attempts to defuse this privilege by claiming that it is meaningless, or at the very least complicated, since Clark has to keep secrets from the people closest to him. But spectators who do not have billionaire friends (or supportive families) must suspect that Clark still has an eerily perfect life for a self-proclaimed outcast. We have to keep in mind, however, that *Smallville* has a highly powerful and enduring originary text with which to contend—a superhero myth that it can adapt but not irrevocably change. Clark Kent in *Smallville* has to be pretty, white, and straight, because Clark Kent within the Superman comics is pretty, white, and straight. And being pretty, white, and straight is an oppressive prerequisite for most popular television shows in North America. Once *Smallville* fulfills this prerequisite (which itself needs to be continually challenged by media critics with strong political investments, and which I am challenging here), it is then free to place its characters in a broad array of situations that trouble or threaten their own systems of privilege. Rather than upbraiding *Smallville* for being so much like other shows aesthetically, I am more interested in looking at what it tries to do (and sometimes does accidentally) in terms of actually challenging televisual stereotypes.

Structurally, *Smallville* owes a lot to previous shows that have been acclaimed as "transgressive," such as *Buffy the Vampire Slayer* (1997–2003) and *The X-Files* (1993–2002). It attempts to incorporate much of the rapid-fire and linguistically inventive dialogue that made *Buffy* famous, although Chloe is the only character who really talks enough within the show to pull this off. And her delivery is often so rapid-fire that spectators can miss the cleverness of what she's saying (or not saying, or trying to say). While *Buffy* thrived on complex dialogic relations, *Smallville* thrives on what isn't said, what gets left out, the blanks and dark spaces that its characters carefully step around. As such, it can never really be as "hip" as other shows because it isn't actually trying to be hip—it's trying to be allegorical. The pilot episode actually conveys a great deal of disturbingly gothic imagery, including the sight of Clark

Kent strung up in a cornfield, cataclysmic meteors crashing into the town, and a teenage villain who returns to his old school (Smallville High), *Carrie* (1976) style, to enact electrical vengeance on the kids who once tortured him. The image of Clark as a scarecrow is a great deal more troubling than it first seems. For queer viewers, this can bring back memories of the murder of Matthew Shepherd, a gay teen who was fatally beaten, tied to a fence, and then left to die in a similarly rural area outside of Laramie, Wyoming. Shepherd's death, in 1998, occurred just three years prior to the debut of *Smallville* in 2001, and although the majority of the show's audience may have conveniently forgotten about the Shepherd case by then, most queer spectators could not possibly have. The result is a peculiar hijacking of real hate-crime imagery, the adaptation (whether unconscious on the part of the writers or not) of an actual murder in order to create as disturbing an image as possible. Most online discussion of this episode reads the Clark/scarecrow image as a crucifixion, and hence a presage of his eventual salvific potential as Superman. I think, however, that it needs to be read as a profoundly disturbing mixture of both.

At its heart, and despite its many missteps, *Smallville* is just as critical and interrogative as shows like *Buffy* and *The X-Files*, although it is not always as well written, and not always as successful in its various interrogations of American ideological practices. Like other shows that draw upon the gothic tradition, it suggests that there is something highly sinister lying beneath the foundations of middle America, beneath the conservative rural core of the countryside, rotting out its Fordist assumptions like a ravenous macrophage. Beneath the town of Smallville lies a cache of radioactive material, kryptonite,[6] which has the power to mutate normal human development (and contributes to the town's skyrocketing mortality rate). Less visibly, *Smallville* itself subsists upon a diet of secrets and lies, of failed relationships and obscured realities, of empty promises, twisted sentiments, and powerful etiolations (to use an Austinian term, which means literally "withering"[7]) of the social interactions that should produce "truth." In this sense, we need to see the show not just as another pretty white offering within the WB lineup (which also gave us *Buffy*), or as a "gothic lite" program like Aaron Spelling's *Charmed* (1998–2006), but as a show that gestures to an American mythology composed almost entirely of secrecy and deception.

With this framework for looking at *Smallville* in place, let us now turn to the relationship between Clark and Lex, upon which so many of the show's narratives depend. It is a bit unusual to find a science fiction show (although *Smallville* fits more under Darko Suvin's heading of "science fantasy": a mixture of the speculative elements of SF with the mythological elements of fantasy) that focuses so intensely on a friendship between two men.[8] Although most mainstream science fiction texts have a male hero pitted against a male villain, few explore the conflicted relationship from which their mutual antagonism must emerge. *Smallville* operates on several overlapping principles of dramatic irony, because it depends upon its audiences to know the backstory between Clark and Lex. What makes their relationship even more complicated is the spectatorial foreknowledge that they will eventually become bitter enemies. Unlike *Lois & Clark*, which had Clark and Lex opposed to each other from the very first episode, *Smallville* is more interested in exploring what first brought these characters together rather than what will someday tear them apart. When Lex, after saving the Kent farm from financial ruin, says in "Phoenix" (2003) "I just hope you'll consider me part of the family," audiences are left to wonder how a surrogate member of Clark's own family could possibly turn against him. Lex himself seems to understand his fatalistic role as the show's antagonist, even as he tries daily to fight it. When Clark asks why their friendship is so important (in the aptly named episode "Devoted" [2004]), Lex's reply is somewhat enigmatic: "There's a darkness in me that I can't always control. . . . I can feel [it] creeping over the corners. Your friendship helps keep it at bay."

Although Clark never explicitly states it thus, he seems to trust Lex, to continually renew his friendship with the troubled young billionaire, because he sees an opportunity to morally recuperate Lex; and Lex seems to be looking for just that kind of moral recuperation from Clark. Although Lex is older by about six years, Clark is the one who appears to be educating him. Yet Lex is also educating Clark, just as a Machiavellian prince might educate his naive young pupil in the ways of cynical society. Both projects, if they are that, seem doomed to fail, since we all know that Lex eventually turns on Clark, and that Clark never exhibits the urbane cynicism, nor the alacrity of self-expression, that Lex is famous for. What we don't know, and what we may never know entirely, is why this happens, and by what complicated circumstances these characters' relationship is so radically and irreversibly transformed.

The Clark/Lex friendship begins with a bang when Lex, speeding as usual, hits Clark with his Porsche (going eighty miles per hour) and both of them tumble off a bridge in "Pilot" (2001). Their first interaction is not verbal at all, but entirely physical. Clark rescues Lex, of course, by peeling open the youth's car like a can of tuna—a feat that Lex spends the next three years trying to explain, since Clark later denies that it ever happened. In fact, Clark makes a regular habit of saving Lex from various threatening forces, so much so that Lex himself becomes more of a damsel in distress than either Lana or Chloe. Although Lana is often Clark's primary "savee," Lex requires a sort of multilayered saving, since Clark is constantly trying to rescue him from both physical and moral peril. And it strikes me as profoundly interesting that, although it takes Clark the entire first season of *Smallville* before he ever dares to kiss Lana, he kisses Lex in the very first episode. Granted, he is performing artificial respiration, but this is still, arguably, the show's very first kiss between two principal characters. And it remains rare, except on a program like *ER* (1994–2009) or *Baywatch* (1989–2001), to see a man resuscitating another man.

Lex assumes the role of patron shortly after this event when he tries to give Clark a new car in return for saving his life. This system of exchange, Lex's money (and other financial resources) for Clark's love and attention, becomes a dominant marker within their relationship, continually reframing them as partners within a fiduciary contract rather than merely as best friends. In fact, it is the character of Pete who most often refers to himself as Clark's best friend, although Chloe claims this position as well.[9] Lex, we must assume, is something different. Even as late as the fourth season, Clark is still trying to explain to Lex that their friendship does not exist solely within these financial parameters. When Lex buys new uniforms for the Smallville Crows football team in "Devoted" (2004) (branded, interestingly enough, with the Luthorcorp logo, just as the stadium itself is branded somewhat transparently by Old Spice), Clark tells Lex that "you can't buy back my friendship." Yet Clark sounds more long-suffering than exasperated when he says this, as if he is merely going through the discursive motions by scolding Lex for his pragmatic understanding of the world. It is difficult to determine whether Clark simply trusts in Lex too

Lex and Clark confer in Smallville *(2001–2011). Credit: Warner Bros. TV and the Kobal Collection.*

much to really cut him out of his life, or if, as Lex hopes, Clark's friendship truly is so thoroughly implicated within their own system of patronage that it really is for sale.

The paranoiac bonds within *Smallville* (and particularly those between Clark and Lex) emerge from the closed-in conditions of the town itself. Although Smallville is surrounded by untapped pastoral wilderness, as exemplified by the pioneering Kent farmers, the *town* of Smallville is an anxious fusion of pastoral and urban that produces both nostalgic and dystopic reactions from its citizens. They are in love with the close-knit atmosphere of Smallville, yet constantly straining against its boundaries and trying to penetrate into the wilderness beyond.[10]

Lex originally comes to Smallville because he has been exiled there by his father, Lionel Luthor. Lionel tells him, "Caesars would send their sons to the furthermost corners of the empire so they could get an appreciation of how the world works," but Lex is unimpressed at having to manage his father's fertilizer plant in Smallville, which he calls the "crap factory" in "Hothead" (2001). This grounding of Lex within classical metaphors—the emperor's son being exiled, the fierce Oedipal relationship between father and son, and Lex's very name, which is short for Alexander (the

Great)—only serves to cement his role as the liberal-humanist influence on farm boy Clark. It also serves to align Lex's own avarice and well-honed sense of pragmatism with his "Renaissance man" education, while aligning Clark's naiveté with his purity as a pastoral laborer. The primary antagonists within Smallville, Lex and Lionel, both have a firm grounding in classical and Renaissance scholarship, whereas even Chloe has a hard time keeping her Greek myths straight and prefers to rely on her "reporter's instinct" for empirical truth rather than on mythological allegories.

But Lex is not simply a walking allegory (although, as the quote that I began this chapter with suggests, there are all sorts of important allegories within *Smallville*). If we want to stay within the classical tradition, then his shortened name, *Lex*, is also a version of the Latinate word for "language." Lex himself is a word, and a word that is constantly being renovated and redacted, always changing, submitting to the ethical/editorial attempts of Clark and his friends. Lex is not simply the conquering figure of Alexander the Great, just as Clark is not simply Kal-El, who is "sent to conquer" by his biological father Jor-El as revealed in "Rosetta" (2003). Lex, through a relationship of patronage that constantly wanders into the territory of erotic friendship, is in effect trying to teach Clark a new *lexia*, a new language, which will modify his wide-eyed and unfailingly optimistic view of the world outside of Smallville. Or he is trying to replace Clark's language with his own, to mold Clark into a utilizable tool. Either way, it is more a question of translation, and less a question of conquering. And if Clark is the only person who can keep Lex's darkness at bay, it remains to be seen why Lex—if he is, indeed, a conqueror—would wish to constrain that darkness in the first place, rather than embracing it as Lionel has.

This coding of Lex as a Renaissance aesthete, and as Clark's cultural educator, also situates him within a queer symbolic tradition that has long been adapted through both classical and pastoral literary modes. Stephen Guy-Bray, in *Homoerotic Space*, observes, "Both Latin and Greek literature provided the educated men of the Renaissance with knowledge about various kinds of homoeroticism . . . [and] many Renaissance writers used classical models to construct their own homoerotic discourses."[11] Although, as Eve Sedgwick insists, we are told "Don't ask; You shouldn't know; It didn't happen"[12] when looking at homoeroticism within premodern literature, the simple fact is that classical myth provides a vast storehouse of queer imagery that cannot simply be written off as "fraternal," or worse, as "pre-homosexual," since homosexuality "did not exist" prior to its inaugural citation during the nineteenth century. Although homosexuality may not have existed as a specific category, same-sex desire has existed for as long as we have historically recorded any type of erotic relationship. And it has existed, at various times, as a constitutive force *for* heterosexuality, or in definitional partnership with it, rather than simply as a transgressive force opposed to it.

I am not saying that Lex's alignment with classical literary models renders him queer by default. But it does situate him within a tradition that has historically (and often covertly) transmitted queer expression, particularly by fixing the male body in a desiring gaze. Clark's queerness, on the other hand, emerges from the pastoral tradition, which Guy-Bray characterizes as a "safe, because carefully demarcated, zone in which homoeroticism can appear."[13] The pastoral poet can express a potentially legible queer desire because s/he is talking about a "golden age" now passed away, a natural utopia that no longer exists, and a community of poor people (pastoral laborers) whose relations occur beyond the pale of aristocratic influence or interest. Despite its reputation as an apolitical literary mode, Guy-Bray argues that pastoral writing is, if anything, overpoliticized, given its unique configurations of legal and civic apparatuses against a backdrop of unspoiled nature. He suggests, "The pastoral's juxtaposition of natural and unnatural might prompt us to consider how it is that we decide which things go in which of those two categories."[14]

Clark's natural grounding within this world pits him against Lex's unnatural civic education, and the full complexity of their relationship is allowed to emerge only within Smallville's pastoral environment. This clash of worlds is evident from the pilot episode, when a nine-year-old Lex, being ferried from Metropolis in his father's company car, is caught in the famous meteor shower (which delivered Clark to Earth) and ends up lying, bald and unconscious, in the middle of a cornfield. Lex is in a position of intense vulnerability. He is a tiny presence curled up within the vast expanse of the cornfield, now bald (as a result of Kryptonian radiation), with just a few strands of orange hair left clinging to the bare skin of his head. Clearly, his ruthless education at the hands of Lionel has not prepared him for this confrontation with nature on a cosmic scale. Clark, however, emerges from his tiny craft as an already-formed pastoral subject, perfectly comfortable as he walks barefoot through the ruined field, smiling, reaching out with his small hands to the Kents in a gesture of welcome rather than desperation. It is Jonathan Kent who finds Lex in his semiconscious state, and who, we later learn in "Lineage" (2002), acts quickly to save Lex while Lionel is still in a state of shock. As, in a moment of rare conjunction, both the Kents and the Luthors cram into Jonathan's truck in order to drive Lex to the hospital, we see that a bond exists between Clark and Lex that predates their reunion (and what Clark thinks is their first meeting) so many years later. As Lex, cradled in Lionel's arms, slips in and out of consciousness, three-year-old Clark reaches out and gently strokes his bald head. Lex seems confused and comforted at the same time, but Clark's look is surprisingly omniscient. He seems to know even this early what Lex clarifies in "Hug" (2002) when they are both much older: "Trust me, Clark—our friendship will become the stuff of legends." Yet this legendary relationship begins with a very small gesture of love on Clark's part, a wise child's attempt to ease Lex's suffering with the barest of touches. We have to assume that even Jonathan, despite his vocal mistrust of Lex, remembers the moment of quiet and unexpected tenderness that first connected them.

As their friendship matures, it begins to organize itself around a complex system of economic exchange, wherein each commodity that changes hands is also limned with traces of emotional desire. Lex offers Clark money on multiple occasions, and specifically offers to buy the Kent farm—which he eventually does in order to keep it from being foreclosed. He lets Clark borrow his Porsche (not quite openly, but he doesn't exactly stand in his way, either) in the episode "Velocity" (2004) and lends him a limousine for his first date with Lana. Although he often frowns upon Clark's snooping around Luthorcorp, he basically gives him an all-access pass to the company grounds and rarely, if ever, asks him to leave. Clark has similar access to Lex's mansion, particularly his intimate office space, and is allowed to come and go—at all hours of the night—as he pleases without Lex so much as raising an eyebrow. Smallville seems especially prone to life-threatening plagues (or character-specific illnesses), but whenever anyone close to Clark so much as develops a cough, Lex offers them free medical care. And when Clark loses his vision in the episode "Whisper" (2004), Lex quickly states that he can make "the world's top ophthalmologists" available to Clark. It is one thing to give your friend the phone number of a competent ophthalmologist, but it is quite another to send a team of the "world's top" experts practically to his doorstep.

It may seem, at first, as if Clark is getting a lot more out of this contractual relationship than Lex. But it remains quite difficult to determine exactly what both men are getting out of it, or if they are indeed "getting" something measurable at all. For, if anything, the more wealth and material goods Lex offers up to Clark and the Kent family, the less substantial all of it seems. And the more Clark tries to pull Lex back from the "darkness" that he sees within himself, the closer Lex seems to move toward it. Yet neither character is wholly willing to sever the relationship, and it is Lex, ever the communicator, who says to Clark in "Bound" (2004), "Don't give up on me." This plea comes after Clark has learned of Lex's various sexual liaisons with women whose names he never bothered to learn—and one woman in particular who decides to punish him for what she perceives as his own inexcusable chauvinism. The episode actually backfires in its feminist intent, repeating hackneyed phrases such as "hell hath no fury like a woman scorned" in order to pathologize Lex's female inquisitor. It recuperates Lex in the end as a tragic figure whose own sexism emerges from his complex problems with intimacy (rather than from the patriarchal atmosphere that inflects most of *Smallville*'s gender relations, or the unconscious patriarchy of the show's virtually all-male writing staff). "Bound," thus, comes to be more about the fraught friendship between Clark and Lex than it is about Lex's mistreatment of women.

It seems, then, that Lex should be saying "Don't give up on me" to the various women in his life—but he says it to Clark. In this sense, his relationship with Clark becomes in part a projection of his failed sexual relationships with women, but also something different. Their friendship has produced a vast and thriving archive of slash (same-sex male pairing) fan fiction on the Internet, which suggests that, even if *Smallville*'s writers never intended the relationship itself to be erotic, many of the show's fans are nonetheless reading it that way. In terms of queer studies and its potential for opening up traditional texts, Guy-Bray notes that, as with queer "misreadings" of classical and Renaissance literature, "a misreading of this kind may on occasion be more productive than a more correct meaning."[15] Although fans may be "misreading" the Clark/Lex relationship as one charged with erotic potential, their misreading reveals a great deal about the show, and is potentially a lot more interesting than the heterosexually "correct" reading of these two characters as close male friends.

The slash tradition—that is, the same-sex pairing of romantic characters, both male and female—emerged from the K/S (Kirk and Spock) slashers who recast the homosocial relationship between Kirk and Spock on the original *Star Trek* (1966–1969). The K/S slash community produced an amazing network of erotic fanzines, made all the more impressive by the fact that they only had access to the most conventional of fan technology—a VCR, a printer, and a public photocopier. Constance Penley discusses this fan community in detail in her book *NASA/Trek*, describing how the slashers, who are primarily heterosexual women, don't radically reposition Kirk and Spock so much as give their relationship the nudge from "homosocial" to "homoerotic"—which always remains the impossible boundary to cross in network television.[16] Keep in mind, too, that Kirk was also raised as a farm boy, a corn-fed Iowa kid like Clark, which makes his "queering" all the more devious and enjoyable to the fans. In her article "*Smallville*'s Sexual Symbolism: From Queer Repression to Fans' Queered Expressions," Anne Kustritz notes the link between Superman and gay culture. She observes,

> Superman also has a long-standing gay male following. Alternately parodied and revered on the television series *Queer as Folk*, Superman presents a prototypical case for why superheroes' lives share important parallels with gay culture. His personality rigidly bifurcated between an ordinary public face and a secret identity kept hidden at any cost, Superman's penchant for changing clothes in small enclosed spaces (phone booths, closets) as he changes personas may metaphorically resemble the closeting of gay identity.[17]

The Clark/Lex relationship in slash fiction takes this one step further, repositioning both the hero and the villain within a queer space that will allow them to express their (and the fans') covert erotic desires. Much of the slash fiction devoted to Clark and Lex seems particularly intent on preserving the pastoral/urban binary between the two of them, which leads me to believe that fans (including myself) see the characters' sexuality as being peculiarly embedded within their own public spaces and economic backgrounds. In "Sleep While I Drive," written by jenn, Lex is described as wearing "his immaculate business best, but the tie's off and curled loosely in one fist, two buttons of the collar undone, revealing traces of pale skin. Pale purple shadows curve beneath his eyes, almost a match for his shirt. Mouth set in a hard line."[18]

Throughout this story, Clark remains easygoing, almost doggishness in his warmth and amiability, while Lex is continually skeptical, edgy, quick to start, always keeping one blue eye on Clark and everyone else. Obviously his sexuality here is linked to his civic/urban identity, his position as a sly Renaissance man, whereas Clark's erotic life is indelibly connected to the farm, to family, and to his celebrated naiveté.

I am not trying, with this discussion, explicitly to queer Lex and Clark, but rather, through their ambiguous and productive relationship, to queer the notion of "close male friends" in general. Patronage systems depended upon male friendships identical to the one shared between Clark and Lex and were equally ambiguous in their language, cultural positioning, and physical expression. It is, I think, manifestly impossible to say of any pairing, same-sex or opposite-sex, that they are "just friends," because "just friends," like "just pastoral" or "just classical," is a fiction that heterosexist and patriarchal culture depends upon for its very survival. The first step in erasing a relationship's transgressive potential is to explain it away through cultural anachronism, through mythical allegory, or through misplaced optimism on the part of the reader.

It is possible that fans see queerness in the Clark/Lex pairing because they want to see it—that I see it because I want to see it. But, consider the wealth of long pauses, significant looks, intimate spatial positioning, physical contact, and amatory language that exists between these characters.[19] It seems more difficult *not* to see an erotic potential emerging from their friendship, as it must emerge from any close friendship. What makes this particular friendship even more interesting is that it is inscribed within traditional models of patronage, and that it is a deliberate rereading of the mythic Superman/Lex Luthor rivalry as set down within the comic tradition. How far we want to take this rereading is up to us, but the show itself has set the wheels of adaptation in motion by rewriting an antagonistic conflict into an intimate friendship doomed to fail.

This is not to say, however, that a show revolving around masculine secrecy is necessarily a bad thing. *Smallville* is a wonderfully engaging show, and part of what makes it engaging is its troubling deferrals and manipulations of the truth. As the quotation by Eve Sedgwick that I began this chapter with states, "closetedness" as a state of being is not founded upon an inaugural or originary silence, but upon a discourse of multiple competing and constituting silences that unite to *produce* the closet. It is not simply performed through speech acts. Rather, it is uniquely articulated through a whole network of secrets, half-truths, unspoken definitions, withheld knowledge, and even hesitations, all of which form the substance of the closet itself. Although it remains historically and politically specific to queer communities (and must remain so), it is also a broader concept that has structured much of homophobic Western discourse for the past several centuries. As Sedgwick observes in *Epistemology of the Closet*, "A whole cluster of the most crucial sites for the contestation of meaning in twentieth-century Western culture" are linked to "the historical specificity of homosocial/homosexual definition . . . [including] the pairings secrecy/disclosure and private/public."[20] Both Clark and Lex have very deep closets, and both live within those closets on a daily basis. What many queer and female fans of the Clark/Lex relationship have done is simply illuminate the obvious conflation of queerness/secrecy that exists within the cultural metaphor of the closet, linking the characters' secrets with their own unvoiced sexuality.

The question, *are they or aren't they?* is ultimately not important. What is important is *Smallville*'s willingness to render these two male characters as vulnerable, as well as its willingness to celebrate their close friendship without shutting down its erotic potential through masculine stereotyping. Most male characters within science fiction texts, we must remember, barely have a physical relationship with their wives and girlfriends, let alone with other men. For *Smallville* to focus so strongly on a friendship that Lex predicts will be "the stuff of legends" is a risky move in itself, but it is a move that has paid off over four seasons' worth of fascinating narrative [at time of original publication]. While Clark remains the invulnerable man who elicits horror from audiences when his body *is* actually violated (as in the episode "Extinction" [2003] when Clark is hit with a kryptonite bullet), Lex's body is constantly being bruised, battered, and assaulted. Lex practically dies in the pilot episode and is constantly being tied up, shot at, or placed on the receiving end of retributive violence (usually at the hands of someone whose life he inadvertently ruined). Clark is, of course, the one who routinely comes to Lex's rescue. But not even

Clark can save Lex from his father, whose attempt to erase Lex's memory through shock treatment in the episode "Asylum" (2004) is startlingly brutal. It may seem like a hackneyed supervillain move on Lionel's part, but it is actually a horrific betrayal that devastates Lionel even as it ruthlessly violates Lex's own body.

This continual pathologizing of the father/son relationship between Lex and Lionel is directly the opposite of the rock-solid relationship between Jonathan and Clark. In this way, *Smallville* presents us with two very real versions of fatherhood, while infusing both with a mixture of ire and tenderness, openness and indecipherability. And, in this particular episode, it juxtaposes Lionel's nearly unbelievable cruelty with a moment of strangely innocent affection between Clark and Lex. Clark is clearly dreading his meeting with Lex after the shock "therapy," since he knows what violence has been inflicted upon Lex's body, whereas Lex is now blissfully unaware of what happened. Yet Lex meets Clark's apprehension with the same curious, almost extraterrestrial certainty that Clark himself demonstrated when, as a child, he first gently touched Lex on the face. "There is one thing I'll never forget," Lex says, "how important your friendship is to me." The two men embrace, and while Clark is visibly anxious, Lex closes his eyes like a child who is totally at peace. Their friendship, whatever it may mean, becomes the one cipher that Lionel's therapeutic invasions cannot eradicate.

By extending the Clark/Lex relationship into an ambiguous and enduring friendship, *Smallville* has effectively rewritten the Superman myth without visibly disrupting it. Although its many attempts to humanize Clark seem at first to emerge from his much-foiled relationship with Lana, Clark seems to be at his most vulnerable when he is interacting with Lex. His connection with Lex remains the one that he trusts, even when Lex has given him no reason to trust it. Their friendship is based upon mutual secrecy, yet it works in a variety of interesting ways, and ways that perhaps the creators of *Smallville* never intended.

It is easy to write off this focus on close male friendship as an antifeminist move on the show's part, or as simply one more gesture to remove Superman from potentially threatening feminine influence. But the relationship between Clark and Lex remains as ambiguous as the one between Clark and Lana, or Clark and Chloe, and we need to acknowledge them as interconnected articulations within the engine of secrecy that powers

Smallville as a show. The female characters on *Smallville* have the same capacity for both vulnerability and heroism as the male characters, and although Lana and Chloe often need to be saved by Clark, he makes it clear again and again that he would be nowhere without the love and support of his friends. And if his friendship serves to keep Lex's darkness at bay, then perhaps Lex also serves to keep Clark's own darkness at bay—for in saving Lex from "himself," Clark is also continually rejecting his role as the conquering Kal-El in favor of the emotionally connected Clark Kent. Lex is, after all, not a megalomaniac following in the footsteps of his father, but a son who, more than anything else, wants his father to love him, as revealed in "Truth" (2004). *Smallville* may never tell us who the "real" hero and villain of this legendary friendship are, but the more we watch that friendship develop, and fracture, and mend, and fracture again, the less able we are to empirically separate hero from villain. It is a secret that will have to remain in Lex's locked room, in Clark's Fortress of Solitude, and in the peculiar closet that forms their connection to each other.

Notes

1. Eve K. Sedgwick, *Epistemology of the Closet* (Berkeley: University of California Press, 1990), 3.

2. Rictor Norton, *The Homosexual Literary Tradition* (New York: Revisionist Press, 1974), 127.

3. We should also remember that the obsessive relations between male heroes and villains within the comic book tradition emerge from a sort of covert homoeroticism. The villain is obsessed with the hero's body, with finding his weakness, with penetrating or shattering or inflicting violence upon him. The villain thus becomes a failed version of the hero who must eradicate the hero in order to validate his own perverse ethical agenda. It is never just about "ruling the world," but also about ruling the hero's body.

4. "Wholesome" tends to be the death knell for media analysis and the glass ceiling against which pop culture scholarship is continually thrust. Generally, for a show to be deemed worthy of academic attention, it needs to encode some sort of exilic, anarchic, or troubling potential (labeled as "transgression"), and it is this *potential* that the analysis is interested in, not the show itself. Once a show is deemed to be too wholesome, or too mainstream (the two are often synonymous), all bets are off in terms of scholarship, and the text is abandoned. The necessary alternative is to study media texts for, rather than in spite of,

their mainstream inclinations, since the transgressive and the mainstream exist in a mutually co-constitutive relationship, and neither could survive without the other. Just because *Disney* movies are wholesome doesn't mean that we shouldn't be worried about their ideological messages, nor that we should discount them as being completely devoid of oppositional potential.

5. *Smallville* tends to shy away from sexual intercourse but has no problem with putting its characters in a lot of heavy make-out sessions. Generally, sex is something that happens *to* Clark, rather than something that he invites. He can only be sexually aggressive when he is under the influence of red kryptonite (which functions much like alcohol), or when he is within the (relative) safety of a dream. Both of his most intense physical encounters with Lana occur either within a dream, "Slumber" (2003), or within a dreamlike memory, "Relic" (2003), whose 1950s backdrop is itself pastoral and nostalgic. [Editor's note: Of course, subsequent to original publication of this chapter, Clark has had several sexual encounters with Lana and other women—as outlined in previous chapters in this volume.]

6. Kryptonite, or "meteor rock" as those not in the know call it, is not just Clark's only real weakness (aside from magic, which doesn't really get explored until the fourth season)—it is also a transparent and valuable plot device that serves as an explanation for every paranormal occurrence in Smallville. In this sense, it is really no different from alien intervention on *The X-Files* or mystical power on *Buffy*. Every science fiction show needs its explanatory substance.

7. J. L. Austin, *How to Do Things with Words* (Cambridge, MA: Harvard University Press, 1975), 22.

8. Darko Suvin, *Metamorphoses of Science Fiction: On the Poetics and History of a Literary Genre* (New Haven, CT: Yale University Press, 1979), 20.

9. What can we say about Pete? Like the character Kendra in *Buffy*, he is apparently the only black person living in Smallville, and none of his storylines involve race elements at all. It appears that rural Kansas is *the* place to live in order to experience racial harmony, since Pete never appears to encounter racism in any form. Pete's chronic lack of narrative attention on the show (does anyone even notice when he leaves?) suggests that neither the audiences nor the writers were interested in a character who was *actually* honest, forthright, and dependable, unless that character was Clark.

10. The town of Smallville appears to consist of one main street, which contains the Talon (with its prominently displayed U.S. flag), a jewelry store, an antique shop, and a few apartments. Like Sunnydale or Capeside, Smallville is designed as a network of safe spaces within which its characters can communicate, if slightly illogical from a city-planning point of view. Metropolis, in general, is represented synecdochally by the Luthorcorp building, which is actually

a government building in downtown Vancouver shot low to the ground in order to make it appear as a towering skyscraper. No one appears to live comfortably in either of these spaces—characters are always trying to escape Metropolis for the pastoral safety of Smallville, or trying to escape the repressive confines of Smallville for the free-living of Metropolis.

11. Stephen Guy-Bray, *Homoerotic Space: The Poetics of Loss in Renaissance Literature* (Toronto: University of Toronto Press, 2002), 5.

12. Sedgwick, *Epistemology of the Closet,* 53.

13. Guy-Bray, *Homoerotic Space,* 15.

14. Guy-Bray, *Homoerotic Space,* 18.

15. Guy-Bray, *Homoerotic Space,* 8.

16. See Constance Penley, *NASA/Trek: Popular Sex and Science in America* (New York: Verso, 1997).

17. Anne Kustritz, "*Smallville*'s Sexual Symbolism: From Queer Repression to Fans' Queered Expressions," *Refractory* 8, no. 1 (Fall 2005).

18. jenn, "Sleep While I Drive," *Level Three Records Room—Smallville Fanfic,* 2005, http://www.smallvillefanfic.com/archive/3/sleepwhile.html (accessed 1 April 2011).

19. In most of the scenes between Lex and Clark, Lex is the one who verbally communicates his own vulnerability, while Clark tends to use ambiguous body language, gestural communication, and positioning. Clark suffers in silence a lot, and is the least emotionally expressive character in the show. He rarely gets angry, and while Lex often seems visibly upset or on the verge of tears, Clark is confined to a perpetually moist expression as he hugs his friends, telling them that everything will be all right. The suggestion here is that Clark doesn't have the luxury of breaking down, since he has a cosmic/comic responsibility to protect his friends, loved ones, and the world in general. But I also suspect that rendering Clark so visibly emotional would disrupt his mythological potential and thus disrupt certain entrenched American ideological practices around heroic democracy and the dream of rugged individualism that Superman represents.

20. Sedgwick, *Epistemology of the Closet,* 72.

CHAPTER FOUR

NO FLIGHTS, NO TIGHTS: *SMALLVILLE* AND THE ROLES OF SPECIAL EFFECTS IN TELEVISION

Rayna Denison

Smallville has come to be defined by the approach-turned-catchphrase first coined by its writers Alfred Gough and Miles Millar: no flights, no tights. Early coverage of the show in *Entertainment Weekly*, for example, quotes Gough as saying, "You should know off the bat what we're *not* going to do: No suit, no glasses, no flying."[1] Just a few months later, in the same publication, the approach driving the show had taken further shape:

> They quickly agreed on a philosophy: *no flights, no tights.* "Our main interest was getting inside Clark Kent's psyche and understanding why he becomes the man he does," says Millar: "Taking away the suit and the glasses was really to strip him away to a more human character and get to the heart of Superman."[2]

Smallville was therefore conceived in terms that distanced it from the more spectacle-driven manifestations of Superman. By "stripping" Superman of his abilities (flight), his costume (the suit), and even the disguise worn by his alter ego Clark Kent (the glasses), *Smallville*'s initial difference to previous incarnations of Superman in film and television is presented through seemingly negative understandings of the franchise's iconography. In denying the centrality of the iconic and "super" aspects of Superman, *Smallville*'s creative team began by denying audiences some of the normal pleasures associated with the franchise.[3]

Many of these iconic and "super" elements, such as flight, are produced in the film and television incarnations of Superman through the use of special and visual effects. Special and visual effects are differently defined by academic theorists, but recent work has tended to emphasize the visual, computer-generated end of the spectrum of effects work.[4] Consequently, this chapter takes a more holistic view of special and visual effects and aims to examine the roles played by different kinds of special effects within *Smallville*. It will examine the show's discursive surround, investigating how this long-running television show's creators have presented their special and visual effects work, and it will then compare those claims with textual examples of special effects as deployed in *Smallville*.

In considering *Smallville*'s production discourses, concerning everything from practical stunts and makeup effects through to newer kinds of computer-generated visual effects across its first nine seasons, this chapter argues that the "super" (or flights and tights) actually plays vital roles within *Smallville*. From creating and managing expectations around the show's production values, to presenting the Superman iconography in new ways, to enabling a slow shift in *Smallville*'s generic identity, special effects work has shaped *Smallville*'s production aesthetics while audiences have been repeatedly told that the show's approach to special effects is tangential, sparing, and purposefully limited. In these ways, *Smallville* makes dissimilar uses of special and visual effects to those frequently discussed in relation to film; for example, making much greater use of repetition and long-term development of visual effects, in addition to balancing between effects used to produce spectacular imagery and those that become routinized and generic aspects of this long-running television text. Therefore, this chapter argues that while Clark Kent may not achieve his alter ego in full until the end of season ten, even from its earliest moments, *Smallville*'s adaptation of the Superman franchise places the "super" at its heart, and with the super, special effects. Furthermore, it argues that television has the potential to experiment with, develop, and utilize special and visual effects in ways that cinema cannot, challenging conceptualizations of special and visual effects generated solely through the examination of cinema.

Special effects arguably took up their most central role within the Superman franchise in the hyperbolic marketing tagline for the 1979 film version of Superman, which proclaimed, "You'll believe a man can fly."[5] Though lower key in nature, subsequent adaptations of Superman have also been noted as pivotal examples of new uses of special effects techniques. For example, Jan Johnson-Smith, analyzing American science fiction television, comments that,

> more recent sfx technology permits Dean Cain to be filmed either in purely analogue (real) time or for the analogue to be supplemented by cgi sfx. The overall image can then be digitally remastered and perfected so that in an apparently analogue setting, Cain's Superman demonstrates both speed and power.[6]

Lois & Clark: The New Adventures of Superman (1993–1997) is, here, conspicuous for its attempts to showcase what Johnson-Smith cites as "supplemented" or hybridized digital-analog space and time, in order to create "apparently analogue" effects that augment the diegetic verisimilitude of the show. In these ways, the creation of groundbreaking special effects technologies, and latterly the adoption and development of new effects technologies across media platforms, has a lingering association with the Superman franchise. *Smallville* can be read in similar ways, and it will be shown hereafter that shifting production discourses about its uses of a range of special and visual effects techniques can be read in relation to the now often hidden impact that special effects are having on the production of television.

As the above quotes imply, and as the work on special effects emphatically demonstrates, there is a common assumption about the use of special effects in the creation of spectacle. This chapter is less concerned with whether or not *Smallville*'s special effects are spectacular, however, and more concerned with the discourses that are generated by and around the notionally "below-the-line" production staff involved in the production of effects in the television show. To this end, several key individuals will be repeatedly referenced in this chapter including Chris Sayour, *Smallville*'s stunt coordinator and stunt double for Tom Welling/Clark Kent;[7] Mat Beck (also sometimes called Matt Beck), the visual effects coordinator and founder of Entity FX; and Bill Terezakis, who appears in DVD commentaries from season eight, for which his company produced practical makeup and creature effects. As these individuals' roles suggest, a considerable amount of *Smallville*'s special effects are outsourced to companies whose associations with the main production have either become embedded over time (Mat Beck has directed "Prototype" [2007] and has staff on set during filming) or remain largely tangential, as with Bill Terezakis. Moreover, their work is often presented as separate despite the fact that a large proportion of *Smallville* effects are composite in nature.

Special effects analyses within academic discourses mirror this discursive division and are still outnumbered by their discussion in technical manuals and popular sources.[8] Instead of grouping around roles or types of special effects, discussions of special effects within academia have tended to group around science fiction film and television and its use of special effects to produce "wonder" or "illusion."[9] While these are certainly useful discussions, and ones that inform this research, their insistence on the role of special effects to produce particular kinds of spectacle (what Pierson refers to as simulation and assimilation techniques)[10] runs contrary to the analysis being attempted herein. Instead of examining special effects (and with them visual effects)[11] as they relate to spectacle, this chapter seeks to examine the range of physical special effects including stunts, pyrotechnics, and in-camera distortions alongside uses of creature effects and computer-generated visual effects in order to assess the ends to which special effects are deployed in *Smallville*.

This decision to holistically focus on *Smallville*'s effects techniques has been taken in light of claims emerging in work around science fiction film and television that question the role of special effects in relation to spectacle. Pierson, for instance, writes,

> One of the less convincing aspects of the claims that all the computer-generated images produced by the film industry have the same aesthetic goal is that it doesn't look at the range of aesthetic functions visual effects fulfil in popular cinema.[12]

Pierson's claim for film chimes with other work on television, for example, Karen Lury's assertion that, in addition to spectacular special effects,

> Increasingly, it seems that television now also uses CGI to substitute for real places and objects for reasons more to do with convenience; in fact, CGI is beginning to substitute for the filming of ordinary locations and its presence may be unknown to the general audience.[13]

The invisibility of some CGI effects in film and television is matched by the relative invisibility in discourse of the composite uses of effects and techniques including stunt work, sound effects, and other seemingly hidden or unrecognized effects technologies. Therefore, while academic discourses have so far been dominated by claims about the emerging technologies of CGI, this chapter seeks to present a case study on how a range of special effects are produced and discussed in order to offer some nuance to academic accounts about the aims of special effects production.

You'll Believe a Man Can't Fly: Limiting the Scope of the Super in *Smallville*

Analyzing *Smallville*'s complex use of special effects is further complicated by the uneven patterns in, and availability of, production discourses. While production sources close to the show provide a broad range of voices from the special effects and visual effects teams, these resources are often patchy and potentially biased. For example, Chris Sayour and Mat Beck are frequently quoted in the *Smallville* companion books, but Sayour and Beck both also feature in "Meet the Crew" segments of the books, providing them with greater personal promotion.[14] Additionally, these professional commentators are frequently called upon to emphasize not their own importance, but the skills of the central cast of *Smallville*. For example, Sayour repeatedly praises the physicality of actor John Glover, *Smallville*'s Lionel Luthor, in one instance saying that, "John Glover is someone I know I can turn to and say, 'John, this is safe for you,' and he gets all excited."[15] Similarly, Beck notes regarding his directorial debut on "Prototype" that "the actors are so strong and willing when it comes to being abused on set in order to make the scene look great. . . . We throw them around, choke them, hang them on wires, and they come back for more. Besides being terrific actors, they are pretty tough when they have to be!"[16]

However, through the hyperbole of these examples, and the obligations of promotion they seem to contain, it is still possible to read something of the on-set hierarchies, and the positions of trust held by stunt coordinators, and visual-effects-turned-director managers.

An interesting discursive split emerges between sources produced for the explicit promotion of the show and those produced by slightly further removed sources. For example, within DVD featurettes on the making of episodes and the companion book series that is now available for seasons one through seven, traditional stunt and physical effects get roughly the same amount of coverage as computer-generated effects. However, visual effects sources are far more plentiful in wider discussions of *Smallville*'s production. This is in part due to the greater presence of *Smallville*'s visual effects house, Entity FX (and subsidiary Entity North FX), online. Unlike other aspects of the show's special effects, such as stunt work and creature effects, Entity FX has its own website (www.entityfx.com), and its founder, Mat Beck, and some of his staff members appear in interviews for specialist trade publications such as the *Animation World Network* magazine and *American Cinematographer*.[17] Entity FX, more so than other outside contractors like Bill Terezakis, who was brought in to design Doomsday and other creature and makeup effects, have a layered online presence relating to their own promotion in addition to their promotional association with *Smallville*. Accordingly, the aim in this section is to analyze as much production discourse as possible, but to compare this discourse with broader comment circulating around *Smallville*.

J. P. Telotte contrasts television production of special effects with film, claiming that,

> Television typically has had to contend with restrictions built into its very media identity: limited budgets, tight schedules, scaled-down effects, and even a very different visual style (one emphasizing the close-up and medium shot rather than the more spectacular long shots and panoramas, for example).[18]

Though wary of the definitive distinction drawn between the cinematic and the televisual in Telotte's work, especially in light of Lury's comments about the normalization of CGI effects within television production, Telotte does present a framework that is helpful in thinking about what affects *Smallville*'s presentation of the super. Budgetary information, however, is difficult to access, although one of the show's initial creators, Gough, has commented that "the visual effects were very important to us in the series and we fought for a rather sizable visual effects budget, because, you know, sort of, in a post-*Matrix* world where you can see Clark moving faster than a speeding bullet, we wanted to be able to do that."[19]

Gough's comments supply a cinematic referent for *Smallville*'s special effects, implying that the benchmark and caliber required by the production team was comparable to that expected of the look of a large-budgeted, special effects laden film. Additional coverage of the show's budget in the trade presses implies a different budgetary story in latter seasons, however. Comments have been routinely made about *Smallville*'s fluctuating viewer figures from record-making highs for the WB (where it debuted to 8.35 million viewers)[20] to a particular low point emerging around April of 2010, with figures reportedly dropping to 2.1 million viewers in its final season.[21] This drop in ratings may well reflect the tailing off of audiences for an aging show, but Lowry does pass comment on the reduction of action television budgets in the wake of the global recession as another potential cause.[22] Writing in 2009, he states, "As a critic, I've already noticed cost-cutting mandates exacting a not-so-subtle toll on series such as 'Terminator' and CW's 'Smallville'—programs that require at least a modicum of special effects and action to keep itchy viewers hooked."[23] This is likely to apply to seasons eight and nine of *Smallville*, with season eight in particular demonstrating a shift from heavy use of computer-generated effects to more use of practical and makeup effects. Therefore, in this instance it is perhaps more instructive to examine the ways that budgetary adjustments across the show have impacted its content, rather than assuming a lesser status for *Smallville*'s special effects based on a comparison with films.

Documentaries about the making of *Smallville*'s villain for season eight, Doomsday,[24] and about the introduction of Justice League of America (JLA) characters into the show in season nine,[25] provided on *Smallville*'s DVDs for those seasons, demonstrate how budgets do affect the content of the show. For example, Brian Peterson, one of the show's producer-writers, claims that Bill Terezakis "brought a pair of wings to the table that I think had been used in some form in another show."[26] Terezakis confirms that the wings he produced for the JSA character Hawkman/Carter Hall in season nine were effectively secondhand and quotes budget constraints as his reason for offering them for use in *Smallville*: "Originally production was trying to find some wings that were already built. They feared that the budget to build these from scratch would be quite high."[27] By contrast, however, sometimes the choice to use Terezakis's creature and makeup effects are explained in less pragmatic terms.

Kelly Souders, another of *Smallville*'s new production-writing team following the departure of Gough and Millar after season seven, for instance, comments that for Doomsday,

> Originally we absolutely thought it would be CGI. One hundred percent thought it would be CGI. That we wouldn't see Doomsday until the finale. . . . We knew that we wanted to see interaction between them. . . . We wanted to see them converse . . . and therefore CGI was not going to give us exactly what we wanted.[28]

However, despite the declared preference for practical creature effects by Souders, the rest of the documentary discusses the fears of the production team about using creature effects within *Smallville*. For example, Turi Meyer, another of the producers, discusses Doomsday's creature effect introduction in "Bride" (2008). He explains how they had a "videographer" character produce handheld footage because,

> by using that device, if we had to we could hide the beast, you know, hide the shark, as it were in the video and keep it all handheld with flashes of images so that if we did not get to a place where, you know, especially the EPs and everyone in post, were happy with how the beast was looking on HD, we could always cut to that.[29]

Again, the referent for experimental techniques is filmic, this time Steven Spielberg's *Jaws* (1975). One of the illuminating things about this comment is the way the postproduction for episodes is shown to have a significant impact on the content of the episodes. Here, however, it is clear that the production team had built (comparatively cheap) redundancies into the production phase in an attempt to contain the risks that they associated with using new kinds of special effects within *Smallville*. In these examples, we can see that budget constraints and changes seem to have the greatest impact on the *types* of special effects used, rather than the *amount* of special effects involved in episodes. However, where CGI usage becomes more limited, it seems that the scale of *Smallville*'s spectacle is curtailed, from CGI worlds to more intimate creature effects and secondhand wings.

Production schedules have also been cited by creative staff as reasons for varying quality in *Smallville*'s special effects. For example, Paul

Simpson, quoting Miles Millar, indicates that *Smallville*'s first season was marked by difficulties in getting visual effects sequences completed within the show's tight broadcast deadlines. He says of "Craving" (2001),

> It was one of those episodes where the production schedule caught up with the airing schedule, and there wasn't time to rectify anything that the producers would have preferred to improve upon. "We had the effect of the deer come in on the day of transmission," Miles Millar recalls, "and we couldn't cut around it. . . . The deer is a little claymation hairless creature, which turns toward the car. . . . It was too late to change it. I think it's the worst effect we've ever done. If we'd known what the effect was going to be like, we would have found a way to cut around it, but there was no time."[30]

The complexity of this effect, which includes physical stunts, computer-generated imagery, and stop-motion animation, is reduced in Millar's memory of the sequence to a problem caused by older, stop-motion, special effects technologies. Moreover, within this narrative it becomes clear that, while special effects sequences may be previsualized or storyboarded, the actual postproduction effects are done on timescales that leave little room for error. Bill Terezakis has, for instance, similarly stated that for the Doomsday creature effects, "Something like this normally takes about five weeks and I think on *Smallville* we had just under two weeks to create this character."[31] Later reports from Entity FX do suggest that short timescales are now offset by a larger staff (in both Vancouver, where the show is filmed, and in Santa Monica, at the headquarters of Entity FX),[32] and by working on batches of episodes simultaneously.[33] The scheduling of effects-heavy production, therefore, can be seen as changing the ways in which ancillary supporting industries like creature effects and computer-generated effects studios work. It also suggests reasons for the sometimes less detailed, more expressive uses of such technologies that can be found across action, science fiction, and fantasy television (of which more in the next section).

Telotte's final claim in his framework is that television offers scaled-down examples of special effects. Indeed, as the examples above indicate, important milestones in film special effects are often cited as the benchmarks against which the makers of *Smallville* judge their work, suggesting a hierarchy of effects production within the industry that places film at the top. Indeed, *Smallville*'s creators have been known to make use of equipment designed for filmmaking, repurposing it to their requirements. For example, the season one finale, "Tempest" (2002), features the wind machines used in the film *Twister* (1996).[34] Adaptation and expansion of effects techniques, or their wholesale adoption from other media as in this instance, provides a different way of thinking about the idea of "scaled-down" effects in television. Michael S. Duffy has provided detailed analysis of instances of special effects reuse in film franchises, using the *Star Trek* films as his main example. Duffy's analysis takes in instances where special effects techniques are reused to ensure continuity across films, and he claims that when *Star Trek* the television show has been adapted to film, "there is clearly an attempt . . . to adhere to an *image and a setting* that is recognizable to Trek fans."[35] The next section picks up on this idea of reused images and settings from the Superman mythology and how these are managed within *Smallville*. At this point, however, the discourses around how the show makes sense of its own internal shifts and changes relate back to Telotte's point about scale within television effects.

This is because, despite reported scaling back in budgets, *Smallville*'s narrative is inexorably moving toward a final reveal of Clark Kent as Superman, able to fly and wearing the Superman costume. The development of *Smallville*'s visual and aural aesthetics along the way, from Clark Kent's introduction as a superfast and superstrong teenager to an adult superhero with a wide range of powers, has been part and parcel of the show's development. Such character and narrative developments have been matched by its special effects. The Entity FX team frequently mention developments in effects within the series, for example. Mat Beck, the company's president, states,

> We started out doing a super-speed effect where Clark runs from here to there. Or an X-Ray effect or a heat-vision effect—those were relatively straightforward things. But now we've reached a point of doing CG versions of Clark, and CG natural phenomena and CG environments—sometimes entire planets.[36]

Trent Smith and others confirm that the series has maintained a continuity within effects, despite gradual developments, which tend to put new twists on established effects:

> When we first introduced heat vision, it was something Clark could not control. Eventually, he learned to control it, and over the years we've fine tuned and even changed the style of the heat beam. . . . Over the years we've moved it with the traditional view of Superman with his heat vision; more of a traditional red color. . . . Nowadays, we do a red beam with heat distortion and hints of fire.[37]

Despite starting from a point of restricted powers, and a resultant low-key approach to visual effects, *Smallville*'s visual effects teams have augmented as well as reused their effects over time, playing with the franchise's history of representations, as well as with *Smallville*'s own standardization of superpower effects. From a starting point of "no flights," then, *Smallville* has become a show in which special effects play a routine role, with a reported 4,382 visual effects shots by the beginning of season ten.[38] Taken together, though, it becomes clear that the discourses around *Smallville*'s special effects are affected by a range of factors, including changes in staff, changes in budgets, and changes in the narrative of the show as it brings Clark Kent closer and closer to Superman. The results of these changes are examined hereafter, taking three types of effects as the basis for analysis.

Old Powers and New Technologies: Digital and Practical Effects in *Smallville*

Smallville is marked by its routinized uses of special effects, and though this is no longer uncommon in "quality" American television, *Smallville*'s management of its repertoire of effects is relatively unusual. The show is unusual for embedding new special effects within narratives of self-discovery, a tactic that helps to suggest readings of these effects as shifting from moments of character "wonder" to moments of mastery. It is also unusual in its slow development of existing visual effects techniques, produced across multiple seasons, as in the example of heat vision Smith outlines above. Therefore, this section argues that *Smallville*'s combination of effects with specific characters, effects that come to act as aural or visual shorthand for their presence on or off screen, provides useful examples of complex combinations of physical effects with visual and aural effects. Four examples make up the remainder of the chapter: the performance of stunts and the contradictory elision of stunt performers; Clark Kent's development of superspeed in the nine seasons of *Smallville* available to date; a repeated combination of visual effects in *Smallville*, namely, Clark Time as it is combined with literal bullet time and latterly heat vision; and, finally, the ability to fly as represented in *Smallville*. The aim is to use these examples to tease out how representations of superabilities in *Smallville* result in a distinctive reworking of the Superman franchise.

Discourses emanating from the stunt teams on *Smallville*, particularly from Chris Sayour, actively discuss stunts used to fool audiences into thinking practical effects are produced through more expensive, postproduction means. For example, describing a stunt in season five in which Clark Kent (Tom Welling) is supposed to perform a superleap over traffic in order to save someone's life, Sayour says,

> I had him run up a bench, jump over a cab, and land thirty feet away and then tackle a guy and prevent him from getting hit by a car. That was all a hundred percent Tom Welling. A lot of fans might have thought it was all CG and visual effects, but it was a hundred percent practical in downtown Vancouver, and a hundred percent Tom. It looks fantastic. I loved it.[39]

While the effect of "landing thirty feet away" was presumably an optical illusion, the practical nature of this effect once again emphasizes the authenticity potentially gained for *Smallville* by emphasizing the behind-the-scenes physical endeavors of protagonist cast members. What it also illustrates, however, is an assumption by Sayour that audiences will assume all spectacular effects are being produced in postproduction and through trickery. In drawing attention to *Smallville*'s stunts in this way, then, Sayour is able to reclaim spectacular production elements for *Smallville*'s practical effects teams.

However, this work belies the unacknowledged moments when stunt teams or performers substitute for cast members. For example, the promotional materials circulated about Doomsday, season eight's central villain, state that the character will be played by Sam Witwer.[40] However, the DVD special feature "*Smallville*'s Doomsday: The Making of a Monster" contains segments on the creation of the Doomsday creature effects that show stunt actor Dario De Iacio being fitted for the costume, and for contact lenses.

Terezakis is the only person to mention De Iacio by name ("we do a test fitting with Dario"), which he does only in passing. Otherwise, Doomsday-as-creature is discussed as a technical process, or as embodied by Witwer, effectively eliding De Iacio's on-screen presence. Moreover, De Iacio is listed only in the "supporting cast" list at the end of episodes in which he features, despite appearing in some of them (such as "Bride"), for longer periods than Witwer, who is included in the opening credits sequence.

While De Iacio's is perhaps the most overt example from the *Smallville* series, stunt performers tend to be left out of discourses almost as a matter of course, appearing unnamed, buried in end credit sequences, and rarely mentioned by academics except in passing.[41] Sayour has been the most visible stunt performer for *Smallville*, largely thanks to his role as its stunt coordinator, and it is notable that even he tends not to name the other stunt performers he works with. Stunt performers and doubles like De Iacio offer a counter to the notion of authored or embodied performances of special effects in film and television, as it is largely their on-screen work but behind-the-screen elision that enables discourses around action stars to be maintained as coherent individuals on-screen. Moreover, with the increasing use of digitally generated doubles and stunt stand-ins for lead actors, even the screen time afforded to stunt performers is increasingly under threat.

The remainder of this section therefore attempts to pick apart particular instances of superpower effects in order to examine their constitution in contemporary action television like *Smallville*. Clark Kent has been getting faster across the *Smallville* seasons (though this does ignore the occasions on which he suffers from loss of powers). For example, in "Rogue" (2002), Clark Kent/Welling is caught in superspeed on video, as a blur, but by season eight, Clark comments to Chloe Sullivan (Allison Mack) that he has to slow down to allow himself to be caught on cameras as the Red-Blue Blur. Both a cost-saving effect that allows Clark Kent to travel between studio-based sets and location shooting without costly interstitial filming, and one of the superpowers long associated with the young Clark Kent (it features in flashbacks in the Superman films, for example), superspeed in *Smallville* is produced via alternately complex and basic combinations of effects.

There are at least two ways in which superspeed has been depicted within *Smallville*. In terms of visual effects, Entity FX regularly uses a range of nonproprietary software packages including Adobe After Effects, which specifically enables filmed elements to be combined on-screen with individual distortion effects and moved independently of backgrounds. Mat Beck has cited the use of high-definition (HD), widescreen footage with programs like Adobe After Effects as the reason for Entity FX's ability to produce a large number of effects shots per episode.[42] This software package appears to be instrumental in the production of Clark Kent's superspeed, enabling the visual effects creators to move Tom Welling through the physical space of a shot at different speeds to the actors around him. These movements are made to look faster by motion-blur effects; hence his superhero name in Metropolis becomes "the Blur." However, just as significant, if not more so latterly, has been the use of physical bursts of air on-set in addition to a wind sound effect that mimics air displaced by Clark's superspeed. Repeatedly, this combination has been used to signal Clark Kent's offscreen appearance at Watchtower, normally with the air blowing into Chloe Sullivan's hair from behind. The actual on-screen time Clark Kent/Tom Welling has spent visualized in superspeed has decreased over the seasons, just as his speed has increased. Instead, the end of a superspeed movement is often implied by the use of on-set air and postproduction sounds effects combined with brief shots of Clark/Welling beginning a superspeed movement going offscreen. In this way, the faster Clark has become, the less superspeed has actually been shown in terms of the relatively expensive and labor-intensive visual effects.

Superspeed is relatively unusual within *Smallville*'s depictions of Clark Kent's superpowers, as it is one of the few powers he has already attained at the show's commencement. Other superpowers have been introduced and slowly developed across seasons, beginning with, surprisingly enough, flight. Clark/Welling is shown hovering over his own bed (and Lana Lang's while he is dreaming) in "Metamorphosis" (2001). Other superabilities have also been introduced slowly, at a rate of about one per season for the first few seasons, before the introduction of new superpowered characters (such as Impulse/Bart Allen and Aquaman/Arthur Curry) began to shift attention away from the development of Clark Kent's superpowers. Among Clark Kent's superpowers, the introduction of X-ray vision and superhearing offer two examples of superpowers whose depictions have helped to differentiate *Smallville* from the rest of the Superman franchise. "X-Ray" (2001) introduces Clark Kent's new eponymous power in a range of ways that looks backward at previous versions of Superman as well as presenting audiences with a genuinely new version of a well-known power. In his struggle to control this new ability after it is first triggered by a kryptonite-infused shape-shifter, three separate versions of X-ray vision are introduced.

The tension in representing X-ray in effects is described by Gough in the following terms: "We wanted X-ray vision to be X-ray vision and not see-through vision. . . . You've actually never seen X-ray vision; you always see, like, craggly-hole-see-through-the-wall."[43] In the first instance, the show's makers demonstrate their new version of X-ray vision using two point-of-view shots from Clark Kent's perspective as he "sees" the world in black, with shapes outlined in blue, mimicking hospital X-ray photographs, but with an added green effect laced through the skeleton of his kryptonite-powered antagonist, Tina Greer (Lizzy Caplan). This is then followed by two shots that fall within three minutes of one another, again motivated by Clark Kent's point of view. The first allows Clark to look literally under the skin of his friend Pete Ross (Sam Jones III), showing Pete's moving muscles as he hangs from a rope in gym class. Shortly thereafter, see-through vision is in fact used, enabling Clark to see into the girls' locker room as Lana Lang (Kristin Kreuk) changes clothes, presumably a nod to previous incarnations of X-ray (or "see-through-the-wall") vision. However, the remainder of the X-ray effects used in the episode return to *Smallville*'s new depiction of the power, as multiple black and blue X-ray shots show the interior of the antique shop owned by Tina Greer's mother, and further shots are created to look under the ground at the local graveyard, all of which are created using CGI. This reimagining of X-ray vision, plus the nodding aside to earlier representations of the power, provides a good example of the ways that *Smallville*'s creative team have playfully utilized and referenced past elements of the Superman franchise.[44]

Superhearing, however, has proven to be perhaps the most changeable of Clark Kent's powers, at least in terms of how it is produced in *Smallville*. The power is first shown in "Whisper" (2004), after Clark is blinded in an accident involving kryptonite. The effect begins as Clark picks up books from his high school, and it is made up of sound effects allied with slow-motion photography to give the sounds real-world referents.

Slowed, reverberating sound effects dominate the soundscape including low, metallic clanging followed by loud footsteps, and more metallic sounds for a zipper closing. These are then followed by CGI shots of the inside of Clark's ear as he "superhears" these sounds and a conversation being had by Chloe Sullivan on the phone somewhere else within the school building. Later examples from *Smallville* only sporadically use the inner-ear CGI shot, but superhearing continues to be implied through the use of actors positioning one ear toward the camera. A particularly good example of this can be found in season nine's "Salvation" (2010), in which the Kandorians superhear General Zod (Callum Blue) whispering as he confesses to having killed the mother of his unborn child. This is shown by filming the actors in groups across multiple shots all turning their ears toward camera, while the soundscape privileges Zod's whispered dialogue. However, while this movement by actors has remained consistent, the effects used to imply superhearing have changed across the seasons, with different kinds of distortion effects being used to imply the filtering of sounds. In this way, superhearing has enabled some complex uses of dialogue and sound effects, again saving the expense of having to recreate inner-ear CGI effects, or of having to show multiple sets (Clark has been shown in latter seasons listening for crime victims scattered around Metropolis while standing on a rooftop, see "Metallo" [2009]), allowing an expansion of *Smallville*'s aural world.

Perhaps some of the most frequently used and complex combinations of effects techniques are sequences that feature Clark Time and bullets (or other projectiles) being fired and then either pushed away, blocked, or melted using heat vision. Clark Time—sequences that are sometimes filmed using HD cameras at 120 frames per second, before additional CGI effects are added—were first introduced in "Accelerate" (2003). However, the first combination of bullets with Clark Time was used in "Rogue" (2002), as Clark's antagonist for the episode, a corrupt Metropolis policeman named Sam Phelan (Cameron Dye), attempts to shoot Clark during a museum robbery that Clark has been blackmailed into attending. The sequence shows a bullet being shot by Phelan and is paced according to the bullet, rather than Clark's speed of movement. Clark is shown in multiple shots moving his head first in one direction and then back again, moving his head out of the way of the bullet just in time to watch it go past him. Within the sequence, the bullet and its casing are CGI-generated objects, as is the distortion of the air shown by ripples that trail behind the bullet. The rest appears to have been shot using high-speed cameras, as is certainly the case for other examples of this type.[45] These sequences are taken to extremes in later seasons, as when Clark melts a rifle bullet shot by his father, Jonathan Kent (John Schneider), using his newly developed heat vision in a similar sequence in "Heat" (2002), or when he rescues Chloe from the White Queen/Amanda Waller's (Pam Grier) castle in "Checkmate" (2010). This latter example provides an experimental variation on this combination of visual effects, coming close to providing a series of comic book–style still panels. In this sequence, the combination of Clark Time, bullets, and heat vision is depicted as flashes of slow-motion movement interspersed with black interstitial frames. The experimental way in which this sequence boils down the key moments from past effects combinations demonstrates the extent to which a special effects shorthand has been developed within *Smallville*.

Where some powers, and even combinations of superpowers, have become so well developed within *Smallville* as to be representable via shorthand techniques, one superpower has gone in the opposite direction. Flight, within *Smallville*, has been the purview of its most threatening and aspiration-invoking characters. The techniques used have been relatively static in terms of visualization, using computer-generated effects to nod backward to the ways in which flight was depicted within other parts of the franchise, particularly the Superman films (Kara-El is shown flying, fist raised above her head, mimicking the performance of Kara-El/Supergirl in *Supergirl* [1984]). Clark Kent/Kal-El's Kryptonian adversaries, including Brainiac (James Marsters) and General Zod, are also shown flying. Motion-blur techniques are carefully combined with color on these occasions, as when Clark becomes Kal-El in "Crusade" (2004). Where Kara-El is depicted wearing red and blue, with a blurring streak of those colors shown in the wake of her flight, Zod, Brainiac, and Kal-El all wear black and are trailed by black visual effects. This creates an aside to the film versions of Superman and Supergirl, replicating the color schemes; whereas evil or threatening characters in *Smallville* are uniformly contrasted to that bright, primary-color-scheme blur. Martian Manhunter's flight is different, in that it is, in the first instance, preceded by a red glow from his eyes, and these points of red light are then intermingled with his flight blur. In subsequent episodes, for example in "Odyssey" (2008), his flight trail is entirely red, and midshots of the Manhunter carrying Clark actually show that surrounding flight light changing from red to golden as they near the sun. In these ways, *Smallville*'s heroic characters in flight tend to echo the franchise's dominant heroic color scheme of blue, red, and gold (the "suit"), providing us with not just flights, but also associative connotations born out of the franchise's "tights."

Conclusions

The "super" in *Smallville* is achieved through a wide range of techniques, some of which have gone almost entirely unremarked in the discourse that surrounds the show. For example, the only articles outside of direct promotional materials that focus on the stunt team of *Smallville* are about injuries suffered by Tom Welling's stunt choreographer and double, Christopher Sayour, after he landed badly in a high-fall stunt.[46] Within production discourses, however, there is a notable shift across the provision of special features on the *Smallville* DVDs, from an emphasis on visual effects in early seasons (especially for seasons two and three) to greater time spent covering creature effects and physical stunts for later seasons (perhaps especially for seasons eight and nine). However, this shift in discourse does not perfectly map onto how special and visual effects are utilized within *Smallville*. Within the show itself there are constant moves to alternately foreground different kinds of specific effects, sometimes physical effects like stunts (for example, when Lex Luthor hits Clark Kent with his Porsche in the pilot episode for *Smallville*, the sequence was largely produced through practical stunts and was reused in later episodes as well as featuring in *Smallville*'s opening credit sequence); sometimes visual effects (as in "Accelerate," which highlights a range of CGI-produced superspeed effects); and sometimes combinations, composited, or even in-camera effects shots (as in the Clark Time, bullet, heat vision combinations discussed above). This, along with the development and refinement of the show's special and visual effects enables a consistent production of spectacular imagery. However, as in the case of flight, that imagery can be grounded in emotional or psychological spectacles and character development, as much as in moments of display or "wonder."

Another important aspect of the show's special effects that tends to go unremarked is the use of visual effects to invisible ends. For example,

Mat Beck claims that "we do have effects where we'll remove somebody from a scene and replace him with somebody else. Or we create a split screen to insert a better performance."[47] Again, in the pilot for *Smallville*, Paul Simpson's companion book quotes Mark Millar as saying that almost all the corn depicted was computer generated because the corn grown specially for that episode had only gotten to be about two feet high.[48] The frequent use of CGI establishing shots for Krypton and the Fortress of Solitude, composited cityscapes (most notably used for scenes set in Metropolis), and CGI-enhanced landscapes found in *Smallville* all concur with Lury's claim that visual effects production is becoming increasingly common, and is going increasingly unnoticed, within television production.

However, television's wide use of other kinds of in-camera, physical, and stunt effects are receiving even less notice in film and television studies. In broaching the topic here, the aim was to suggest just some of the reasons for these elisions and some tantalizing ways in which special effects have been harnessed by television producers. Rather than attempting to be exhaustive, the hope is that this chapter can point to some of the ways that television uses special effects to traditionally "cinematic" and traditionally televisual ends. For example, the "supervision" superpowers depicted in *Smallville* tend to start from close-ups of Welling's eyes with added CGI light effects (initially yellow in his irises for heat vision, but the series has shown numerous others including red for red kryptonite, and rainbow shades were even used in season nine's Valentine's Day episode "Persuasion" [2010]). This alternative use of close-ups offers just one example of how techniques often associated with television production are being manipulated in *Smallville*, how they are being used to foreground the importance of special effects in televisual terms. Therefore, despite its "no flights, no tights" motto, *Smallville*'s new incarnation of Superman is redolent with special effects—special and visual effects which, as with earlier versions of the franchise, demonstrate key developments in the technologies of the "super."

Notes

1. Josh Wolk, "*Smallville*," *Entertainment Weekly* 612–613, 7 September 2001, 66.

2. Jeff Jensen, "Shows of Strength," *Entertainment Weekly* 627, 23 November 2001, 28.

3. For more on these, see Richard Berger, "'Are There Any More at Home Like You?' Rewiring Superman," *Journal of Adaptation in Film & Performance* 1, no. 2 (2008): 87–101.

4. See, for example, Dan North, *Performing Illusions: Cinema, Special Effects and the Virtual Actor* (London: Wallflower Press, 2008); Michele Pierson, *Special Effects: Still in Search of Wonder* (New York: Columbia University Press, 2002); Stephen Prince, "True Lies: Perceptual Realism, Digital Images, and Film Theory," *Film Quarterly* 49, no. 3 (Spring 1996): 27–37.

5. Advertisement, "*Superman: The Movie*," *Variety*, 3 January 1979, 33.

6. Jan Johnson-Smith, *American Science Fiction TV: Star Trek, Stargate and Beyond* (Middletown, CT: Wesleyan University Press, 2005), 58.

7. Lauro Chartrand was initially the named stunt coordinator for season one, but by season four, Chris Sayour is the central named stunt coordinator. See Paul Simpson, "Meet the Crew," *Smallville: The Official Companion, Season 1* (London: Titan Books, 2004), 150–151.

8. For just a few examples, see Ray Harryhausen and Tony Dalton, *Ray Harryhausen: An Animate Life* (London: Aurum Press, 2003 [2009]); Vincent Kehoe, *Special Make-Up Effects* (Boston: Focal Press, 1991); Richard Ricketts, *Special Effects: The History and the Technique* (London: Aurum Press, 2006); Francis Ridley, *Stuntmen and Women* (Tunbridge Wells: TickTock Books, 2009).

9. For excellent précis of these arguments, see Scott Bukatman, *Matters of Gravity: Special Effects and Supermen in the 20th Century* (Durham, NC: Duke University Press, 2003) and Pierson, *Special Effects*, or North, *Performing Illusions.*

10. Michele Pierson, "CGI Effects in Hollywood Science-Fiction Cinema 1989–95: The Wonder Years," *Screen* 40, no. 2 (Summer 1999): 175.

11. Pierson, *Special Effects*, 103.

12. Pierson, *Special Effects*, 63.

13. Karen Lury, *Interpreting Television* (London: Hodder Arnold, 2005), 18.

14. See Craig Byrne, "Meet the Crew," *Smallville: The Official Companion, Season 4* (London: Titan Books, 2007), 146–148, and Craig Byrne, "Meet the Crew," *Smallville: The Official Companion, Season 6* (London: Titan Books, 2008), 148–150.

15. Chris Sayour quoted in Byrne, *Smallville: The Official Companion, Season 4*, 47.

16. Mat Beck quote in Byrne, *Smallville: The Official Companion, Season 6*, 107.

17. Tara Bennett, "Keeping Superman Flying on *Smallville*," *Animation World Magazine*, 15 January 2009, http://www.awn.com/articles/production/

keeping-superman-flying-ismallvillei/page/2%2C1 (accessed 5 April 2011); Bill Desowitz, "*Smallville* Takes Final Flight," *Animation World Magazine*, 29 September 2010, http://www.awn.com/articles/article/smallville-takes-final-flight/page/2%2C1 (accessed 5 April 2011); Ellen Wolff, "*Smallville*: Greater Superpowers from Entity FX," *Animation World Magazine*, 20 September 2006, http://www.awn.com/articles/production/ismallvillei-greater-superpowers-entity-fx (accessed 5 April 2011); Jean Oppenheimer, "Young Man of Steel," *American Cinematographer* 88 (May 2007): 54–63.

18. J. P. Telotte, "Introduction: The Trajectory of Science Fiction Television," in *The Essential Science Fiction Television Reader*, ed. J. P. Telotte (Lexington: University Press of Kentucky, 2008), 5.

19. "Faster Than a Speeding Bullet," *Smallville* Season Two DVD.

20. Rick Kissell, "'Smallville' Bow Super for the WB," *Variety*, 18 October 2001, News, 1; Rick Kissell, "'Smallville' Gets Big for WB on Tuesdays," *Variety*, 17 October 2002, News, 4; Rick Kissell, "Leaps Tall Ratings," *Variety*, 26 January 2006, Special Report 2: *Smallville*'s 100th Episode, B1.

21. James Hibberd, "'Miami Medical,' 'Smallville' Drop in Friday Ratings," *Hollywoodreporter.com*, 30 November 2010, http://www.hollywoodreporter.com/blogs/live-feed/miami-medical-smallville-drop-friday-53419 (accessed 6 April 2011).

22. James Hibberd, "CW Downsizes: Sheds Comedy Division," *Hollywoodreporter.com*, 4 March 2008, http://www.hollywoodreporter.com/news/cw-downsizes-sheds-comedy-division-106143 (6 April 2011).

23. Brian Lowry, "Feeling Thin and Bargain Bin," *Variety*, 25 May 2009–31 May 2009, Television, 9.

24. "*Smallville*'s Doomsday: The Making of a Monster," *Smallville* Season Eight DVD.

25. "Absolute Justice: From Script to Screen," *Smallville* Season Nine DVD.

26. "Absolute Justice: From Script to Screen," *Smallville* Season Nine DVD.

27. "Absolute Justice: From Script to Screen," *Smallville* Season Nine DVD.

28. "*Smallville*'s Doomsday: The Making of a Monster," *Smallville* Season Eight DVD.

29. "*Smallville*'s Doomsday: The Making of a Monster," *Smallville* Season Eight DVD.

30. Simpson, "Craving," *Smallville: The Official Companion, Season 1*, 46.

31. "*Smallville*'s Doomsday: The Making of a Monster," *Smallville* Season Eight DVD.

32. Tara Bennett, "Keeping Superman Flying High on *Smallville*," 2009; Rick DeMott, "Entity FX Adds Effects to *Vampire Diaries*, *Smallville*, *Hellcats*," *Animation World Magazine*, 10 September 2010, http://www.awn.com/news/

television/entity-fx-adds-effects-vampire-diaries-smallville-hellcats (accessed 6 April 2011).

33. Ellen Wolff, "*Smallville*: Greater Superpowers from Entity FX," *Animation World Magazine*, 20 September 2006, http://www.awn.com/articles/production/ismallvillei-greater-superpowers-entity-fx (accessed 6 April 2011).

34. Gregg Beeman, quoted in Simpson, *Smallville: The Official Companion, Season 1*, 102.

35. Michael S. Duffy, "'Blow Up the Damn Ship!': Production Redesign and Special Effects Reuse in the *Star Trek* Films," in *The Influence of Star Trek on Television, Film and Culture*, ed. Lincoln Geraghty (Jefferson, NC: McFarland, 2008), 140–141.

36. Wolff, "*Smallville*: Greater Superpowers from Entity FX."

37. Desowitz, "Smallville Takes Final Flight." See also Bennett, "Keeping Superman Flying High on *Smallville*."

38. Desowitz, "*Smallville* Takes Final Flight."

39. Chris Sayour, quoted in Chris Byrne, *Smallville: The Official Companion, Season 5* (London: Titan Books, 2007), 103.

40. James Hibberd, "Witwer, Freeman Two New 'Smallville' Villains," *Hollywoodreporter.com*, 20 June 2008, http://www.hollywoodreporter.com/news/witwer-freeman-two-new-smallville-114285 (accessed 6 April 2011).

41. See, for example, Lisa Bode, "No Longer Themselves? Framing Digitally Enabled Posthumous 'Performance,'" *Cinema Journal* 49, no. 4 (Summer 2010): 46–70. Bode's interest in posthumous stardom preferences even dead stars over their living stand-ins. While this is perfectly understandable given her focus, it does highlight the fact that there has been little perceived need to study the stunt performer or double in depth.

42. Wolff, "*Smallville*: Greater Superpowers from Entity FX."

43. "Faster Than a Speeding Bullet," *Smallville* Season Two DVD.

44. Such referencing is not limited to special effects. It can also be seen and heard in the repetition of earlier catchphrases and in stunt casting. See Ian Gordon, "Superman on the Set: The Market, Nostalgia and Television Audiences," in *Quality Popular Television*, ed. Mark Jancovich and James Lyons (London: BFI Publishing, 2003), 148–162, for more on intertextual referencing within the Superman franchise.

45. Jean Oppenheimer, "Young Man of Steel," 62.

46. Lila Holland, "*Smallville* Stuntman Hospitalized," *TV.com*, 27 July 2005, http://www.tv.com/smallville-stuntman-hospitalized/story/491.html?print=1 (accessed 6 April 2011).

47. Wolff, "*Smallville*: Greater Superpowers from Entity FX."

48. Simpson, "The Pilot," *Smallville: The Official Companion, Season 1*, 22.

Part Two
AUDIENCES AND METATEXTS

Playing Superman. Picture courtesy of Van Norris.

CHAPTER FIVE

SMALLVILLE: SUPERHERO MYTHOS AND INTELLECTUAL PROPERTY REGIMES

Ian Gordon

On October 16, 2001, *Smallville* debuted on the WB, a network owned by the Time Warner Corporation. The WB was a fledgling network that focused on the teen young adult market and was at various times the home to such teen-focused series as *Dawson's Creek* (1998–2003), *Roswell* (1999–2002), *Buffy the Vampire Slayer* (1997–2003), and *Gilmore Girls* (2000–2007). *Smallville*, too, aimed at that teen market. The series set in the mythical Kansas hometown of Clark Kent/Superman contained the basic features of the Superman story, such as his parents having sent him as an infant in a spaceship to escape the doomed planet Krypton, Martha and Jonathan Kent finding him in the ship, and his super strength and speed. Some other aspects of the series came from the Superboy comics, the adventures of Superman as a teenager. For instance, just as in the Superboy comic book and the Superman movies, Lana Lang was Clark Kent/Superman's initial love interest. And, as in the Superboy comic books, Clark and Lex Luthor were friends and Lex was not predestined for evil. But in *Smallville*, Clark Kent did not don the familiar Superman suit, nor in general did he fly. The conceit of the series, at least in the first few seasons, was that Clark's powers were only just developing and that he, like a pubescent boy, was trying hard to adjust to the changes in his body. Although the series underplayed the superhero aspect of the character, the press nonetheless described *Smallville* variously as "Superboy redux," a "teenage Superman series," and "a teen friendly update of the Superboy saga." As this latter article suggested, it was a series "located just a mile or so upstream from *Dawson's Creek.*" The series, then, was both a teen angst–filled drama and part of the Superman mythology.[1]

Smallville is the third live television series of Superman. The first series in the 1950s, *The Adventures of Superman* (1952–1958), began as something akin to a hard-boiled detective series with Superman cracking the jaws of criminals, but after the first season the producers lightened the tone somewhat for a younger audience. That show ran for six seasons, although from the third season on only thirteen episodes, and not the usual twenty-six, were produced. Deborah Joy LeVine, the producer of the 1990s series *Lois & Clark: The New Adventures of Superman* (1993–1997), originally conceived of it as a light action-romance series along the lines of the Bruce Willis–Cybil Sheppard series *Moonlighting* (1985–1989). For various reasons, she soon had to add more action and somewhat less romance, muddying the focus of the series and losing some of its broad demographic appeal. As a result, the series only lasted four seasons. These two series and the film versions of Superman showed that the potential audience for a seventy-year-old comic book character is large and diverse, stretching from current comic book fan boys to those with a passing interest in the character. At the same time, segments of that potential audience are easy to lose if some aspects of a particular incarnation do not meet their expectations from prior encounters. The challenge for *Smallville* was to hold teen drama fans, which were a core of the WB's audience, and hopefully add Superman fans. A series with a "no flights, no tights" rule, that is without either the iconic Superman suit with its distinctive chevron (the crest symbol on the chest), nor the fully realized superpowers of the character, would at first instance seem to have an uphill battle to connect with fans of the superhero. But the series grounded itself in the Superman mythos, that is, a symbolic version of American beliefs and practices expressed or remembered in a "particularistic and idiosyncratic" fashion, even as the producers and writers sought to avoid putting off its teen audience with an overt display of superness.[2]

Smallville: Mythos Meets Derivation

The *Smallville* series producers used colors, symbols, and associations to tie *Smallville* to a larger Superman mythos. By tying *Smallville* to that mythos, the producers and writers clearly derived much of their settings and characters from long-standing features of Superman. One of the key elements of Superman over many years has been his superhero costume of a full-body blue skin-tight suit (once popularly known as a union suit but increasingly called spandex), red trunks, boots, and cape. This ensemble is set off by the red and yellow *S* crest on his chest, and in some incarnations also on his cape. Without the emblematic Superman costume, *Smallville*'s producers still replicated the color scheme of dominant red and blue simply and nonintrusively by having Clark Kent wear blue jeans with a red T-shirt. When Warner released seasons of *Smallville* in DVD box sets, red and blue dominated the design or was a key element. *Smallville* always appears in the same bold red as Superman's costume on the DVD covers, and Tom Welling, who plays Clark Kent in the series, more often than not appears in a blue T-shirt, or if not, then in a red one.

There are numerous other connections to the Superman mythos in the series. These include Annette O'Toole, who played Lana Lang in the movie *Superman II* (1980), playing his mother in *Smallville*. Guest appearances by Christopher Reeve, Margot Kidder, and Terence Stamp, respectively Superman, Lois Lane, and General Zod in the movies, also established a connection to earlier versions. Although these actors play different characters, in Stamp's case swapping from Superman's enemy to his father Jor-El, their presence evokes broader dimensions of Superman. Numerous playful references in the series link it to Superman. In the pilot, Clark Kent carries a copy of Friedrich Nietzsche's collected works including *Thus Spoke Zarathustra* (1885), which introduces the concept of the "superman," and Lana Lang asks him whether he is man or superman. In the first-season episode "Reaper" (2002), Lex Luthor says he received a copy of Nietzsche's *Will to Power* (1910) for his tenth birthday. In "Drone" (2002), Lex suggests to Clark that he run for student president under the slogan "Man of Tomorrow," and Clark says he stands for "truth, justice, and other stuff." The "Man of Tomorrow" was an alternative moniker for Superman in the 1950s, and "Truth, Justice, and the American Way," first used in the 1940s radio serial and later in the 1950s television series, is perhaps the most famous slogan associated with Superman. In the second-season episode "Nocturne" (2002), Lana refers jokingly to Clark Kent as "Man of Steel." In season two, many of the episodes feature music that "quotes" the *Superman* movie theme by John Williams. In season three, a police chief says to journalist Perry White,

"Don't call me chief," which references the 1950s television series' Perry White telling Jimmy Olsen not to call him chief.

And the list goes on, with key phrases, powers, and events from Superman's back catalog trotted out at regular intervals. Catchphrases from Superman's many incarnations such as "What is it? A bird? A plane?" "faster than a speeding bullet," "powers and abilities far beyond those of mortal men," "up, up, and away," "truth, justice, and the American way," "strange visitor from another planet," and "able to leap tall buildings at a single bound" appear in numerous episodes.[3] Likewise, references are made to other versions of the characters: Lois Lane cannot spell (as in the movies), a character is told to "kneel before Zod" (a favorite fan line from *Superman II*), Princeton scouts come to view Clark play football (Dean Cain who played Superman in the series *Lois & Clark* went to Princeton where he played football), Clark squeezes coal into a diamond (an oft-repeated trick in the comic book), and Chloe wonders what next, "spin the earth backwards on its axis?" a reference to *Superman* (1978).[4] In addition, appearances by numerous characters from DC Comics locate the series within the mythos. Characters such as the Flash, Green Arrow, Aquaman, and Bruce Wayne have also appeared in the show. And in one episode, a dog, seemingly with superpowers, arrives at the Kent house, and for a moment Clark toys with naming him Krypto, the name of Superboy's super pet dog in the 1950s and 1960s comic books. All of this suggests that *Smallville* is not just highly derivative of the original Superman, but part of a broader circulation of the Superman mythos. Moreover, the writers of the series work this mythos so that, as Angela Ndalianis has argued, "the *telling* of the myth has become *as* important as the myth that is told."[5]

Paul Ricoeur reminds us that through memory, the absent can be present; *Smallville* relies on the whole Superman mythos to remind us of the character, even though some of that mythos is not present. Once we have enough references, we can fill in the gaps. But what references, and what is enough for any given person? And each of us probably fills in the gaps in our own way, importing those bits from the Superman we remember, be it the 1980s film versions or the 1990s television versions, or the comic book versions from numerous eras. *Smallville* raises the question of what needs to be included and what can be left out for Superman to be Superman. And this in turn raises the issue of what makes Superman, Superman. Superman is a narrative in process to which we all bring our individual memories. Narrative shapes Superman because there, as Ricoeur notes, memories in the plural and memory in the singular are articulated, and differentiation is joined to continuity. But another part of the question is answered legally. Superman is Superman because the copyright and trademark owners say he is and mark him as such. *Smallville* is not simply derivative in a discursive sense, but also in a technical legal sense.[6]

Smallville uses one of the most distinctive popular fiction icons of America in a manner that stretches the mythos surrounding the character beyond the familiar. The significance of the series, then, is that it shows how many disparate narrative genres can be brought together under the rubric of Superman. At the same time, it raises questions about how far Superman can be stretched before the character is distilled beyond recognition. Such a dilution is a literal concern, as Superman is a trademarked and copyrighted piece of intellectual property, and distilling the character potentially distills the brand. But if Superman is also representative of an American ideology, as I have argued elsewhere, *Smallville* raises the question of how far the character can be stretched before it ceases to hold the symbolic value ascribed to it. *Smallville* is derived from Superboy comic books, which in turn were derivative and an adaptation of Superman comic books.[7] Just how much the series is derivative of Superboy and Superman is subject to legal determination as part of an ongoing battle between Superman cocreator Jerry Siegel's widow and daughter, and DC Comics, that began in 2004. Although the level of derivation is unlikely to be strictly enumerated, it is one of the issues raised in that case.

Mythos and Intellectual Property

The late Joanne Siegel and Laura Siegel Larson, Jerry Siegel's widow and daughter, have been trying to regain their share of the Superman copyright.[8] As the case has unfolded in the courts, the Siegels and their lawyers have argued for a particular construction of the Superman mythos and their opponents another. The case pits them against the Time Warner conglomerate and its comic wing, DC Comics. The case entails many complexities of intellectual property law, corporate structures, legal technicalities, and court procedures. Indeed there are two separate cases: one about Superman and one about Superboy. Because of issues of derivation, the Superboy case has been set aside until the various aspects of the Superman case are decided. As of March 2011, the cases are still before the court and may well be for some time. But on March 26, 2008, the court did rule that as of April 16, 1999, the Siegels had recovered the copyright to their half of Superman as he appeared in *Action Comics #1*. Joe Shuster, the cocreator of Superman, has no direct family heirs, and so the estate has not been part of this case because although the Copyright Term Extension Act of 1998 added the possibility of estates reclaiming rights, which enables a claim by Shuster's estate, the grounds for an estate are not as strong as for direct family members. Just exactly what that recovery of copyright meant is why the matter is still before the courts, but one key aspect is to show what parts of Superman in *Action Comics #1* are essential to the post–April 1999 Superman. At stake before the courts now are issues of adaptation and derivation. And that involves a determination of just what constitutes Superman. In this case, the Siegels have tried to show how the various incarnations of Superman in comics, television, and movies rely on Siegel and Shuster's original concept and realization of the character. As part of their case, they have explicitly argued in a submission to the court that DC-Warner's "Superman revenues are from *licensing* the Superman mythos" and that the key elements of this mythos were present in *Action Comics #1*.[9] What this entails according to the Siegels are his name, character, compatriots, origins, mission, and heroic abilities. These features extend further to "his square jaw good looks, dynamic costume, glasses, conservative dress, Lois's personality and the large city within which the action is set." Even the key themes and formats "for further episodic Superman stories" were present in the dual identity of Superman/Clark Kent, played out as a masterful/awkward bifurcation, the love triangle between these two identities and Lois, and the gruff editor assigning his reporters.[10] Superman stories, the Siegels have contested, exist "not in a vacuum but in the context of this well-known and beloved Superman story."[11]

DC-Warner's response was that "the Superman character and mythology have been significantly expanded with new characteristics, characters and story elements in the decades since *Action Comics #1* was published, and those new elements—which were never owned by Siegel and accordingly were not recaptured by Plaintiffs [Siegel's heirs]—permeate all of the post-termination works in various amounts."[12] The case, then, turns on differing views of mythos and on a determination of what characteristics were present at the beginning and how much these shaped what was to come. A key point may be that an idea cannot be copyrighted, only its execution or realization, and not all ideas contained in the early stories were fully realized. Also some elements of Superman are copyrighted, and other elements are trademarked, and a mix of the two elements permeates every appearance of the character. The constant appearances of numerous elements from the long history of Superman in *Smallville*, then, at the very least served the case of DC-Warner because it surrounded the character of Clark Kent, indisputably a creation of Siegel and Shuster, with an array of important markers not of their creation. So, for instance, although Siegel and Shuster had Superman able to "leap 1/8 of a mile" and "hurdle a twenty story [*sic*] building" in *Action Comics #1* in June 1938, this does not quite translate to "able to leap tall buildings in a single bound," a phrase that first appeared in the radio serial and attributed by radio historians to producers Allen Ducovny and Robert Joffe Maxwell.[13] Indeed the opening narration to the radio series, and later the television series, provided many of the key epithets associated with Superman. It ran: "Faster than a speeding bullet! More powerful than a locomotive! Able to leap tall buildings at a single bound!" Voices: "Look up in the sky! It's a bird! It's a plane! It's Superman!" Announcer: "Yes, it's Superman, strange visitor from another planet who came to Earth with powers and abilities far beyond those of mortal men. Superman, who can change the course of mighty rivers, bend steel in his bare hands, and who, disguised as Clark Kent, mild-mannered reporter for a great metropolitan newspaper, fights a never ending battle for truth, justice, and the American way."

Working many of these phrases into *Smallville* both heightens the association with the Superman mythos and weakens the series' connection to the Siegel and Shuster copyrighted elements. It also of course plays to the memory of those who saw the series in the 1950s and in its many reruns in the years that followed. By incorporating these phrases into *Smallville*, the producers and writers mesh the memory of an individual, say me, to a collective memory of Superman, which through this utterance is further associated with *Smallville*. Ducovny and Maxwell created these catchphrases as work for hire, and so the copyright for them belongs to DC-Warner. As of 2011, these issues have not been tested in court, but DC-Warner had the legal right to create derivative works based on Superman when it had these phrases authored and so owns these phrases free and clear of any claims by the Siegels.[14] Such ownership will help DC-Warner defend their trademark use of the word "Superman."

Those without legal training frequently misunderstand copyright and trademark. DC Comics argues that it holds both copyright and trademark ownership of Superman. Copyright and trademarks are both regimes of intellectual property, but their purpose and origins differ. Copyright, as originally conceived in the United States by the Copyright Act of 1909, provided authors with incentive to create artistic works by affording them protection, or ownership, in that work for twenty-eight years from the date of first publication, with one renewal period of twenty-eight years for a living author or immediate family. Trademarks as codified in acts of 1881 and more crucially 1905 allow corporations to register distinct marks as symbolic representations of their goods and services, the justification for which is that such marks provide citizens with a guarantee of certainty, at least in terms of the supplier of the product and presumably a uniformity of quality. The intention of this legislation was to protect consumers from fraudulent and dangerous products, and it was part of a package of progressive legislation that included the Pure Food Act of 1906. The basis of copyright is protection of the author (creator) of a work. The justification for trademark law is the protection of consumers because the mark acted as a guarantee that they could assume the same value and quality in goods so marked. But the practice of this law is that it protects the owners of trademark from infringers, and whatever the justification for the law, the key to property law is that it creates value (property) that can be commercially exploited, which is the case with both copyright and trademark, particularly when authors assign copyrights to publishers. The expansion of Superman into serial form, such as television series and the like, ensures the trademark protection of the character under a legal doctrine of secondary meaning, which offered protection for commercial signs based on use and popularity.[15] In part, DC argues that they own Superman under trademark law because they and they alone have continually reproduced the figure in series of ongoing works, or authorized such reproductions. This argument may have some weight in determining shares of revenue, but a 2003 Supreme Court case made clear that copyright trumps trademarks constitutionally. But since a good number of people would associate Superman with the distinctive opening phrases from the radio series and television series, part of the copyright that underpins the trademark will remain in DC-Warner hands regardless of whether or not the Siegels' recapture of the copyright to the original comic book appearance stands.[16]

The copyright history of Superman is useful in understanding the issues of derivation now under consideration. In a serial narrative that has run for over seventy years and had multiple authors and numerous incarnations in different media, how can Siegel's heirs have recovered their part of the copyright, apparently signed away by Jerry Siegel and Joe Shuster in 1938, from the company that can lay claim to being the one constant in the character's history? Siegel and Shuster first toyed with the idea of a superman in a January 1933 self-published short story, "The Reign of the Superman."[17] In this story, the superman was Nietzschean in concept, and the pair soon after redeveloped the concept creating a series of comic strips featuring a costumed hero, Superman, which they tried to sell to comic strip syndicates. This creation was not picked up by any of the syndicates, and Siegel and Shuster moved on to producing comic book material featuring other characters for the embryonic industry. In 1938 the two submitted the 1933 Superman strips to DC, which was looking for material for a new comic book, *Action Comics*. DC apparently required some revisions but accepted the material and in March sent Siegel a release form that contained clauses transferring to DC the first Superman story and "all good will attached thereto and exclusive right to the use of the characters and story, continuity and title of the strip . . . to have and to hold forever and to be your exclusive property" in exchange for a one-time payment of $130. In 1947 after some years of unhappiness with the nature of their contract, Siegel and Shuster attempted to have the March 1938 release declared void by the New York Supreme Court. Judge J. Addison Young's decision in this case declared that the March 1, 1938, release transferred all right to DC, which consequently "became the absolute owner of the comic strip Superman, including the title, names, characters and concepts." In the case of Superboy, Siegel submitted a script to DC in 1940, but the company apparently did not use this script when it eventually published a Superboy story in 1944. The 1947 case resulted in DC paying $94,000 to Siegel and Shuster as part of a negotiated settlement to ensure all rights to Superman and Superboy, which was formalized in a stipulation signed by the parties on May 19, 1948, and issued as a consent judgment by Judge Young on May 21, 1948.[18] That DC did not control the copyright to Superboy before May 21, 1948, is implicit in that case because the court found that DC controlled all rights to Superman, and the $94,000 was a sum exchanged in consideration for the rights to Superboy. And so it would seem the matter was closed. But the U.S. Copyright Act of 1909 that granted copyright protection for twenty-eight years on registration also provided that a copyright holder could renew copyright for a further twenty-eight years during the final year of the initial registration. Siegel and Shuster used this provision to launch another legal action against DC.

In this action, which was eventually decided in DC's favor in 1974, Siegel and Shuster argued that the 1948 settlement had not transferred the renewal rights to DC. The pair further argued that since the Superman strip they submitted to DC in 1938 was a fully developed work, it could not be, as DC argued, "work for hire" under the terms of the Copyright Act. In its judgment, the Second Circuit Court of Appeals found that DC controlled the renewal rights and found in favor of DC. But in doing so the court reversed a lower court's decision in this case that the 1948 settlement had deemed Siegel and Shuster's initial work in creating Superman as work for hire on the basis that, regardless of the fact that DC had required the pair to revise the work, Judge Young had found as a matter of fact in 1947 that Siegel and Shuster were "the originators and authors of the cartoon character Superman of the title Superman and first created cartoon material in which the said character and title first appeared in 1934." In 1974 this finding might have been a rather abstract point of law since it gained Siegel and Shuster nothing in legal terms. But ensuing changes in the U.S. Copyright Act gave this decision, along with the 1948 acknowledgement of Siegel's creation of Superboy, an unforeseen legal weight.[19]

In 1976, Congress passed a new Copyright Act, perhaps reflecting the general reform mood of the country following the turmoil of the Nixon presidency. The act incorporated some generous protection for the individual creators of intellectual property. Section 203 (a) (5) granted authors the right to terminate rights that they had transferred "not withstanding any agreement to the contrary." Because the act excluded work for hire from this termination right, the 1974 decision became particularly important for Siegel and Shuster, as did the 1948 case and the implicit recognition that Siegel created Superboy. Successive copyright acts culminating in the Copyright Term Extension Act of 1998 have extended the term of copyright protection so that now it is for the life of the author plus seventy years. This action obviously makes the Superman property more valuable; since Siegel died in 1996 and Shuster in 1992, the said copyright lasts at least until 2062 under the current law, and Siegel's share possibly until 2066. In their case against DC-Warner, the Siegels at first gained a ruling on March 23, 2006, that they had recaptured the copyright to Superboy due to renewal claims, but a later decision by Judge Stephen G. Larson on July 27, 2007, put this judgment aside and determined that the key to ownership turned on whether Superboy was a work derivative of Superman. Importantly Larson provided a detailed legal rationale why the decision in the 1948 case that Superman was not a work for hire must apply as a matter of collateral estoppel, which basically means that although the judge's decision was put aside in favor of a settlement between the two parties, the effort expended by the court and the better factual evidence before it requires that the decision hold weight in subsequent legal explorations of the nature of Superman's creation.[20]

There is some irony in DC-Warner's attempts to fend off derivation claims from Siegel's heirs. In its initial efforts to prevent competitors from duplicating the success of Superman in particular, and the new superhero genre in general, DC defended Superman and other copyrights. A series of cases beginning in 1939 saw DC argue in the courts that companies that published characters who were similar to Superman, in that they were endowed with superpowers and wore a superhero-type outfit, had breached DC's copyright with such derivative characters. In a 1940 case, *Detective Comics Inc. v. Bruns Publications Inc.*, the U.S. Court of Appeals Second Circuit upheld the lower court decision in *Detective Comics Inc. v. Bruns Publications Inc.* that Bruns's comic book character Wonderman had infringed DC's copyright in Superman. Handing down the decision of the judges, Augustus Hand determined that "the pictorial representations and verbal descriptions of 'Superman' . . . embody an arrangement of incidents and literary expression original with the author" and were the "proper subjects of copyright." The ink was scarcely dry on Hand's judgment before Fox Publications, a renamed Bruns, tested the meaning of Hand's "closely imitating" with two comic book characters, "the Lynx" and "Blackie the Mystery Boy" (clones of the Batman and Robin the Boy Wonder), published in Mystery Men Comics in August and September 1940. The

District Court of New York admonished Fox for not having learned its lesson in the early case and awarded $2,000 in damages to DC.[21]

In a case against Fawcett Publications that began in 1945 and dragged on to 1952, DC's copyrights of Superman were at first found to be faulty by the New York District Court, but on appeal were deemed to subsist by the Second Circuit Court of Appeals. Nonetheless, in his judgment for the court, Learned Hand insisted that although Fawcett was a "deliberate and unabashed" infringer of copyright, DC had to show exactly what copyright material had been reproduced before matters of infringement could be determined.[22] The judgment caused sufficient enough confusion that the court had to issue an explanatory *per curiam* in which it made clear that for matters to be determined, "a comparison of each strip put in suit by the plaintiff [DC] with Fawcett's strip" that allegedly copied a DC strip would have to be made and that each strip would need to be determined individually as to whether copyright subsisted.[23] When Hand issued his clarification of the judgment, comic books were somewhat on the wane, and Fawcett shut down its comic book line and paid DC damages. But this judgment must have raised some concern for DC because it suggested that each and every instance of Superman's appearance was subject to copyright testing, which might have proved a financially exhausting litigious process. Seemingly in control of its copyright, DC had registered the word "Superman," in a stylized form, as a trademark in 1939 and went on to register his general likeness and the distinctive chest logo as trademarks. Since trademarks can be renewed indefinitely, these property rights were and are more readily defendable.[24] But a trademark is simply a symbol or distinct likeness meant to provide a guarantee of uniform quality. The ability to derive a profit from reproducing a trademark rests on some value intrinsically linked to that trademark. In Superman's case, the trademark is a semiotic sign of Superman's qualities and character, things that are expressed in stories, which are subject to copyright. If the court in the current case was to follow the logic DC argued for in the early case, any incarnation of Superman is derivative of the original.

Smallville = Superman Redux?

In *Smallville*, the issue is not whether the series is derivative of Superman or not, but rather how much it is derivative. Legally the issue is how to determine the appropriation of copyright and trademark to any monetary value associated with the character through its use in the series. The status of the Superman crest, or chevron, is a useful example to show how the issue of intellectual property relates in an immediate monetary sense to *Smallville* and to issues of mythos and memory. The red and yellow crest on Superman's chest is an integral part of his costume. It is also a trademark registered by DC comics. The key marketing image of *Smallville*'s first season shows Tom Welling, naked from the waist up, as Clark Kent with a big red *S* drawn on his chest. To be sure, the *S* stood for Smallville in this instance, but the marketing was deliberate to create the connection to the *S* crest. The DVD of the first season used this image as a cover photograph, and the box used the stylized Superman *S* chevron, complete with the TM (trademark) symbol. Each subsequent box set also contains this mark. This *S* chevron cropped up again and again in the series, with the plot device being that it was akin to Superman's Krypton family crest. For instance, in an episode in the third season of the series, Clark has the *S* symbol burned into his chest. By season nine, Clark Kent wore a T-shirt with this symbol, albeit a black shirt with the symbol in white. The use of this symbol not only tied the series, which never used the word "Superman" except in jest, to the comic book character but also bound it to the intellectual property trademarked by DC. Indeed, the crest is such a key indicator of the character that issue 875 of *Action Comics*, the comic in which Superman originated, used the symbol on the cover, without any other appearance of Superman, to represent the character.

The success of *Smallville*, which according to court papers had generated over $300 million in "gross receipts after accounts receivable" (most likely this is Hollywood speak for profit) by June 30, 2006, made a share of the revenue from it something worth fighting over.[25] Although the case is by no means finalized, the court has held that the Siegels are only entitled to a share of the licensing fee of $45,000 per episode that DC receives from Warner Bros. Television Production under a December 5, 2000, agreement. This decision is a result of the complex corporate structure of the Time Warner Corporation and its many interlocking subsidiaries. The Siegels had tried to question the validity of one part of the corporation licensing the character to another part for below market value as a means of diverting profits. The court held that DC had acted appropriately and received market value.[26] Cut off from this avenue, the Siegels are still pursuing other aspects of the case. In an earlier submission to the court, the Siegels argued that "the Superman crest in *Action Comics* No. 1 and in its subsequent derivative form, with its unique and striking design and color combination is clearly copyrighted material" because it meets legal standards of having "'some value' as a composition [and] is no longer a 'mere label.'" They further argued that the crest trademarked by DC Comics in 1976 was clearly derivative of the original crest. Because in the Siegels' view the crest constituted "a derivative work under the Copyright Act, its exploitation in new post-termination works constitutes a 'mixed use' of copyright and trademark for which" DC must account to the Siegels.[27] In this view, DC-Warner would owe the Siegels money for the use of the crest on the DVD box sets. How much money would depend on how much the crest depended on copyright for its trademark status and how much the trademark is worth because of DC-Warner's keeping it in circulation. Beyond these legal issues, what else is at stake is how much the use of the crest tied *Smallville* to the larger Superman mythos and how much tying it to that mythos was worth in terms of sales of the DVD.

The use of the chevron on the DVD box set raises the issue of just who DC-Warner thought would buy boxed sets of *Smallville*. Given that the series played on the youth-oriented WB Network, perhaps DC-Warner clearly identified the box set as part of the Superman mythos to attract an older audience who missed it in broadcast mode. At the same time, as Rayna Denison points out, DC-Warner covered its bases by including on the DVD a comic intertext, "The Chloe Chronicles," accessible by playing the DVD on a computer with an Internet connection, in an effort to appeal to an information technology savvy, and presumably younger, audience.[28] Denison draws on the work of Aaron Barlow to argue that "DVD offers us not just the opportunity to reaccess film and television *post facto*, but also to access our memories of it and to have these memories reinscribed by the materials accompanying the text." She further notes that DVDs that contain a range of special or additional features are multitexts "of layered, competing yet combined narratives," which means that the DVD of *Smallville* added yet more layers to the Superman mythos beyond those added by the series in broadcast form.[29] The inclusion of the chevron means that the process of remembering might call on memories otherwise outside the frame of *Smallville*, but intrinsically and legally key to the Superman mythos.

DC-Warner released the first-season DVD box set in September 2003 almost two years after the initial run in broadcast. At that time the entertainment industry corporations discovered that a boxed set of a television series season was a handy earner as sales of compact discs declined in the face of consumers sharing digitized music. Marketing strategies were, if not entirely hit or miss, not well worked out and articulated. Indeed, given the flurry of new technology platforms through which to obtain and view a current series over the ten years of *Smallville*'s run—such as digital video recorders (DVR), TiVo, online streaming, iTunes, and torrent downloads—positioning the box sets in any year's marketing strategy seems to have been a work in progress and in constant flux. For instance, a long piece on DVDs in the *New York Times* in November 2004 scarcely mentioned boxed sets of television series, but did note that "executives in Fox's television division [have] discovered the tremendous revenue that a season on DVD can bring in."[30] Having released season one of *Smallville* in October 2003, Warner released season two in May 2004 and season three in November 2004. By December 3, 2004, the third-season box set ranked tenth in all DVD sales in the United States, one of two television series sets in the top ten.[31] So successful were Warner Bros. in marketing television DVD box sets that in 2005 this endeavor contributed a billion dollars in revenue to the corporation.[32] At the same time, Nielsen Media Research showed that owners of DVRs watched *Smallville* at twice the rate of those who did not possess the machine, which suggests that many fans of *Smallville* regularly recorded the series.[33] Such data raise the possibility that some fans at least collected the DVD not so much to have access to previously broadcast episodes, but because they wanted the DVD itself.[34] From 2005 to 2010, the company used the release of the previous season's DVD box set as a tie-in promotion to the launch of the current season of *Smallville*.

In a market in flux, the trademark symbol of Superman at least provided some consistency in the nature of the product being marketed; Warner was not in the business of selling DVDs so much as in the business of selling Superman on whatever media platform was available. The 250,000 units of *Smallville* it could sell for most seasons and the $10 million or so in revenue per season added to both the series' and the corporation's bottom lines, but also to the circulation and memory of the Superman mythos and a broader bottom line.[35] The business model was tried and tested for DC. Informing Jerry Siegel in 1940 that he had sold the film serial rights for Superman to Republic Pictures for $8,000, DC executive Jack Liebovitz noted that DC felt "assured that all the publicity we will receive as a result of this venture would aid us materially in building up the radio end and promoting the sale of licensed merchandise."[36] Because the DVD carries the Superman chevron, its circulation helps tie *Smallville* more closely to the Superman mythos than the broadcast of the series alone would, given that the chevron is mostly absent in individual episodes, and in doing so adds further value to the chevron as a symbol of Superman. And the chevron most likely broadens the audience for the DVDs and so adds value to *Smallville* based on the Siegels' and DC-Warner's shared intellectual property. The complexities of the legal case and the difficulties in determining apportionment of the recaptured copyright, accounting for shared copyright, and complex mixes of copyright and trademark are perhaps the reason the trial judge urged the parties to seek mediation and settle the matter out of court.[37] The symbolism of colors, the trademarks, and the various references to the world of DC comics define the character in *Smallville* to the point that anyone with any memory of Superman will recognize him in this series even without many of the usual points of reference. Such is the strength of the Superman mythos.

Notes

1. "The People Beat," *San Antonio Express-News*, 18 July 2001, G2; Phil Rosenthal, "A Lot of Nerve," *Chicago Sun-Times*, 16 May 2001, 54; "Frankenvision," *Toronto Star*, 26 October 2002, J2; Walt Belcher, "Here's Reality: 14 Days of Meeting Stars," *Tampa Tribune*, 16 July 2001, 3; Charlie McCollum, "ABC, WB Schedules Get Major Retooling," *San Jose Mercury News*, 16 May 2001, E1.

2. For more on *Lois & Clark*, see Ian Gordon, "Superman on the Set: The Market, Nostalgia and Television Audiences," in *Quality Popular Television: Cult TV, the Industry and Fans*, ed. Mark Jancovich and James Lyons (London: British Film Institute, 2003), 148–162; Hal Boedeker, "A New Lease of Life for the Teen of Steel," *Courier Mail*, 23 July 2001, 22. I borrow this idea of mythos from Faith Davis Ruffins, "Mythos, Memory, and History: African American Preservation Efforts, 1820–1990," in *Museums and Communities: The Politics of Public Culture*, ed. Ivan Karp, Christine Mullen Kreamer, and Steven D. Lavine (Washington, DC: Smithsonian Institution Press, 1992), 506–611.

3. See season four's "Crusade" (2004), "Run" (2004), and "Onyx" (2005); season five's "Thirst" (2005) and "Mercy" (2006); and season six's "Crimson" (2007).

4. See season four's "Gone" (2004) and "Spell" (2004), season five's "Reckoning" (2006), and season six's "Zod" (2006).

5. Angela Ndalianis, "Enter the Aleph: Superhero Worlds and Hypertime Realities," in *The Contemporary Comic Book Superhero*, ed. Angela Ndalianis (New York: Routledge, 2009), 286.

6. Paul Ricoeur, *Memory, History, Forgetting* (Chicago: University of Chicago Press, 2004), 16, 97.

7. Ian Gordon, "Nostalgia, Myth, and Ideology: Visions of Superman at the End of the American Century," in *Cultural Studies*, ed. Michael Ryan (Malden, MA: Blackwell, 2008), 1009–1021.

8. Joanne Siegel died February 12, 2011, when I was working on a final draft of this chapter; Bruce Weber, "Joanne Siegel, the Model for Lois Lane, Dies at 93," *New York Times*, 16 February 2011, B20.

9. *Siegel v. Time Warner et al.*, United States District Court—Central Division of California—Eastern Division, Case Nis. CV 04-8400 SGL (RZx), Plantiffs Submission, 21 July 2008 submission, 23.

10. These details are paraphrased from the Plantiffs' 21 July 2008 submission (23–24), but quotes and ellipses would make the text ungainly.

11. *Siegel v. Time Warner et al.*, Plantiffs Submission, 21 July 2008 submission, 23.

12. *Siegel v. Time Warner et al.*, United States District Court—Central Division of California—Eastern Division, Case Nis. CV 04-8400 SGL (RZx), Defendants Submission, 21 July 2008 submission, 35.

13. Anthony Tollin, *Superman on Radio* (Schiller Park, IL: Radio Spirits, 1997), 8.

14. Title 17 of the United States Code codifies American copyright law as enacted in numerous statutes; see chapter 1, sections 103 and 106.

15. Jane Gaines, "Superman, Television, and the Protective Strength of the Trademark," in *Contested Culture: The Image, the Voice, and the Law* (Chapel Hill: University of North Carolina Press, 1991), 213.

16. *Dastar Corp v. Twentieth Century Fox Film Corp.*, 539 U.S. 23 (2003).

17. Aldo Regalado, "Unbreakable and the Limits of Transgression," in *Film and Comic Books*, ed. Ian Gordon, Mark Jancovich, and Matthew P. McAllister (Jackson: University Press of Mississippi, 2007), 116–136.

18. *Siegel v. National Periodical Publications Inc.*, 364 F. Supp. 1032 (1973) gives details of the 1948 action.

19. *Siegel v. National Periodical Publications Inc.*, 508 F.2d 909 (1974).

20. Dave McNary, "Super Snit in 'Smallville'; Skein Faces Copyright Infringement Charges," *Daily Variety*, 4 April 2006, 1.

21. 111 F.2d 432 (2d Cir. 1940); 28 F. Supp. 399 (D.N.Y. 1939); *Detective Comics Inc. v. Fox Publications Inc. et al.*, 46 F. Supp. 872 (D.N.Y. 1942).

22. *National Comics Publications Inc. v. Fawcett Publishers Inc.*, 93 F. Supp. 349 (1950); and *National Comics Publications Inc. v. Fawcett Publications Inc.*, 191 F.2d 594 (1951).

23. *National Comics Publications Inc. v. Fawcett Publishers Inc.*, 198 F.2d 927 (1952).

24. Superman trademark: U.S. Trademark Serial No. 71410024 registered 10 October 1939.

25. Expert report of Steven D. Stills filed 10 December 2007 in *Siegel v. Time Warner et al.*, United States District Court—Central Division of California—Eastern Division, Case Nis. CV 04-8400 SGL (RZx), CV 04-8776 SGL (RZx).

26. *Siegel v. Time Warner et al.*, United States District Court—Central Division of California—Eastern Division, Case Nis. CV 04-8400 SGL (RZx), Honorable Stephen G. Larson, U.S. District Judge, "In Chambers Findings of Fact and Conclusions of Law Following Trial," 8 July 2009, 5, 29.

27. *Siegel v. Time Warner et al.*, United States District Court—Central Division of California—Eastern Division, Case Nis. CV 04-8400 SGL (RZx), "Plantiffs' Memorandum of Points and Authorities on Pre-Trial Issues Filed Pursuant to the Court's July 3, 2008 Order," 11 August 2008, 56–57.

28. Rayna Denison, "It's a Bird! It's a Plane! No It's DVD!" in *Film and Comic Books*, ed. Ian Gordon, Mark Jancovich, and Matthew P. McAllister (Jackson: University Press of Mississippi, 2007), 162.

29. Denison, "It's a Bird! It's a Plane! No It's DVD!" 163, 178.

30. Jon Gertner, "Box Office in a Box," *New York Times Magazine*, 14 November 2004, 104.

31. "Best Sellers—Video," Associated Press wire, 3 December 2004, Factiva: Document APRS000020041202e0c3007eq (accessed 20 February 2011).

32. David B. Wilkerson, "Time Warner Beats View, Confirms Adelphia Bid," *MarketWatch*, 4 February 2005, LexisNexis (accessed 20 February 2011).

33. David Bauder, "TV Executives Defend Effectiveness of Ads," *Philadelphia Inquirer*, 18 November 2005, E12.

34. This effect can be seen in the desire to own and the purchase of the Universal Horror films box set as described in Peter Hutchings, "Monster Legacies: Memory, Technology and Horror History," in *The Shifting Definitions of Genre: Essays on Labeling Films, Televisions Shows and Media*, ed. Lincoln Geraghty and Mark Jancovich (Jefferson, NC: McFarland, 2008), 216–228.

35. Exact sales figures are not so easily come by, and DC-Warner did not produce detailed information of these during the court case. But a website, http://www.the-numbers.com, shows that in most years since 2006, *Smallville* sold about this many copies (accessed 22 February 2011). See http://www.the-numbers.com/dvd/charts/weekly/2010/20100926.php (2010), http://www.the-numbers.com/dvd/charts/weekly/2009/20090927.php (2009), http://www.the-numbers.com/dvd/charts/weekly/2008/20080928.php (2008), http://www.the-numbers.com/dvd/charts/weekly/2007/20071007.php (2007), and http://www.the-numbers.com/dvd/charts/weekly/2006/20061001.php (2006).

36. Jack Liebovitz to Jerry Siegel, 2 May 1940. *Siegel v. Time Warner et al.*, United States District Court—Central Division of California—Eastern Division, Case Nis. CV 04-8400 SGL (RZx), Document 353-3.

37. At the time of writing (24 February 2011), the copyright case has not been resolved. On 21 September 2009, the Siegels agreed to the court serving as a mediator since they had been unable to reach a settlement of issues with DC-Warner. Following that, Judge Stephen G. Larson resigned from the court to re-enter private practice. With matters remaining unsettled, DC-Warner fired their lawyers and then with a new team of lawyers led by Daniel M. Petrocelli sued the Siegels' lawyer Marc Toberoff for enticing the Siegels into what they termed a series of unlawful agreements that would leave Toberoff with a controlling stake in Superman. Matters are now tied up in court on legal technicalities: "'Superman' Lawsuit Delayed by Appeal," *Hollywood Reporter*, 18 October 2010, http://www.hollywoodreporter.com/blogs/thr-esq/superman-lawsuit-delayed-appeal-31344 (accessed 24 February 2010).

CHAPTER SIX

VIDS, VLOGS, AND BLOGS: THE PARTICIPATORY CULTURE OF *SMALLVILLE*'S DIGITAL FAN

Juli Stone Pitzer

Smallville's series finale on May 13, 2011, ended its ten-year run as the longest-airing Superman comic book adaptation on American television, beating earlier shows such as *The Adventures of Superman* (1952–1958), *Superboy* (1988–1992), and *Lois & Clark: The New Adventures of Superman* (1993–1997). As a popular television series, *Smallville* was able to find long-term reception among its new-millennium audience of dedicated fans. This chapter provides an overview of *Smallville*'s digital fan studies that explores some of the factors that have contributed to the successful generation and retention of *Smallville* fans. It looks at the relationship between networks and fans, and how new technologies affected the formation, participation, and sustainability of online fan communities. Studies of *Smallville*'s fandom have multiplied recently due to the contemporary nature of fan practices and technologies highlighted here. Further evidence can be found in this collection's section on fans and the metatext.

The so-called digital revolution has given unlimited access to a new form of participation in the consumption and production of media. Lev Manovich writes, "Today we are in the middle of a new media revolution—the shift of all culture to computer-mediated forms of production, distribution, and communication."[1] Digital fans are not limited to collecting *Smallville* merchandise and attending events like the San Diego Comic-Con, although they may do this regardless. This generation of fans is able to interact with the show through new digital media avenues.

Digital technologies have changed fan consumption, production, and ultimately fan identification, and they allowed for unprecedented outlets for storing, archiving, distributing, and exhibiting content. This chapter will identify and analyze the ways *Smallville* fans have used the Internet and new media resources to organize, discuss, and manipulate the series in order to interact with and produce new texts, thus enabling a self-sustaining fan community and prolonging the life of the series. Fans in the digital age are participating in the sustained formation of a global *Smallville* fan community. To borrow a phrase from Nancy Baym, fans are "tuning in, logging on," and creating relationships between themselves, the broader audience, and the *Smallville* franchise. *Smallville*'s success as the longest Superman television adaptation may owe itself to the new digital fandom of the twenty-first century.

Henry Jenkins writes that fans must translate their "viewing [or consumption experience] into some kind of cultural activity, by sharing feelings and thoughts about the program content with friends, by joining a 'community' of other fans who share common interests. For fans, consumption naturally sparks production."[2] Jenkins' definition of fans requires specific fan actions that he has defined as follows: having a distinct mode of reception, creating interpretive communities, engaging in consumer activism, extending fan partialities into everyday life, becoming producers in a particular art world, and ultimately creating an alternative social community.[3] Within this social community is what Mark Jancovich calls fans' subcultural identity—the distinction between an authentic and inauthentic fan.[4] Together fans create their own tastes, interests, language, and metatexts, ultimately defining a specific *Smallville* fan identity.

While other popular shows such as ABC's *Lost* (2004–2010) have generated an enormous fan following that participated in online fan communities, *Smallville*'s online fandom was one of the first programs whose online marketing and fan participation was both supported and sanctioned by its creator the Warner Bros. (the WB) Television Network. The WB's role as a complicit catalyst in generating online fan formation was truly vital to the evolution and retention of *Smallville* fans. This chapter focuses on the relationship between the network and fans, as well as the ways digital technologies and new media have enabled collective fan communities to interact in new spaces, such as the Internet. This chapter begins with an overview of the WB's marketing strategies for generating and sustaining online fan communities for *Smallville* in the network's attempt to monitor fan behavior. It illustrates how the WB and the digital fan community's relationship operates in the give and take of maintaining successful and collective support of the show. The next section identifies *Smallville*'s digital fan base and the formation of a fan community identity. The third section defines and characterizes *Smallville*'s online fan community, subcultural identity, and fan activities. It focuses on fan practices as producers of new media texts and as consumer activists sharing a direct or indirect dialogue with network producers. Finally, the fourth section acknowledges digital fan art productions and some of the legal issues that fans have faced when distributing content online.

The WB's Strategies in Marketing to Its Digital Audience

While many theorists in the 1990s looked to the digital revolution as a mechanism that would change and ultimately replace older media forms, Jenkins writes instead about the digital transition and media convergence. "Convergence," he says, "alters the relationship between existing technologies, industries, markets, genres, and audiences. Convergence alters the logic by which media industries operate and by which media consumers process news and entertainment."[5] Jenkins focuses on old and new media convergence rather than one replacing the other, and he emphasizes the ways that convergence changes both the production and the consumption of media. José van Dijck indicates that the result of this convergence is a "participatory culture which increasingly demands room for ordinary citizens to wield media technologies—technologies that were once the privilege of capital-intensive industries—to express themselves and distribute those creations as they seem [*sic*] fit."[6] Quoting Anne Friedberg, Dan Harries adds, "The movie screen, the home television screen, and the computer screen retain their separate locations, yet the types of images you see on each of them are losing their medium-based specificity."[7] As these technologies converge, audiences are exercising more options in how they choose to consume television programming and other media.

Historically, both old and new media have affected how fans consume television programming. The introduction of the VCR in the 1980s created "convenient consumption," providing audiences with the freedom to record and watch favorite shows at their convenience. New media devices such as the digital video recorder (DVR) and TiVo have further improved convenient consumption. According to Bear Stearns Equity Research, in the United States, DVR usage has risen from 1 percent of households using the technology in 2001 to about 40 percent with DVRs in 2009.[8] The Internet has opened pathways to consume television programming from sites such as Hulu.com, Netflix.com, and also from the network sites themselves. TheWB.com continues to make full episodes of *Smallville* available online, while CWTV.com, the new network site for *Smallville*, offers streaming episodes from the current season for those who missed the show live or wish to watch it multiple times. The Internet and new computer software have allowed for instantaneous fan participation as both consumers and producers, something that the WB Network realized with *Smallville*'s first season and found a way to create their own fan space where the studio could monitor the behaviors of fans.

Cary M. Jones' article "Twenty-First Century Superman: *Smallville* and New Media Mythmaking" provides a contextual narrative of how the WB, Warner Bros.' original television network, used marketing strategies to generate an online fan following during the premiere season of *Smallville* in 2001. She outlines a three-tiered strategy that included (1) pursuing a young audience, (2) drawing upon the cultural capital of a character associated with both Americanness and comic book fandom, and (3) encouraging an active participatory culture by extending the metatext of the show into familiar formats of fandom.[9]

Outlining the first two strategies, the WB Network's target audience was females eighteen to thirty-four years old, with successful, youth-oriented shows like *Dawson's Creek* (1998–2003) and *Buffy the Vampire Slayer* (1997–2003). However, Jones emphasizes the struggle the network faced in trying to adapt a show about a male comic book hero, Superman, for a primarily female audience. The WB turned the focus onto the young actor Tom Welling, who would play Clark Kent. Using Welling's "sex appeal," the network marketed the shirtless pre-Superman to the young female audience.[10] The network also wanted to draw in a strong male viewership. In dealing with their two presumably divergent target audiences, the show was cross-marketed as an interwoven narrative of relationships for its female audience and the Superman icon with action-packed CGI sequences for its male viewers.[11] This strategy allowed the network to develop the new story of Clark Kent's adolescent and young adult experiences while building on the Superman comic franchise and its established fan base.

The third aspect of encouraging an active participatory culture may have been the most important marketing tool for activating a fan space online. Referencing Jenkins' article on interactive audiences, Jones demonstrates how "media consumers relate to each other, to media texts, and to media producers"[12] by way of new participatory trends that began at the turn of the century with more access to online venues and increasing new digital capabilities. Jones writes, "The WB's success in marketing *Smallville* on the Internet can be attributed simply to teenagers' familiarity with the act of going online for information, [and] viewers' comfort level with the computer interface itself plays a significant role in the context of the show's structure."[13] The WB used young people's comfort with online interaction to create a network of sites that would draw fans toward interactive, multimedia platforms. This strategy also called for a more synergized approach between the network and its soon-to-be fan market.

From 2001 to 2004, the WB created and ran an online network of Internet sites that would help draw fans into interactive multimedia platforms called Smallville.net. Smallville.net is a network of series-related sites that allow fans to explore multiple facets of the world of *Smallville.* Its main page or entry page, Smallville.net, allows visitors to virtually explore the town of Smallville through an interactive map. By using the mouse to roll over hot spots, users can be hyperlinked to places like the Talon and the Kent family farm for more information. On its sidebar, Smallville.net has links to four other *Smallville*-related sites. One link takes users to an online version of Smallville High School's student newspaper called *The Torch*, edited by Clark's schoolmate, Chloe Sullivan. During the first few seasons when Clark was in high school, the page was updated with information like Chloe's tracking of mutations through her "Wall of Weird." Similar to *The Torch*, a third site called *The Ledger*, Smallville's weekly newspaper, was also updated weekly to reflect events from regular episodes. Luthorcorp, a fourth site, was dedicated to the business aspects of Lionel and Lex Luthor's enterprise.

The WB also created a separate space for *Smallville* fans on its network website. It utilized online forums to entice fans with the latest gossip at TheWB.com. Bringing the fan community to the network allowed the WB to monitor fan behaviors and control fan access to online environments in order to become more "knowledgeable about their fan communities."[14] *Smallville* fans participating in the WB's forums had to create their own user identity in order to gain access to the forum. The network's forums allowed fans to participate in online discussions on the latest gossip about the cast or characters, or to exchange their opinions about recently aired episodes. Website administrators could then distribute collected information to studio executives, following a similar format used with focus groups. After the merger with CBS, creating the CW Television Network (the CW) in 2005, online fan communities generated by the WB were turned over to the CW's website to create new *Smallville* fan content. The WB's original decision to take the show online on its own website and create sites for fans encouraged an interaction between media, producer, and fan, as stewards of a *Smallville* fan community. This interaction extends further when fans begin to generate their own online communities creating a larger tree of participatory culture.

Identifying *Smallville*'s Fan Base

By identifying specific fan groups and fan activities, generalizations can be made about how *Smallville*'s online fan world functions as both a supportive and critical mechanism for the television series, aiding in *Smallville*'s longevity and creating what Pierre Levy calls "collective intelligence," or consumption that has become a collective community process.[15] Every television series has a specified target audience from which a fan base can be cultivated. Though data can be collected and analyzed by the Nielsen Company to generate viewer demographics, it is difficult to pinpoint the "typical" *Smallville* fan online. For the purpose of this chapter, fans are generally defined as the viewing audience who continually watched the show and participated in online fan communities. Both males and females actively create fan sites, blogs, vlogs, and discuss *Smallville*-related content in forums, but the typical fan is difficult to identify due to the anonymity of Web activities. However, there are specific fan activities online that help pinpoint things like gender, age, and ethnicity. Fans that vlog, or make personal video Web logs, are identifiable by their on-camera, videotaped diaries, such as those found on YouTube.com. There are also pockets of fans, such as vidders—fan music video makers—that are historically female fans. This research attempts to identify *Smallville*'s gendered online community where it is necessary and able to do so, but is more interested in defining how online activities help create a unified fan body, a collective community that sustains the television program by satisfying current fans and bringing new fans to *Smallville*.

Smallville fan participation is defined by user agency expressed through interactions online. José van Dijck defines Internet users as "active internet contributors, who put in a 'certain amount of creative effort.'"[16] In her article "Users Like You? Theorizing Agency in User-Generated Content," she references a survey of American participation online that categorizes user participation into six tiers of online activity. In the first, only 13 percent of online users are considered to be "active creators," or those who produce and upload content (like fan art, vlogs, or vids). In the second, 19 percent are considered "critics" who rate or give evaluations of online content. Another 15 percent make up the third group called "collectors" who bookmark URLs, join groups, and save content for later retrieval. People who join groups like Facebook but do not contribute to these social networks make up 19 percent of users in the fourth group, called "joiners." It may come as no surprise that the majority of users in the last two groups—33 percent termed "passive spectators" and 52 percent termed "inactives"—may read materials but do not actively engage in online communities.[17] Though *Smallville* may have generated a couple million viewers per episode, a very small share of these viewers may be considered true fans by Jenkins' definition, and of these only a small percentage could be considered active online users or fan producers.

The focus here is on the small percentage of fans that make up *Smallville*'s digital fan community of online users who both produce and distribute content in online fan communities—fan sites, forums, blogs, vlogs, digital fan art, and vids.[18] These fans express user agency in ways that Mark Jancovich explores among "authentic fans." Authentic fans may consider themselves to be ultimate fans that adhere to a set of shared fan values and may consider themselves guardians of the original Superman metatext. These fans also use computer software and other technologies to produce fan art and music videos or vids and distribute these works online. It is through these fan production activities in forums, blogs, vlogs, and fan sites that the participatory nature and formation of the particular *Smallville* fan collective identity or collective community can be understood.

Fan Participation and Consumer Activism

In *Fans, Bloggers, and Gamers: Exploring Participatory Culture*, Jenkins writes,

> As early participants [in new fandom] spread news about emergent fandoms, supporters quickly develop the infrastructure for supporting critical dialogue, producing annotated program guides, providing regular production updates, and creating original fan stories and artwork. The result has been an enormous proliferation of fan websites and discussion lists.[19]

As Jenkins illustrates, the Internet has created a "new digital environment [that] increases the speed of fan communication, resulting in what Matthew Hills calls 'just in time fandom' . . . so that fans now go online to discuss new episodes immediately after the episode's transmission time or even during ad-breaks [*sic*] perhaps in order to demonstrate the 'timeliness' and responsiveness of their devotion."[20] Fan sites of both general and focused orientation have created a place where fans can engage and interact with the television program within their own online communities. Though the WB created its own fan-friendly websites for devoted *Smallville* fans to explore and engage in, fans were also active online creating their own "interpretive communities" that help to form the basis for "consumer activism," two of Jenkins' six fan actions highlighted by Janet Staiger in her text *Media Reception Studies* and mentioned above in the introduction.[21] These interpretive communities offer a place where fans can interact with the program, engage with one another, and distribute content or fan-generated material productions.

Some of the most common interpretive communities, or places where "groups discuss, debate, and for newcomers, teach perceptions of variation among the formulas, explanations for aspects of the text or performance, and predictions of future encounters with [*Smallville*],"[22] are *Smallville*'s fan-generated devotee sites that focus on specific characters, actors, or aspects of the show. Fan devotion sites from all over the world have been created to dote on Clark Kent, Lois Lane, Chloe Sullivan, Lana Lang, and Lex Luthor, as well as actors Tom Welling, Erica Durance, Allison Mack, Kristin Kreuk, and Michael Rosenbaum. DevotedToTomWelling.com, for example, contains facts, photos, behind-the-scenes information, forums, and a place for fan-created media. Fans can unify themselves through general *Smallville* community sites or more specialized *Smallville* online networks, as both serve as informative mechanisms and speculative avenues for online community interaction.

Popular fan community sites like Kryptonsite.com include cast member bios, episode guides, the latest news and gossip, and discussion boards. Kryptonsite was once devoted to *Smallville* exclusively but has expanded its fan community to include information for series like ABC's *V* (2009–Present), the CW's *Vampire Diaries* (2009–Present), NBC's *Heroes* (2006–2010), and Fox's *Human Target* (2010–Present). The site continually deletes or adds new network programs to its repertoire based on each new season, and it provides gossip to potential comic spin-off programs like the new Wonder Woman series.

Kryptonsite was a pioneer fan site for knowledge transfer about the *Smallville* series, aiding in the further cultivation of fan identity and community participation online.[23] Cornel Sandvoss writes that the "projection of self-identity on to a collective, resulting in a distinct sense of belonging, illustrates the ambiguity of identity construction between self and community in fandom."[24] The function and role of the online fan community thus becomes important in creating both an individual and a collective identity. Acknowledging Pierre Bourdieu's work in cultural distinction, Nancy Baym writes, "The locus of community or culture is in the ordinary practice of its members. It is their habitual ways of acting that support, maintain, and continually recreate a group's norms, values, and belief systems."[25] There are four communicative practices identified by Baym that can be attributed to other television and media fan cultures including *Smallville* fan sites. These practices of informing, speculating, criticizing, and reworking together build an individual and collective *Smallville* fan identity or culture.

According to Baym, fans inform the community by sharing information about the television series: its cast, story and plotlines, and related material that new or current fans need to know.[26] Like other television series' fans, *Smallville* fans can "draw on information beyond the [media producer's] texts" such as "magazines, star appearances, commercial computer networks, and other sources" to provide their own interpretation of the series.[27] Likewise, online communities offer fans avenues to discuss and speculate about the television program. They treat "the story like a game in which they try to discern what a character is like, what could happen, what should happen, what will happen, how it will happen, and what the ramifications throughout the [*Smallville*] community should be."[28] Spoilers, or inside information about future episodes, may also be given out. Sites like Kryptonsite contain internal links (links to information found within the Kryptonsite website) to general information about *Smallville*. Forums, however, are where fans, or users of the site, can inform, discuss, and speculate about current and past episodes and characters.

Forums operate under certain guidelines generally accepted as proper fan behavior. These guidelines often outline what is acceptable language, terms, and usage pertaining to specific websites and discussion forums. These group values can be seen in Kryptonsite's forums. The forum itself has its own rules that govern what can and cannot be posted; yet the individual message boards within the forum also include more site-specific guides for users. Kryptonsite's operators post many forum rules, but users can post their own concerns or suggestions that can ultimately be turned into guidelines for other user-fans. These rules may address language used in posts, topics allowed in the forum or discussion threads, and distribution of copyrighted material. Fans who serve as informers may help instruct current and new fans of the proper *Smallville* online fan etiquette. This etiquette also crosses into the final two aspects of Baym's fan community interactions: criticism and reworking. Both practices of criticizing and reworking occur within fan communities and in forums, and they can also form the basis for what is termed "consumer activism."

Fans criticize the show "at multiple levels including internal consistency and quality of props, sets, acting, writing, and ideological content among other criteria."[29] They can rework the program to illustrate what would or could happen if changes were made. Fans who become consumer activists may campaign to save programs or change or alter storylines and character depictions that they dislike. Mark Jancovich writes of this subcultural fan behavior as becoming "authentic fans" in which fans see themselves as ultimate fans that govern the authenticity of the program as well as dictating and deciphering other fan behaviors.[30] Janet Staiger points out how this activism can sometimes generate an "interaction with media producer and fan in online communities."[31] However, this interaction can often be difficult to pinpoint, and direct impacts on series' constructs are difficult to quantify. Yet these odds do not keep "authentic fans" from voicing their opinions in both direct and indirect dialogue with networks.

One example of consumer activism and fan protest was demonstrated online through *Smallville*'s seasons one and two. These seasons incorporated the "villain of the week" or "freak of the week" format, where Clark faced and defeated a new kryptonite-generated villain in each episode. Though these initial *Smallville* seasons gained a significant viewership share from the major networks, fans complained about the staleness of the plot in sites like Television without Pity (televisionwithoutpity.com), an early fan-generated online community. By season three, the nature of the show's narrative had changed, following a more continuous and connected storyline where each episode built to the season's finale and ultimately contributed to the longevity of the series. Whether the activism of online fans generated these changes is difficult to prove, but online fan communities may influence media producers in multiple media platforms. As demonstrated by the WB, media producers and studio executives are paying attention to fan activities online, and fans themselves believe that their activities online are worthy of their attention.

Another example of Jancovich's "authentic fan" behavior is an active fan group called the Red Jacket Defenders. The Red Jacket Defenders positioned themselves as active resisters of the studio's storyline and character development. They organized an online campaign in the fall of 2007 called Operation Save Clark Kent (OSCK) in order to "tell the executives at DC Comics and Warner Brothers how [they] felt about the dis-respect [*sic*] being shown to the Superman legacy."[32] The main purpose for their attack was due to their belief that,

> The character portrayed on *Smallville* during the end of season 6 and into season 7 bore little resemblance to the character defined for over 70 years in American popular culture. They believed that *Smallville*'s Clark Kent can be written to restore faith in the character and give hope, a staple of the Superman character, to future generations of Superman fans.[33]

The Red Jacket Defenders used their collective cultural agency as authentic fans—invested in upholding the history, storyline, and what they deem as the true character of Superman—to attack the network's portrayal of the young Clark Kent. Since these fans did not feel that the studio upheld their vision of the metatext, they believed their protest could help shift the program back on track, while dismissing the show's portrayals as inauthentic. The Red Jacket Defenders believed their efforts played a role in the series shift in management and creative direction in 2008 and commended season eight for its back-to-his-roots Clark Kent. The direct relation between the advocacy of the group and network decision making is unclear, but fan groups like the Red Jacket Defenders feel a sense of validation when they perceive that their ideas are taken into consideration and reflected in series' changes.

Blogging and vlogging have also become online tools for direct interaction between media producer and fan consumer. Fans who blog (a word short for "Web log") or vlog (fans who "video log") share common authentic fan behaviors online. Jenkins categorizes bloggers as those who "take knowledge into their own hands, enabling successful navigation within and between these emerging knowledge cultures."[34] A vlogger, for example, videos him/herself providing personal insights and commentary in discussing aspects of *Smallville* in terms of story, plotline, and character. Both bloggers and vloggers can function as interpreters, reactors, informers, and consumer activists participating within the online fan community.

Blogging and vlogging can also lead to general fan identification. As previously noted, it is often difficult to identify online demographics of *Smallville*'s fans due to the nature of online anonymity. Since vlogs involve the direct recording of the individual or individuals (as some vlogs are shared experiences between multiple people on camera), age, gender, and race help define the fan through his/her visual characteristics. Blogs, moreover, are generally personal sites in which the blogger may also be more likely to identify him/herself. Blogging may have preceded vlogging, due to the file size and availability of hosting Web video, but sites like YouTube have enabled vloggers to express fan agency by providing them with both a space and a voice. In addition, the increased affordability of digital video and Web cameras has enabled fans to utilize this area for expression with greater frequency.

From October 2007 to May 2008, the CW teamed with Sprint in putting out a call for fans to submit vlogs as part of a contest called the *Smallville*/Sprint Vlogger of the Month Competition. The winning vlogger was deemed "Vlogger of the Month," and his/her vlog was showcased on the CW site, upon which their thoughts and opinions on any aspect of the show aired that season were portrayed.[35] Of course the network had the ultimate say over which vlogs would be posted online, but users still had a network-sponsored window of communication. Fan participation and interaction in online communities—from fan sites to vlogs and blogs—helps form the basis for the greater *Smallville* fan community. Fan sites serve as places for current fans to speculate, criticize, and rework aspects of *Smallville* while providing a place to collect and inform new fans about their favorite show, while also providing producers with valuable information about consumer demands.

Fan Productions and the Legal Environment

The proliferation of digital devices has transformed fan art, music, and video creation and increased production. Photoshop and other image-generating software, mp3s and digital audio, and affordable nonlinear video editing programs have enabled fan producers to create their own *Smallville* avatars (graphic icons), banners, images, online video games, filk (fan produced music), and vids (fan music video). Even fan sites like Kryptonsite have special forums for sharing ideas and distributing fan productions. Kryptonsite's forum "Smallville Fan-Created Media" has two designated areas: one for fan art and the other for music videos or vids. In the fan art section, there are numerous message boards where users can show their works. Some fans might even ask others to create art for them for their personal site, like banners or image art, or user icons called avatars. Avatars are generally made up of single or multiple still images that move in sequence. Many feature pictures of fans' favorite *Smallville* character or actor. Avatars, for example, may become representative of the individual users' online fan identity as the image icon becomes recognizable alongside the username. The *Smallville* fan art community works as both a place of production and distribution for the sharing of ideas that both cling to the Superman metatext as well as allow for its expansion.

In 1997, Marc Davis wrote, "Over the next 50 years we will witness an explosion of access and production and distribution of video by communities that could not earlier afford to produce video in their homes, schools, and offices. . . . [C]omputational video technology will enable these and new communities to make video a part of their daily communication."[36] Despite articles from writers such as Jake Coyle, who attributed fan vidding as having been the brainchild of YouTube, fans have been actively producing vids since the 1970s.[37]

Francesca Coppa, a vidder and professor at Muhlenberg College, has written about the early development of vidding in her article "Women, *Star Trek*, and the Early Development of Fannish Vidding." Coppa attributes the first fan vid to a woman named Kandy Fong who in 1975 put still images of outtakes from the *Star Trek* television series to music for a fan convention.[38] From there, vidding became an underground, predominantly female fan culture, which used available electronic devices to edit together fan vids from popular television shows.[39] Coppa defines fan vids as music videos that are edited from pieces taken from favorite programs and other sources, such as interviews, and combining these elements and music to create something new.[40] For Coppa, vidding is more than merely selecting random images and video clips from television programs. She suggests that there is a conscious process involved that is balanced between the music and careful selection and arrangement of video clips in producing "a story, an essay, a mood piece, a love note."[41]

Vidding has continued to evolve and develop through the 1980s, 1990s, and into the new millennium, and sites like YouTube have provided an easy alternative to video distribution. Fans of television, film, and other media have used YouTube as a platform for showcasing their creative artworks in public since it went online in 2005.[42] There are other sites that host vids from television and film fans such as RabidShare.com, MegaUpload.com, and YouSendIt.com. However, most of these sites do not have nearly the file storage capacity that YouTube offers.[43] Vidders.net is a vidder and fans-of-vids network, requiring user registration. The recently updated site boasts that it has a predominately international female membership of over 15,000 users who can post and distribute vids on its site. Vidders.net has numerous group pages dedicated to both film and television shows such as *Star Trek* (1966–1969), the *Twilight* series (2008, 2009, 2010), *The X-Files* (1993–2002), *True Blood* (2008–Present), and *Smallville*. The site's forums also allow vidders and fans of vids to interact online.

Smallville vidding fans have created exclusive online communities for generating, cultivating, and appreciating one another's productions. They formed their own Do-It-Yourself (DIY) community, instructing one another and providing technical and aesthetic tips.[44] Kryptonsite has a special forum called "*Smallville* Music Videos," allowing producers of vids and vid fans to participate and network with one another. Users who do not create vids themselves can make suggestions for videos they would like to see and often request specific songs. Fans have also coined their own language to reference certain characters, relationships, or love interests in communicating about the show that allow for a quick exchange of information in forums. Terms like "Clana," for Clark and Lana Lang, and "Clex," referring to Clark and Lex Luthor, are character name combinations often used in online *Smallville* fan communities and have become reference points for fan-generated vids. Clana vids, for example, may pay homage to favorite moments in Clark and Lana's romantic relationship.[45]

Vidding has aided in creating an "alternative social community," one of Jenkins' fan actions. Along with other fan productions, it has enabled fan interaction online. The visibility of fans as producers, whether they work in vidding, digital fan art, blogging, or vlogging, can help generate fan visibility, spark enthusiasm for the series, rekindle interest among former fans, or introduce new males and females of all ages and demographics to the series by way of contagious online fan enthusiasm. Those browsing YouTube may stumble on a *Smallville* vid, leading to an interest in the series. The active online presence that vidding brings to the show can help sustain and prolong the life cycle of the series and cultivate a new set of fans that tune in to the program each week.

Recently, vidding has begun to surface in fan studies and commentary on fan activities in academia as part of the interpretive fan art community. Scholars have begun to acknowledge the work of vidders as early fan video artists, including fan editors, in the discussion of fan media production. However, vidders and vids should not be confused with fan editors who rework entire storylines and edits of original works (more often attributed to motion pictures than television series) into either spoofs, parodies, or retellings of the narrative. Fan editors have targeted films such as S*tar Wars Episode I: The Phantom Menace* (1999), *The Matrix* (1999), and the *Lord of the Rings* trilogy (2001, 2002, 2003) in efforts to "make the film better." The products of fan editors often resemble a reconstructed film that reflects the way they felt the original narrative should have flowed—cutting scenes or characters, reordering dialogue, or making other changes.[46] Vidders, on the other hand, pay tribute to the show and its characters through the intertwining of music and images, creating something new that more closely resembles a music video.

As both nonlinear video editing software and storage become more affordable and accessible, digital fan production in online communities and networks increases. Editing programs such as Microsoft Windows Movie Maker, Adobe Premiere and Premiere Elements, Sony Vegas, and Apple iMovie have become more affordable for a variety of budgets, allowing vidding to become more widespread between age groups and gender, though it is still predominately a female fan activity. Storage has also become less of a concern, as hard drives have increased in size and decreased in cost. Vidders are able to store full episodes and seasons on their computers for easy access.

In the past, distribution of vids was usually channeled through fan conventions and compilation VHS tapes made by the artists themselves. Intellectual property rights and copyright have become obstacles that online vidders face due to the public nature of video circulation that YouTube and other streaming sites offer today, something their 1970s and 1980s counterparts did not have to worry about as much due to limited distribution channels. In her article "Copyright Law, Fan Practices, and the Rights of the Author," Rebecca Tushnet discusses some of these dilemmas. Tushnet acknowledges that "most fan fiction, particularly that [which is] disseminated on the Internet, would be classified as fair use under U.S. copyright law."[47] However, this freedom is not always perceived online. Vids are often challenged by musicians, studios, networks, and show producers and blocked or "taken down" from sites like YouTube. Many vidders have been prompted to include disclaimer statements and credit original authorship.[48] *Smallville* vidders (and also fan art, filk, slash, websites, etc.) are not excluded from copyright and authorship concerns. Despite setbacks that individual vidders have faced with videos being removed from sites, the production and distribution of vids and other fan-generated media continues.

Conclusion

In analyzing *Smallville*'s online fan community, fan consumption, production, and distribution are used to illustrate how digital technologies have transformed fan participation as both a consumer and producer of new media texts. As the longest-airing Superman television series, *Smallville* has benefitted significantly from new digital technologies in generating and maintaining a strong male and female audience, and an active fan community. Sanctioned by its producers at the WB and the CW television networks, *Smallville* was destined to have fan participation online. From network sites to the creation of fan community and devotion sites, fans can inform, speculate, criticize, and rework the program to meet the needs of the individual or collective fan body. Sometimes this reworking demands fan consumer activism and indirect or direct communication between fan and network producers.

Fan activity online is also not limited to its host audience in the United States, as *Smallville* fan sites, fan art, blogs, vlogs, and vids have online fan communities engaging through sites like Kryptonsite and YouTube from all parts of the world, creating a unified *Smallville* online community and subcultural identity. The increased accessibility and affordability of digital technologies like video cameras and computer graphics and video editing software, combined with new distribution avenues online, has created vlogging, enabled digital fan art sharing, and opened new channels for fan vidders to expose their works where they historically remained relatively inaccessible.

The Internet has become an agent for cultivating fan participation as both consumers and producers, whose use and familiarity with new digital technologies and the ability to instantaneously distribute new media content enables vibrant online activity. Online activity of the collective fan audience has helped to sustain the longevity of the series because the movement of fan activity from private venues such as individual memorabilia collections and conventions has become more publicized by way of the Internet. Existing and new fans can network together to help bring recognition to the show through their devotion online. *Smallville*, the WB, and the CW owe some part of their longevity to what online fandom has done in generating interest in the series while maintaining loyal viewership for its decadelong storyline and characters.

Notes

1. Lev Manovich, *The Language of New Media* (Cambridge, MA: MIT Press, 2001), 19.

2. Henry Jenkins, *Fans, Bloggers, and Gamers: Exploring Participatory Culture* (New York: New York University Press, 2006), 41.

3. Janet Staiger, *Media Reception Studies* (New York: New York University Press, 2005), 98–107.

4. Mark Jancovich, "Cult Fictions: Cult Movies, Subcultural Capital and the Production of Cultural Distinctions," *Cultural Studies* 16, no. 2 (2002): 306–307.

5. Henry Jenkins, *Convergence Culture: Where Old and New Media Collide* (New York: New York University Press, 2006), 15–16.

6. José van Dijck, "User Like You? Theorizing Agency in User-Generated Content," *Media, Culture & Society* 31, no. 1 (2009): 42–43.

7. Dan Harries, "Watching the Internet," in *The New Media Book*, ed. Dan Harries (London: British Film Institute, 2002), 171.

8. David B. Yoffie and Michael Slind, "TiVo 2007: DVRs and Beyond," Harvard Business School, http://monashsingapore.pbworks.com/f/Assignment+1+(Case+Study)+-+TiVo+2007.pdf (accessed 15 October 2007), 20.

9. Cary M. Jones, "Twenty-First Century Superman: *Smallville* and New Media Mythmaking," *Jump Cut: A Review of Contemporary Media* 48 (Winter 2006).

10. Jones, "Twenty-First Century Superman."

11. Jones, "Twenty-First Century Superman."

12. Jenkins, *Fans, Bloggers, and Gamers*, 136.

13. Jones, "Twenty-First Century Superman."

14. Jenkins, *Fans, Bloggers, and Gamers*, 145.

15. Cited in Jenkins, *Convergence Culture*, 5.

16. van Dijck, "Users Like You?" 42.

17. van Dijck, "Users Like You?" 44.

18. The author acknowledges that there are numerous other fan-generated artifacts such as fan fiction, slash, sculpture, paintings, drawings, filk (or fan music), and so forth. For the purpose of this chapter, only fan productions and activities traced to the Internet and new digital technologies will be analyzed. For further reading, see Staiger's *Media Reception Studies* and Henry Jenkins, *Textual Poachers: Television Fans and Participatory Culture* (New York: Routledge, 1992).

19. Jenkins, *Fans, Bloggers, and Gamers*, 142.

20. Jenkins, *Fans, Bloggers, and Gamers*, 141.

21. Staiger, *Media Reception Studies*, 99–101.

22. Staiger, *Media Reception Studies*, 99.

23. Kryptonsite is just one *Smallville* community site online, and many other comprehensive *Smallville* fan sites exist including DevotedtoSmallville.com, AllThingsSmallville.com, SmallvilleDedication.com, and SmallvillePH.com.

24. Cornel Sandvoss, *Fans: The Mirror of Consumption* (Cambridge, MA: Polity Press, 2005), 64.

25. Nancy Baym, "Talking about Soaps: Communicative Practices in a Computer-Mediated Fan Culture," in *Theorizing Fandom: Fans, Subculture, and Identity*, ed. Cheryl Harris and Alison Alexander (Cresskill, NJ: Hampton Press, 1998), 112.

26. Baym, "Talking about Soaps," 115.

27. Baym, "Talking about Soaps," 117.

28. Baym, "Talking about Soaps," 119.

29. Baym, "Talking about Soaps," 122.

30. Jancovich, "Cult Fictions," 312.

31. Staiger, *Media Reception Studies*, 101.

32. Kate, "About OSCK," *OSCK Fans of Smallville Blog*, 2008, http://osck.wordpress.com/about (accessed 12 February 2010).

33. Kate, "About OSCK."

34. Jenkins, *Fans, Bloggers, and Gamers*, 151.

35. "CWTV.com Searches for *Smallville* Vlogger of the Month," *The CW*, 2007, http://blog.cwtv.com/2007/10/30/cwtvcom-searches-for-smallville-vlogger-of-the-month/ (accessed 2 February 2010).

36. Cited in Henry Jenkins, "What Happened before YouTube?" in *YouTube: Online Video and Participatory Culture*, ed. Jean Burgess and Joshua Green (Cambridge, MA: Polity Press, 2009), 109.

37. Francesca Coppa, "Women, *Star Trek*, and the Early Development of Fannish Vidding," *Transformative Works and Cultures* 1 (2008), http://journal.transformativeworks.org/idex.php/twc/article/view/44/64 (accessed 2 November 2009), para., 1.2.

38. Coppa, "Women, *Star Trek*, and the Early Development of Fannish Vidding," para., 1.4.

39. Jenkins, "What Happened before YouTube?" 117.

40. Jesse Walker, "Remixing Television: Francesca Coppa on the Vidding Underground," *Reason*, August/September 2008, http://reason.com/archives/2008/07/18/remixing-television (accessed 8 January 2010).

41. Walker, "Remixing Television," para., 1.

42. Jenkins, "What Happened Before YouTube?" 109.

43. New video hosting sites continue to emerge, such as Vimeo.com, in attempts to challenge YouTube's popularity.

44. Coppa, "Women, *Star Trek*, and the Early Development of Fannish Vidding," para., 1.5.

45. There are other character reference examples used in fan vids, fan fiction, slash, art, etc., like "Clois" for Clark and Lois, "Chlark" for Chloe and Clark, and "Lexana" for Lex and Lana. References like these help add to the fan terminology and language. Fans create, use, and teach others the specialized "lingo" for others

to become knowledgeable in the series. This "lingo" helps connect fans together in a way that separates them from the general viewing public.

46. There has been little scholarship written on fan editing specifically, but authors have acknowledged the impact that edits like *The Phantom Edit* (2001) have made on *Star Wars* fan cultures. See Henry Jenkins, "Quentin Tarantino's Star Wars? Digital Cinema, Media Convergence, and Participatory Culture," http://web.mit.edu/cms/people/henry3/starwars.html, and Joshua Wille (forthcoming).

47. Rebecca Tushnet, "Copyright Law, Fan Practices, and the Rights of the Author," in *Fandom: Identities and Communities in a Mediated World*, ed. Jonathan Gray, Cornel Sandvoss, and C. Lee Harrington (New York: New York University Press, 2007), 60.

48. Tushnet, "Copyright Law, Fan Practices, and the Rights of the Author," 63.

CHAPTER SEVEN

"I'VE A FEELING WE'RE NOT IN KANSAS ANYMORE": EXAMINING *SMALLVILLE*'S CANADIAN CULT GEOGRAPHY

Lincoln Geraghty

This chapter addresses the notions of cult television and fan tourism, arguing that *Smallville* (2001–2011) is a Canadian TV text (despite its being made by a Hollywood studio) because, being filmed in Vancouver, its fictional locations have become real sites of pilgrimage for its many devoted fans—both North American and international. As with other science fiction series shot in Vancouver, including *The X-Files* (1993–2002), *Stargate SG-1* (1997–2006), and *Battlestar Galactica* (2003–2009), fans of *Smallville* participate in this fan tourism and record it for public display by creating online pictorial travelogues of where important locations and scenes have been shot, adding their own personal commentary and reflections on their visit. The local communities of those towns and locations used for filming within the metropolitan area of Vancouver also contribute to this online discourse by organizing special tours and yearly events for fans keen to make the trip over. For example, the local business association of Cloverdale (a small town outside Vancouver where downtown Smallville scenes are filmed) advertises on their website that Cloverdale is the "Home of *Smallville*"—a statement backed up by the road sign that welcomes drivers as they pass through. Investigating the cult geography of Vancouver, British Columbia, as Smallville, Kansas, reveals important changes in genre programming, whereby American TV series are becoming increasingly international in production and reception, and allows us to interrogate the ever-changing nature of global television fandom where boundaries of economic and cultural capital are becoming blurred through the use of new media technologies, and concepts of place and space are evolving as a result of fan interaction.

Moreover, the following analysis of fan blogs found on the visitor guest book on the Cloverdale town website provides an interesting example of how the spaces and places of cult TV fandom may not necessarily lie in the physical geography. For a greater and richer appreciation of fan spaces, it is perhaps more helpful to consider the link between the real places of fan pilgrimage (sets and locations within the geographical environs of Vancouver) and the virtual spaces of fan communities (the Internet). Using the work of phenomenological geographers and models of understanding fan practices developed and applied by scholars of popular culture such as Henry Jenkins, Will Brooker, Matt Hills, Jonathan Gray, and others, I would argue that through the example of *Smallville*, it is clear that scholars need to cast their nets widely to provide a rich and detailed appreciation and analysis of contemporary television fandom. This means that we must recognize the various affective mechanisms for fan interaction, both between the text and fan and between the fan and the virtual environment. Bloggers who write about their experience in Cloverdale, visiting the *Smallville* filming locations, are associating themselves with the real town and, by extension, drawing connections with the fictional town of the series—yet both hold equal meaning for them. Furthermore, through the practice of blogging, a third space is visited when fans click into the website to leave their comments. Thus, all three spaces of *Smallville* fandom allow for interaction across and beyond the series—giving fans more opportunities to extend the narrative of the series into their real lives, virtual lives, and the life of the text.

The first steps toward a wider consideration of cult TV, fandom, and the relationship between fans and their object of affection is to acknowledge the prominent position of media *paratexts* as opposed to the centrality of specific films or television series as the *text*. Indeed, we are now accustomed in fan studies to state that the productivity of fans and their related fan practices represent an appropriate and worthy text to study just as much as the media text to which they are related or by which they are inspired; so, rather than studying *Star Trek* as cult text, we might study fan-produced videos on YouTube as important texts of fan activity that carry inherent meaning and significance in and of themselves. Jonathan Gray's *Show Sold Separately: Promos, Spoilers, and Other Media Paratexts*

(2010) defines media paratexts as all that come with and inform the text. For example, *Star Wars* carries with it meaning within and outside the narrative—from an analysis of its mythic story structure using the work of Joseph Campbell to studies of its fans who actively engage in their own meaning making by dressing up, making videos, and writing fan fiction. However, the peripheral texts—those associated with the commercialization of the franchise such as the lunchboxes, toys, video games, and websites—are so much part of the meaning-making process that they become texts to study in their own right. A paratext "is both 'distinct from' and alike" the original, but also "intrinsically part of—the text." Yet Gray is also keen to point out that paratexts "are not simply add-ons, spinoffs, and also-rans: they create texts, they manage them, and they fill them with many of the meanings that we associate with them."[1]

Studies of *Smallville* paratexts are varied and add to the expansive body of scholarship on the series. These studies shy away from concentrating on the televisual text, even the metatext of the Superman mythos that informs it, and focus on the tangible products of fandom such as the blogs and travelogues and the official convergent and transmedia texts such as the DVDs, studio websites, and television adverts. These studies follow in the tradition of what Gray terms "off-screen studies"—or a "call for a screen studies that focuses on paratexts' constitutive role in creating textuality, rather than simply consigning paratexts to the also-ran category or considering their importance only in promotional and monetary terms."[2] Eric Freedman's "Television, Horror and Everyday Life in *Buffy the Vampire Slayer*" (2005) uses *Smallville* to introduce and discuss notions of genre, seriality, and the shifting boundaries between the television text and everyday life. His analysis of both *Smallville* and *Buffy the Vampire Slayer* (1997–2003) as flagship series of the WB Network launched in 1995 to target the niche youth audience[3] reveals that they are "examples of how the fantastic and the real via genre and form are linked to ideology, myth and commerce."[4] The officially produced websites that extend the series beyond what is shown on screen (*The Torch*, which replicates Chloe Sullivan's high school newspaper, and *The Ledger*, which acts as a virtual map of the town of Smallville), and the DVD extras that allow you access to secret information designed to be read alongside the episodes, reinforce "the narrative dynamic of the show" and embed "the programme's fundamental plot points in a new architecture that invites interaction."[5] Thus, the fictional text seeps into the media environments of everyday life—the Internet—imbuing the real with a sense of immediacy to what is happening in the town of Smallville at any given moment.

Cary M. Jones in "Twenty-First Century Superman: *Smallville* and New Media Mythmaking" (2006) continues this analysis of the new media texts surrounding *Smallville* and discusses the WB websites in conjunction with Henry Jenkins' theory of convergence culture. Jones asserts that *Smallville* fan practices, such as blogging and contributing to *The Torch* and *Ledger* websites and their own fan fiction sites that offer new episodes to read as part of the series, evidence a turning away from subversive revisions of the official text and now form part of the "explicitly stated goal of the show's producers."[6] Fans are now active in the mythmaking processes of television seriality, and the studios and producers rely on this interaction to promote and extend the life cycle of their show: "[I]t's becoming clear that the confluence of factors surrounding the transition to a culture of convergence encourages *all* fans, cult or mainstream, to invest time, effort, and money in a narrative that extends far beyond the TV screen."[7] Likewise, in Rayna Denison's "It's a Bird, It's a Plane! No, It's DVD! *Superman*, *Smallville*, and the Production (of) Melodrama" (2007), an analysis of the varying production discourses from advertising, press releases, and DVDs allows us to "rethink the shifting relationship that Superman's stories have to the genres of action and melodrama."[8] The extras that form the special-feature elements of the *Smallville* DVD box sets, documentaries that go behind the scenes, and fictionalized handheld camera interviews produced by Chloe (played by Allison Mack) that continue her investigation of the weird and mysterious goings-on in Smallville supplement the wider narrative but are all bound up in one volume spread across six to eight discs. Corresponding to Gray's more recent conception of paratextuality, Denison's chapter expands upon "the importance of the DVD, seeing it not just as a means of remembering and contextualizing film and television, but as a forum in which new narratives can be inserted, and new meanings created."[9]

Vancouver's Runaway Success: The Phenomenological Geography of *Smallville*

Meaning is important to a text like *Smallville*. As has been explored in depth throughout this collection, *Smallville* can mean so much and so many different things to various people that no one meaning can be ascribed to it. As a text that has a history, being part of the Superman mythos and canon, *Smallville* could seemingly be identified as an ideologically American text, inherently part of the American cultural landscape and located very much in the geographic heartland of the United States. However, as I stated in the introduction to this chapter, it is entirely possible to think of *Smallville* as a Canadian television series—funded by Hollywood for sure, but also one that sits within an increasingly transnational industry of film and television production. For Jason Mittell in the conclusion to his study of television and American culture, the model of the "runaway" production[10] raises doubts about notions of brand identity and the continued Hollywood dominance of the media industry, and, importantly, it invites the question, "Is a show shot outside the United States truly an American program?"[11] I would agree that such is the impact of Vancouver as "Hollywood North," we need to be more careful when considering the origins of contemporary television series, particularly those genre series like *Smallville* where its longevity makes the show a valuable part of the local economy and thus means more to the residents and its employees in Vancouver than it does to studio executives based in Los Angeles.

Jane Landman rightly highlights some of the problems associated with the "runaway" production, those being seen in Hollywood imperialism and the dependency created by Hollywood in some countries who are so keen to attract overseas productions that they are coerced into deals that may not necessarily benefit the local industry or provide long-term investment. Yet Landman also points to the multiplicity of meaning created in series that are filmed abroad and which actively points to this distancing from Hollywood in the generic nature of the text. In *Farscape* (1999–2003), for example, a series whose narrative concerns an American astronaut lost in space and which is filmed in Australia, constant references to *The Wizard of Oz* (1939) (with Oz metaphorically standing for Australia) and John Crichton feeling that he is "not in Kansas anymore" encourage "audience recognition and complicity."[12] With countries like Canada and Australia becoming such important sites of production for different types of film and television, notions of local identity are becoming blurred. There is a "plasticity of place" that characterizes those countries and cities that can stand in for America or any other international location.[13] For example, Will Brooker believes that Vancouver's "perceived anonymity" accounts for its being used as a stand-in for mainstream USA: "Its streets are considered generic and unrecognisable to a US audience."[14] Yet, in terms of the *Farscape* example, the very nature of its narrative about the territorial advancement of an intergalactic colonial empire parallels the encroachment of American industry and practice into the Australian economy.[15] While Landman focuses on the Australian situation, similarities to *Smallville*'s production in Vancouver are clearly definable and are applicable to the fan blogs that talk about the filming of an American TV show on the streets of Cloverdale and what implications this has for the local economy, the residents of a small Canadian town, and the fans that travel there. She argues that "the contemporary global studio's range of locations offerings blur distinctions between 'reality, artifice, superficiality and verisimilitude.'"[16]

It would be remiss not to mention *Smallville*'s concurrent series, *Supernatural* (2005–Present), in the context of Vancouver's preeminence in the production of "runaway" telefantasy. A series about two brothers that travel America hunting ghosts and demons may sound problematic in terms of finding the diversity of filming locations around the Vancouver area that can stand in for towns in Kansas, Minnesota, Wisconsin, Montana, and New York, but it works due to the nature of contemporary television production, the viewing contexts, and the audience's ability to see beyond the reality of filming and work within the narrative of the text. For Alison Peirse, *Supernatural* creates a dialogue of in-jokes and intertextuality with its fans who recognize the transnational nature of the series but take pleasure in its being flagged up in certain episodes. References to the "unusual weather" for having a swimming pool when the brothers are supposed to be in Los Angeles signal the self-reflexivity of the writers in acknowledging their colder Canadian location but also the increasingly sophisticated ways in which fans understand the television series they watch and how they watch them. Filming details and insider knowledge of locations provide those extratextual details that make DVD box sets so appealing to own, and the relationships between different series, their references to popular culture, and the actors who star in them[17] create an intertextual web of meaning for fans across different media texts and paratexts: "The popularity of *Supernatural* as a cult television text creates a transnational language that moves beyond national boundaries, undercutting specific local cultures and viewing practices."[18]

Recognizing the contemporary importance of the "runaway" production to the city of Vancouver, both Will Brooker and Matt Hills have discussed how fans of television series made there treat visiting shooting locations as a form of pilgrimage. Traveling to sites once glimpsed or overtly identified becomes a way of getting closer to the text and ascribing personal meaning to it, making the intangible tangible by achieving a proximity to the "real" Kent farm (a private dairy farm in the Fraser Valley) if you are a *Smallville* fan or to a "real" Caprican building (the Vancouver Public Library for example) if you are a fan of *Battlestar Galactica*. This liminal positioning of the fan is described by Brooker as offering an experience where they "hover on the borders between actual and fictional, holding both in a double-vision of alternate realities."[19] The allusion to the religious pilgrimage has also been investigated; both Hills and Roger C. Aden ascribe some of the language of religious ritual and pilgrimage to the practices of traveling fans who must touch or be on the spot where their favorite character/actor once stood. Thus, as Cornel Sandvoss asserts, "The physical places of fandom clearly have an extraordinary importance for fans."[20] However, for Aden, the idea of pilgrimage is more a symbolic act featuring "individuals ritualistically revisiting powerful places that are symbolically envisioned through the interaction of story and individual imagination."[21] Fans, therefore, create a map of their favorite text that means something on a personal level, whether it is through the watching or rewatching of specific episodes or the emotive relationship created within a community of fans that share those experiences with others. The text, the story, becomes somewhere to go to, a "promised land," when fans want to escape the material world.[22] Hills contests this reading to the extent that he suggests the metaphor is not adequate to take into account the desire of fans to travel to the places where their "promised lands" are filmed, suggesting that "'inhabitation' of extratextual spaces . . . forms an important part of cult fans' extensions and expressions of the fan-text relationship" and is "an affective-interpretive process which spills into and redefines material spaces."[23] Vancouver, then, acts as an "urban imaginary,"

> where a single point of geography—an alley, a building, a street—can, with an adjustment of "frequency"—a certain way of looking, a stretch of imagination and a leap of fan faith—transport the visitor to another,

> fictional world. One pilgrim sees this quad of Simon Fraser University as Earth-*X-Files*; the other sees it as Earth-Caprica; and the same pilgrim is quite capable of switching between the two, with a reprioritizing of investment, a different imaginary angle, a shifting of vision, a change in "vibration," a retuning.[24]

However, it is not simply being there that counts. What fans do there seems to make the traveling worthwhile. So, whether it is recreating the moment Scully was kidnapped in *The X-Files* on Grouse Mountain (just outside the Vancouver metropolitan area) by tying someone up, putting them in the trunk of the rental car, and taking a picture[25] or finding out where filming will happen on a certain night and standing in the freezing cold and rain just to get a picture of Tom Welling, the activity is of utmost importance. The Cloverdale blogs I discuss in the next section also reflect a sense of "doing" and "activity"—whether it be watching a movie in the local cinema that stands in as *Smallville*'s Talon coffee shop, watching the crew shoot a town parade, or literally moving to the town—and thus conform to those fan practices discussed elsewhere. Then again, the going and the doing are only two stages of a three-part process that also includes the return. Once fans return from their Cloverdale trip, they can post on the town website just how much they enjoyed it, loved the small-town atmosphere, and why they think *Smallville* is the greatest show on TV. Will Brooker's work on fan viewing and notions of Aden's "symbolic pilgrimage" takes into account both the physical traveling to and placing oneself in a location from a television series but also extends the metaphor to include the idea of "traveling without moving" when watching and rewatching episodes on DVD well after original broadcast. For him, fans may not necessarily take a physical pilgrimage to a place but instead make a symbolic "homecoming" when returning to a text and the fan community that they may not have been part of for some time—particularly if the series has long since been canceled: A "sense of returning, of immersion in a place of belonging, that fits the broader definition of pilgrimage."[26] Therefore, bearing in mind Brooker's work, those fans that post their memories of being in Cloverdale to get closer to the *Smallville* they know and love are getting closer still to both the text and physical space they once occupied—returning to a place to which they now feel they really belong.

Much of the work surveyed so far contextualizes the movement and practices of fans in geographical spaces within notions of "affective play"[27] and social interaction. Meaning, attachment, and a sense of belonging are created through physically being in the city where a television series is filmed, recreating moments of viewing, and sharing the experience with other fans after the event. Thus we might be able to view this work and fan tourism through the lens of phenomenological geography which concerns the study of place and space, taking into account "practical and emotional aspects of day-to-day existence . . . habitual movements and unselfconscious senses of place."[28] For David Seamon, phenomenology is "the description and interpretation of human experience. A major effort of phenomenology is to identify and describe broader, underlying patterns—e.g., the lived expressions of environmental embodiment—that give order and coherence to the richness and 'chaos' of human experience as it is lived as everyday life."[29] The way we react and interact with our natural and built environment helps define a sense of identity through place. The media we use in those spaces also contributes to this sense of place, whether it is talking on one's mobile phone while walking through town or taking pictures of famous landmarks. But that again is focusing on the physical, the being there and the doing. Shaun Moores, in his article on media usage and environmental experiences, considers the virtual spaces of new media as equally important in the conceptualizing of place. Websites, e-mails, texts, blogs, and VR games all create a sense of place in that you interact with both the medium and those you communicate with through them. We may not be speaking to a person face to face or interacting in a physical location like a coffee shop, but we are still communicating and interacting. Therefore, we might understand the *Smallville* blogs on the Internet in the same way and see the fans as interacting with other fans, the website, and the town of Cloverdale through a media environment that acts as a place for all things to happen at once: being back in Cloverdale, remembering the shooting locations, and taking pleasure in the *Smallville* text once more. For Moores,

> Instead of dismissing technologically mediated communications as a threat to "face-to-face contact" and "place-based communities," [his] preference would be for a fuller exploration of those apparently automatic *uses of media in the habitual movements of the daily round*—in what

> Seamon calls time-space routines, body and place-ballets—and also for an appreciation of what could be best thought of, in general terms, as *everyday experiences of media environments*.[30]

Extending Moores' concepts of media environments and the phenomenological geography of media experiences, we should now turn to the blogs themselves in order to appreciate the relationship between virtual space and physical space in *Smallville* fandom.

Come to Cloverdale: Confessions and Expressions of Public and Private *Smallville* Fandom

Taking the form of a guest-book blog, the Cloverdale Business Improvement Association's page on the town website asks *Smallville* fans to leave their messages of support and affection. Following the prompt "Smallville is great because . . . ," fans are expected to fill in a blank box, leave their name, and say where they come from before submitting the contribution to the site. The Cloverdale website is clearly trying to start a dialogue with *Smallville* fans; the town after all has a vested interest in attracting fans as visiting tourists, and what better tourists are there than devoted fans who want to buy a piece of *Smallville* memorabilia? Yet the Cloverdale Web pages also try to attract filmmakers and studios, advertising "Destination Cloverdale" and that along with *Smallville*, other cult films and television series shot there include *Stargate SG-1*, *The Muppets' Wizard of Oz* (2005) and the miniseries *Taken* (2002).[31] The film and television industries, as well as fan tourists, are important contributors to the local economy and the character of the town: "'Destination Cloverdale' is a concerted effort to promote cultural and heritage events that bring visitors to the community plus attract specialty businesses."[32] When shooting occurs on the streets, pictures are posted on the town website showing how versatile it is as a set, but also how much the community supports the activities of the filmmakers. Cloverdale's identity as a small town in British Columbia is as much defined by the filming that goes on there as it is by local attractions and events that have been held there for decades, such as the Blueberry Festival and Rodeo. The Business Improvement Association pages describe Cloverdale as historic, "known for its agricultural roots, its railway History of Surrey [the county it is in] and country influence" while also advertising that "historic facades, heritage homes and country hospitality characterize the community." But alongside this endorsement of its history, the website declares, "Because it has retained its small town ambiance, Cloverdale is a popular location for the film industry and has become the home of the hit TV series *Smallville*."[33] Fans that post on the town website and share how much they like the show also directly reference this notion of "small town ambience"; thus they become in some form a proud temporary resident—someone with a vested interest in promoting the town and supporting its local economy through their *Smallville* fandom.

There is a tremendous amount of scholarship written on the cultural implications of the Internet blog, and *Smallville* fans' blogging activities have been discussed before. Melanie Kohnen's "The Adventures of a Repressed Farm Boy and the Billionaire Who Loves Him: Queer Spectatorship in *Smallville* Fandom" (2008) examines the blogs devoted to discussing a particular form of fan fiction, slash, based on the interrelations between Clark Kent, played by Tom Welling, and Lex Luthor, played by Michael Rosenbaum. In their messages and responses to each other and some particularly memorable episodes, the fans debate the extent to which Lex and Clark's friendship may be more than just platonic. Following similar scholarship that focuses on female fans of *Star Trek* who have read a homoerotic relationship between Kirk and Spock, Kohnen suggests that fan discourses surrounding *Smallville*'s hero and antihero "underline how *Smallville* fans take up an attitude towards heteronormativity that reflects academic discussions on the same subject."[34] These fans, blogging on the "Television without Pity" website, "do not consider the nominal heterosexuality of the show's characters as something that is self-evident in *Smallville*'s narrative. Rather, fans perceive that the adolescent Clark Kent and Lex Luthor's heterosexuality needs to be continually established and repeated, and if it is not, viewers in turn celebrate the very lack of such stabilizing repetition."[35] So, fan blogs in this instance are indicative of the subversive practices of fandom and signal the extent to which blogging has become a means through which fans can offer an alternate voice to that of the producers. Yet, as Kohnen states, fan desires "may cross gender and sexual divisions [straight women seeing queer relations between men]," where "a separation between sexual and spectatorial identification is also imperative."[36]

Blogs, wikis, and social networking sites have been described in mainstream coverage as "narcissistic domains for one's own individual opinion." Yet blogs can be political, and bloggers "have repeatedly demonstrated themselves as technoactivists favouring not only democratic self-expression and networking, but also global media critique and journalistic sociopolitical intervention."[37] For S. Elizabeth Bird, "Blogs have an exhilarating capacity to deconstruct the texts of the powerful"[38] and as such equip "audiences with knowledge to question media conglomerates and other powerful interests."[39] The blogs analyzed by Kohnen clearly reflect a certain kind of intervention and knowledge as fans discuss the counter-readings of Clark and Lex's relationship. This is framed by a particular discourse concerning identity and sexuality. A similar study of queer blogging by Tyler Curtain (2007) emphasizes how the online practice is a form of "queer knowledge production" where bloggers "perform identity through content and form—how links, for example, become vital props in the performance of what we might term the 'blogself.'"[40] The guest blog entries on the Cloverdale website do signify a certain "blogself," but one that is not necessarily based on revealing your sexual preference, sexuality, or an alternate reading of the text. Instead, the Cloverdale blogs are predominantly about place and connecting with Cloverdale as the place where *Smallville* is filmed. As such, the online discourse constructed by fans there is not concerned about revealing individual and personal identity through story or critique but is more about getting closer to the text, the actors, the crew, and the physical locality of the town of Smallville.

Curtain states that "a blog creates from the intractable cultural-archive space of the net a story about its readers, a shared cultural-discursive space, and its relationship to them."[41] In terms of the Cloverdale blog, the online space forms a relationship with the series, its fans, the cast, and the producers, but also with the physical space of Smallville, Kansas, or downtown Cloverdale, British Columbia. From fan messages that describe their affection for representations of small-town America to entries that express desires to travel to Cloverdale to get the real experience of the show, the town website acts as a virtual portal that can connect fans from around the world to the Canadian locale and some of its real-life inhabitants—who are, they write, very happy and excited to be living in the same place where *Smallville* is filmed. Indeed, writing is all about the practice of being a fan; having the chance to write, blog your opinion, or describe your thoughts and feelings is the impetus for the creation of fan communities. For, as Ken Gelder argues, "Subcultures are brought into being through narration and narrative: told by the participants themselves, as well as by those who document them, monitor them, 'label' them, outlaw them, and so on."[42] *Smallville* fans are simply taking advantage of this virtual site to connect through the written word with the place of Smallville.

While the Cloverdale town blog offers fans a virtual space to connect with the real place of Cloverdale and the fictional space of Smallville, it also offers visitors and potential future visitors a chance to communicate with each other. To share memories of the town, the series, and to indicate when they might yet visit Cloverdale. In this sense, the blog is ever changing; it is constantly evolving as more people contribute to it, from people who have just been to those who are planning to go. As such, the Cloverdale visitor blog conforms to what Paul Booth sees as vital in the continued popularity of blogs as a form of Internet communication and community building: "The 'writer' of the blog is ultimately a group, not an individual. . . . Blogs, consequently, are never finished. They are in a constant state of revision and rewriting, as more and more comments contribute more and more information to the blog."[43] Yet while fans can access a virtual tourist guide in preparation for their visit, in a sense it is a guide that literally offers nothing new to the reader; whether fans have been to Cloverdale or not, they have all been to the fictional town of Smallville and thus are fully aware of the relevant sites of importance and know where they must go to get the full *Smallville* experience. As a consequence, the blog acts as a site of local and physical familiarity despite its international and virtual audience. Those people who post on it are talking to others who are at the same time strangers across the globe as well as fellow fans who have a shared affinity for the *Smallville* text and, by extension, that small town in British Columbia.

Booth's analysis of digital fandom and the use of blogging, ranging from *Doctor Who* to *Battlestar Galactica*, centers on media texts that attract devoted fan audiences. Therefore, applying his work to the *Smallville* blog is not necessarily problematic. Indeed, his work extends that of media theorists Jonathan Gray and Jason Mittell who have themselves built upon Henry Jenkins' concept of "convergence culture" to explore the interrelated nature of fandom, cult television, and transmedia storytelling.[44] For Jenkins, Gray, and Mittell, "contemporary television media texts are becoming more akin to Barthesian intertexts, as cult television shows have started to spread out the 'text' of the show across different media platforms," while Booth further argues that viewers of cult television, of which *Smallville* is obviously a key example, move "across media to construct the narrative intertextually. . . . The reader moves between discursive texts, actively constructing the story."[45] The Cloverdale blog is just another platform on which to extend the *Smallville* text, offering fans another text to consume and alter, but it is also another narrative, another story, that the visiting fans have the power to write. When writers "write on a blog, they not only intertextually contribute to the ongoing discussion about the extant media object, but they also intra-textually construct that text itself through their own playful contributions."[46] Intratextuality, for Paul Booth, "examines the meaning that occurs *inside* the transmediated text itself"[47] and therefore, as with the *Smallville* blog, is defined by writers who write "not just to reference an original text, but also to playfully build a fan-community, a fandom, of other blog writers through agreeable, non-critical comments about a mutually shared media text."[48]

The blogs on the Cloverdale site are posted by people from all over the world[49] and fall into several categories: those that focus on the series itself, those that focus on actors, and those that respond to the town and the Canadian environs. Some people's blogs cover a range of those topics, and some respond to what was posted before. They all, however, imply a sense of *Smallville* community that transcends geographical distance between bloggers and yet identifies Cloverdale as a physical small-town location that connects them. John Nations from Orlando, Florida, posts,

> I love Smallville because it is a modern retelling of a classic fantasy, a superhero who grew up in a small town like most of us in the United States (and Canada too) and then became a world-traveling hero. . . . I can relate to the character of Clark Kent, who puts on a costume and "performs" for a global audience. No matter how many times I go to Oslo, or Sydney, or Paris, or Cologne, or London, I can come back to Greenville South Carolina and it's still small and slower-paced, like Smallville is whenever Clark comes back to his old stomping ground.[50]

Similarly, Terry Harris from Newport, Ohio, posts that they like *Smallville* because, "What else it has Tom Welling! I was fortunate enough to visit Cloverdale on two separate occasions and am planning another visit in a couple of weeks. It is a beautiful little town and it reminds me of the small towns where I am from."[51] The connections made between small-town USA and Cloverdale serve to underline the nature of shooting in *Smallville*. Cloverdale was picked as a location exactly because it could stand in for a small town in Kansas; therefore, fans are clearly drawn to the generic nature of the streets, buildings, and local cinema (the Clova Theatre, aka The Talon).[52]

Yet Cloverdale is also clearly positioned as Canadian. *Smallville* fans who have the privilege of living in the town, or nearby, are keen to stress in their blogs that there are inherent qualities that make it a special place, and that is what makes the series so great. This, in effect, casts the series as somehow embodying the local character of the town and thus perhaps makes it just as much a Canadian show as it is American. From fans such as Leah Stow from Cloverdale who confesses that "Tom Welling is so hotttt!!!! The show is also very good and it is filmed in my home town of cloverdale, bc!!!!" to Christine from Pitt Meadows, British Columbia, who posts, "All of the actors, and the episodes are unique and good in different ways. plus it doesn't hurt that tom welling is a totalll babe!!!! I think i'm in love lol. forget Lana Lang, I live near Cloverdale . . . ," their fandom is defined through physical attraction to Tom Welling and a form of local pride and loyalty to the town.[53] This is taken further to encompass a form of regional and national identity as several bloggers post details of where they live in relation to other filming locations—"Name = J, Location: 10 minutes from Lex's Mansion (Hatley Castle)"[54]—or that they moved from one location in Victoria, British Columbia, to be near another. KC, describing Cloverdale as "the real Smallville," declares that they "just moved from Victoria where Lex's mansion was a mere 10 min walk away to the real Cloverdale, I've been lucky enough to see them shoot right in front of the theater also known as the famous Talon."[55] Affirming the series' Canadian credentials, Terry Ladd from Fort McMurray, Alberta (but originally from New Brunswick), simply puts that they think *Smallville* is great "Because it is made in Canada."[56] This short blog parallels that underlying awareness of local identity and pride that characterizes the "Welcome to Cloverdale" website through which you have to click to get to the *Smallville* blog. So, while *Smallville* acts as an advertisement for the town's economy and history, it also acts as a symbol of national identity for Terry Ladd who associates its real production, not its fictional narrative, to notions of Canadianness.[57]

Confessions of a personal nature, whether they be about a fan's infatuation with one of the actors or their desire for the world to be more like *Smallville*, make up the majority of blogs on the website. Dawn, from Cloverdale, posts in quite revealing prose that "there is no man on earth hotter than Tom Welling, I would like to do very bad and nasty things with that man,"[58] and likewise, Angel from Germany believes "Tom Welling is the hottest Clark Kent in the world!!!"[59] As I have argued elsewhere in connection to *Star Trek* fan letter writing, a television series can act as inspiration for its fans whereby it "reproduces a historical narrative," providing "fans a framework" for their own understanding of history, morality, and social interaction.[60] In the same way, these blogs indicate a strong emotional bond shared between fans and the *Smallville* text, the physical filming locations, and the themes of the show identified as integral to what makes it successful and inspirational for fans. For example, Erica Lalak from Monroeville, Alabama, writes,

> I am absolutely infatuated with the smallville series. At first my life long dream was to become a chef and cook in some big fancy restaurant . . . but i dont think i could handle something that crazy, hot, and sweaty. So the Talon inspired me to own my own chain. I fell in love with the "in"-and "ex"-terior of the talon as soon as I saw it. I just know that if I get the chance, i'd love to own my own Talon one day. and even then i'd still get to cook if I wanted to. . . . Over all, Smallville is very inspiring.[61]

Similarly, Elle from Salisbury, Maryland, describes how the series inspired her so much she started her own fan website and raises money for charity:

> Well, I loved it so much I started my own Smallville/Superman fansite! It inspired me to start the site, get involved in various charities related to the show and Superman and even walk with John Glover in his annual Alzheimer's walk in my hometown. Superman is such great icon and I am glad we have a show that can continue this legend![62]

The Cloverdale town blog acts as more than a connecter between fans and location. It becomes a personal sounding board for feelings of pride, affection, and longing. Rebecca from England posits that "The world needs heroes now, more than it ever has before. Smallville brings the best of them to us in a realistic enough way that the people of today can relate to it." For her, the real town and the fictional town provide "a great escape with wonderful stories, and it's a place where everything is alright in the end."[63] These feelings are shared by Colleen from Johannesburg, who says, "I echo everything that Rebecca from England says, the world needs heroes! The Smallville series, season 1–6 got me through 6 weeks of sick leave so I am a dedicated fan!"[64] Several fans concur with each other: Joyce from Columbus, Ohio, and Steve from New York both say it "raises my spirits,"[65] and Luis Colomo from Mexico philosophizes that "Smallville is great because it helps us become better persons by following the moral principles of all the actors . . . it teaches you many good things and it helps you relax and think about people."[66] A sense of aspiration is also contained in Whitney Clayton's blog, which posits, "This show is great because it makes you believe that anything is possible and that we set our own destiny's and we follow our own road to greatness."[67] Despite the writing errors and "texting speak," it is clear from these few examples that *Smallville* remains a very personal text for fans, even though it is shared by millions, and that the locality of Cloverdale as Smallville is an important place through which they can express feelings, desires, and aspirations. A narrative, shared between fans from across the globe, is constructed through group contributions. These fans are individuals, but they speak as one, building layers of personal meaning on top of the *Smallville* text and the town of Cloverdale. Space is important—the town and the virtual website—but so too is closeness and proximity. Some fans enjoy reciting their stories about going to Cloverdale and seeing it for real, getting a sense of being close to the actors and producers, while other fans communicate that the series brings them closer to other people, through a shared knowledge and love for the episodes and characters. In both respects, the Cloverdale Business Improvement Association's website represents a real place and a virtual space for fans of *Smallville*.

Conclusion: Real Places, Virtual Spaces, and *Smallville* as Fan Heterotopia

In discussing Vancouver's importance to both TV fans and Hollywood, I noted that Matt Hills contests Roger C. Aden's notion that fan pilgrimages to so-called "promised lands" are symbolic, that geography is more a metaphor for textual representation than it is a physical space. Instead, for

Hills, being in a place matters more because it allows fans access to extra-textual pleasures and affords them the opportunity to reinterpret the text since "*the media cult cannot be entirely reduced to metaphors of textuality.*"[68] I agree with Hills to the extent that the *Smallville* fans I have discussed in this chapter do travel to places like Vancouver and Cloverdale as part of their fandom, reordering the physical space according to their desires, feelings, and personal memories of the text. Still, reading the blogs on the Cloverdale town website presents us with different perspectives on how space is used, consumed, and manipulated by fans—fans that have a working knowledge of the real place (Cloverdale) and the fictional place (Smallville). Indeed, what we have seen from the blogs is that fans from all over the world shrink distances between those places by using the virtual space as a meeting point with other fans; this meeting point, at the same time, also becomes a site for revisiting Cloverdale. An individual's memory of being in Cloverdale to see it for oneself, attempting to get closer to the *Smallville* text, becomes a signpost of recognition for other fans that have done the same, or plan to do it in the near future. As blogs do, fan memories are built up as an extra layer of meaning on top of the original *Smallville* text, and thus fans must interpret and interact with them at the same time they engage with the TV series. One person's experience of traveling to Cloverdale, then, adds to and frames another person's who went there (or will go there) for similar reasons but may not have necessarily seen or done the same things.

In reconciling the contradictory nature of *Smallville* fan experiences—the relationship with the fictional text, travel to the physical place, blogging on a virtual space—we might use the work of Michel Foucault and his conception of the heterotopia. In opposition to the nonphysical spaces of utopias, which Foucault feels are "unreal spaces," heterotopias are

> real places—places that do exist and that are formed in the very founding of society—which are something like counter-sites, a kind of effectively enacted utopia in which real sites, all the other real sites that can be found within the culture, are simultaneously represented, contested, and inverted. Places of this kind are outside of all places, even though it may be possible to indicate their location in reality.[69]

Following Foucault, Ken Gelder sees the heterotopia as imagined, "but it also has some kind of realisation, somewhere."[70] For *Smallville* fans, then, the heterotopia is realized in the text itself as it combines and simultaneously represents, contests, and inverts the physical real place of Cloverdale, the virtual space of the Web, and the fictional universe of a young Clark Kent living in Smallville, Kansas. *Smallville*'s Canadian cult geography is all three things at the same time. Ultimately, all spaces that *Smallville* fans inhabit are lived spaces, spaces of possibilities that are at the same time nonplaces and real places. They offer a dialectic space important to communal life and community: absolute, relative, and relational.[71] For fans of popular television series like *Smallville*, place and space are in constant flux as individuals within the community move between the TV text and the multiple paratexts. Concepts of the fixed space are no longer relevant, particularly in an age of convergence where all things and all people can play with and interpret media in different ways. Contemporary television series are heterotopias, real places in which and through which fans can access new worlds, meet new people, and travel to different geographic spaces.

Notes

1. Jonathan Gray, *Show Sold Separately: Promos, Spoilers, and Other Media Paratexts* (New York: New York University Press, 2010), 6.
2. Gray, *Show Sold Separately*, 7.
3. Valerie Wee, "Teen Television and the WB Television Network," in *Teen Television: Essays on Programming and Fandom*, ed. Sharon Marie Ross and Louisa Ellen Stein (Jefferson, NC: McFarland, 2008), 43.
4. Eric Freedman, "Television, Horror and Everyday Life in *Buffy the Vampire Slayer*," in *The Contemporary Television Series*, ed. Michael Hammond and Lucy Mazdon (Edinburgh: Edinburgh University Press, 2005), 160.
5. Freedman, "Television, Horror and Everyday Life," 169–170.
6. Cary M. Jones, "Twenty-First Century Superman: *Smallville* and New Media Mythmaking," *Jump Cut* 48 (Winter 2006).
7. Jones, "Twenty-First Century Superman."
8. Rayna Denison, "It's a Bird! It's a Plane! No, It's DVD! *Superman*, *Smallville*, and the Production (of) Melodrama," in *Film and Comic Books*, ed. Ian Gordan, Mark Jancovich, and Matthew McAllister (Jackson: University Press of Mississippi, 2007), 160.
9. Denison, "It's a Bird, It's a Plane!" 163.

10. The "runaway" production defines those film and television projects that are funded by and launched in Hollywood but shooting and other special effects work are outsourced and done in another country, taking advantage of lower production costs, beneficial exchange rates, and local tax incentives.

11. Jason Mittell, *Television and American Culture* (New York: Oxford University Press, 2010), 445.

12. Jane Landman, "'Not in Kansas Anymore': Transnational Collaboration in Television Science Fiction Production," in *Production Studies: Critical Studies of Media Studies*, ed. Vicki Mayer, Miranda J. Banks, and John Thornton Caldwell (New York: Routledge, 2009), 140.

13. Landman, "'Not in Kansas Anymore,'" 143.

14. Will Brooker, "Everywhere and Nowhere: Vancouver, Fan Pilgrimage and the Urban Imaginary," *International Journal of Cultural Studies* 10, no. 4 (2007): 427.

15. Landman, "'Not in Kansas Anymore,'" 149.

16. Landman, "'Not in Kansas Anymore,'" 144.

17. *Smallville* and *Supernatural* are linked both through filming location and a central cast member. *Supernatural*'s Jensen Ackles (Dean Winchester) first appeared in season four of *Smallville* as Lana's new boyfriend, Jason Teague. Teague lasted for only one season, but his short run was apparently not brought about by his casting in *Supernatural*: "Jason's role in the series evolved, though contrary to fan rumors, most of Jason's arc was planned in advance, and Jensen Ackles' casting in the TV series *Supernatural* did not change the overall plan." See Craig Byrne, *Smallville: The Official Companion, Season 4* (London: Titan Books, 2007), 124.

18. Alison Peirse, "*Supernatural*," in *The Essential Cult TV Reader*, ed. David Lavery (Lexington: University Press of Kentucky, 2010), 261.

19. Will Brooker, "The *Blade Runner* Experience: Pilgrimage and Liminal Space," in *The Blade Runner Experience: The Legacy of a Science Fiction Classic*, ed. Will Brooker (London: Wallflower), 13.

20. Cornel Sandvoss, *Fans: The Mirror of Consumption* (Cambridge, MA: Polity Press, 2005), 61.

21. Roger C. Aden, *Popular Stories and Promised Lands: Fan Cultures and Symbolic Pilgrimages* (Tuscaloosa: University of Alabama Press, 1999), 10.

22. Aden, *Popular Stories and Promised Lands*, 4.

23. Matt Hills, *Fan Cultures* (London: Routledge, 2002), 144.

24. Brooker, "Everywhere and Nowhere," 438–439.

25. Hills, *Fan Cultures*, 149.

26. Will Brooker, "A Sort of Homecoming: Fan Viewing and Symbolic Pilgrimage," in *Fandom: Identities and Communities in a Mediated World*, ed.

Jonathan Gray, Cornel Sandvoss, and C. Lee Harrington (New York: New York University Press, 2007), 163.

27. Hills, *Fan Cultures*, 112.

28. Shaun Moores, "Media Uses & Everyday Environmental Experiences: A Positive Critique of Phenomenological Geography," *Particip@tions* 3, no. 2 (November 2006).

29. David Seamon, "*A Geography of Lifeworld* in Retrospect: A Response to Shaun Moores," *Particip@tions* 3, no. 2 (November 2006).

30. Moores, "Media Uses & Everyday Environmental Experiences."

31. "Filming in Cloverdale," *Destination Cloverdale*, http://www.itsmysite.com/cgi-bin/itsmy/go.exe?page=20&domain=1&webdir=cloverdale (accessed 5 April 2011).

32. "Historic Cloverdale," *Welcome to Cloverdale*, http://cloverdalebia.com/ (accessed 5 April 2011).

33. "Historic Cloverdale."

34. Sharon Marie Ross and Louisa Ellen Stein, "Introduction: Watching Teen TV," in *Teen Television: Essays on Programming and Fandom*, ed. Sharon Marie Ross and Louisa Ellen Stein (Jefferson, NC: McFarland, 2008), 23.

35. Ross et al., "Introduction," 22–23.

36. Melanie E. S. Kohnen, "The Adventures of a Repressed Farm Boy and the Billionaire Who Loves Him: Queer Spectatorship in *Smallville* Fandom," in *Teen Television: Essays on Programming and Fandom*, ed. Sharon Marie Ross and Louisa Ellen Stein (Jefferson, NC: McFarland, 2008), 208.

37. Richard Kahn and Douglas Kellner, "Technopolitics and Oppositional Media," in *The Cybercultures Reader*, 2nd ed., ed. David Bell and Barbara M. Kennedy (London: Routledge, 2007), 627.

38. S. Elizabeth Bird, *The Audience in Everyday Life: Living in a Media World* (New York: Routledge, 2003), 183.

39. Bird, *The Audience in Everyday Life*, 184.

40. David Bell, "Cyberidentities: Introduction," *The Cybercultures Reader*, 2nd ed., ed. David Bell and Barbara M. Kennedy (London: Routledge, 2007), 271.

41. Tyler Curtain, "Promiscuous Fictions," in *The Cybercultures Reader*, 2nd ed., ed. David Bell and Barbara M. Kennedy (London: Routledge, 2007), 327.

42. Ken Gelder, *Subcultures: Cultural Histories and Social Practice* (London: Routledge, 2007), 66.

43. Paul Booth, *Digital Fandom: New Media Studies* (New York: Peter Lang, 2010), 43.

44. See Henry Jenkins, *Convergence Culture: Where Old and New Media Collide* (New York: New York University Press, 2006); Gray, *Show Sold Separately*; Jason

Mittell, "Narrative Complexity in Contemporary American Television," *The Velvet Light Trap* 58 (2006): 29–40.

45. Booth, *Digital Fandom*, 50.

46. Booth, *Digital Fandom*, 51.

47. Booth, *Digital Fandom*, 43.

48. Booth, *Digital Fandom*, 44.

49. Visitors to the site come from Canada, America, the UK, Ireland, Germany, Russia, Poland, Chile, South Africa, Cyprus, Mexico, Brazil, Italy, Belgium, Malaysia, Kenya, Argentina, Australia, and Spain. The global reach of *Smallville* is clear but again suggests that through a common affinity for a television series and the practice of online blogging, Cloverdale literally becomes a global town, virtually connected and physically symbolic.

50. John Nations, "I Love Smallville because . . . ," *Cloverdale Business Improvement Association*, http://www.itsmysite.com/cgi-bin/itsmy/go.exe?page=21&domain=1&webdir=cloverdale (accessed 5 April 2011).

51. Terry Harris, "What else . . . ," *Cloverdale Business Improvement Association*, http://www.itsmysite.com/cgi-bin/itsmy/go.exe?page=24&domain=1&webdir=cloverdale (accessed 5 April 2011).

52. Interestingly, one fan helps identify themselves by adding after saying they come from Nottingham, UK, that it is the home of Robin Hood. One might see this as an extension of those blogs that proudly state that Cloverdale is the home of *Smallville*. See Sam Oldham, "Smallville is great . . ."; Christina, "All of the actors . . . ," *Cloverdale Business Improvement Association*, http://www.itsmysite.com/cgi-bin/itsmy/go.exe?page=21&domain=1&webdir=cloverdale (accessed 5 April 2011).

53. Leah Stowe, "Tom Welling is so hotttt!!!! . . . ," *Cloverdale Business Improvement Association*, http://www.itsmysite.com/cgi-bin/itsmy/go.exe?page=21&domain=1&webdir=cloverdale (accessed 5 April 2011); Christina, "All of the actors . . . ," *Cloverdale Business Improvement Association*, http://www.itsmysite.com/cgi-bin/itsmy/go.exe?page=21&domain=1&webdir=cloverdale (accessed 5 April 2011).

54. Name = J, "Where have I been?! . . . ," *Cloverdale Business Improvement Association*, http://www.itsmysite.com/cgi-bin/itsmy/go.exe?page=24&domain=1&webdir=cloverdale (accessed 5 April 2011).

55. KC, "It shows those common struggles . . . ," *Cloverdale Business Improvement Association*, http://www.itsmysite.com/cgi-bin/itsmy/go.exe?page=24&domain=1&webdir=cloverdale (accessed 5 April 2011).

56. Terry Ladd, "Because it is made in Canada," *Cloverdale Business Improvement Association*, http://www.itsmysite.com/cgi-bin/itsmy/go.exe?page=24&domain=1&webdir=cloverdale (accessed 5 April 2011).

57. Brett Mills discusses a similar working through of local and national identity for fans of BBC's *Torchwood* (2006–Present), specifically drawing attention to the distinction between traveling to Cardiff as a tourist unaware of any local knowledge about shooting locations and the superior status of living in the city that serves as the backdrop to the narrative. See Brett Mills, "My House Was on *Torchwood*! Media, Place and Identity," *International Journal of Cultural Studies* 11, no. 4 (2008): 379–399.

58. Dawn, "Smallville is awesome because . . . ," *Cloverdale Business Improvement Association*, http://www.itsmysite.com/cgi-bin/itsmy/go.exe?page=24&domain=1&webdir=cloverdale (accessed 5 April 2011).

59. Angel, "It is a amazing story! . . . ," *Cloverdale Business Improvement Association*, http://www.itsmysite.com/cgi-bin/itsmy/go.exe?page=24&domain=1&webdir=cloverdale (accessed 5 April 2011).

60. Lincoln Geraghty, *Living with Star Trek: American Culture and the Star Trek Universe* (London: I. B. Tauris), 29.

61. Erica Lalak, "I am absolutely infatuated . . . ," *Cloverdale Business Improvement Association*, http://www.itsmysite.com/cgi-bin/itsmy/go.exe?page=21&domain=1&webdir=cloverdale (accessed 5 April 2011).

62. Elle, "Well, I loved it so much . . . ," *Cloverdale Business Improvement Association*, http://www.itsmysite.com/cgi-bin/itsmy/go.exe?page=24&domain=1&webdir=cloverdale (accessed 5 April 2011).

63. Rebecca, "The world needs heroes . . . ," *Cloverdale Business Improvement Association*, http://www.itsmysite.com/cgi-bin/itsmy/go.exe?page=24&domain=1&webdir=cloverdale (accessed 5 April 2011).

64. Colleen, "I echo everything . . . ," *Cloverdale Business Improvement Association*, http://www.itsmysite.com/cgi-bin/itsmy/go.exe?page=24&domain=1&webdir=cloverdale (5 April 2011).

65. Joyce, "This show raises . . . ," *Cloverdale Business Improvement Association*, http://www.itsmysite.com/cgi-bin/itsmy/go.exe?page=21&domain=1&webdir=cloverdale (accessed 5 April 2011) and Steve, "I would like to echo Joyce . . . ," *Cloverdale Business Improvement Association*, http://www.itsmysite.com/cgi-bin/itsmy/go.exe?page=24&domain=1&webdir=cloverdale (accessed 5 April 2011).

66. Luis Colomo, "Smallville is great . . . ," *Cloverdale Business Improvement Association*, http://www.itsmysite.com/cgi-bin/itsmy/go.exe?page=24&domain=1&webdir=cloverdale (accessed 5 April 2011).

67. Whitney Clayton, "It shows the trail of a teenage boy . . . ," *Cloverdale Business Improvement Association*, http://www.itsmysite.com/cgi-bin/itsmy/go.exe?page=21&domain=1&webdir=cloverdale (accessed 5 April 2011).

68. Hills, *Fan Cultures*, 145.

69. Michel Foucault, "Of Other Spaces," *Diacritics* 16, no. 1 (1986): 24.
70. Gelder, *Subcultures*, 81.
71. David Harvey, "The Kantian Roots of Foucault's Dilemma," in *Space, Knowledge, and Power: Foucault and Geography*, ed. Jeremy W. Crampton and Stuart Elden (Aldershot: Ashgate Publishing, 2007), 45.

CHAPTER EIGHT

SACRIFICE OR SALVATION? *SMALLVILLE*'S HEROIC SURVIVAL AMID CHANGING TELEVISION TRENDS

Michael S. Duffy

Tess Mercer[1] arrives on the scene in the opening moments of the eighth season of *Smallville*, the enormously successful contemporary take on Superman's origins, chiding a lower-ranking official: "What have you been doing all this time, building snowmen?" The line functions not only as a strong introduction to the personality of Tess herself, but as a nice in-joke for the shifting creative direction of the show, which had ended the previous season at a creative standstill. While *Smallville* had successfully instituted itself as a strong and creative genre production in its first few seasons on the air, seasons five, six, and seven began to struggle with stretching the internal complexities of the show's own premise and legacy ("no flights, no tights," among other elements) beyond what most observers had thought to be possible—or even probable. However, with the departure of the show's original creators and show runners, Alfred Gough and Miles Millar, at the end of *Smallville*'s seventh year, and a genre production that was becoming, in ratings and revenue terms, increasingly inexhaustible, the show was forced to reassess its own creative conception and methodology.

This chapter will discuss how *Smallville* continued to renew and reinvigorate itself in its eighth and ninth seasons, despite broadcast network transformations, creative upheavals, cast shake-ups, and character ownership rights entanglements. Even as it concluded its tenth and final season in May 2011, it remained one of the most reliable genre hours on television for audiences worldwide. Though the program's "prime-time" ratings diminished from an average of 5 to 6 million viewers in its first four seasons to a balance of around 2.5 million during its ninth and tenth years on the air, it is likely that the show could have continued in one form or another if Warner Bros. Television, the producers/show runners, and certain cast were willing. While its primary narrative—that of establishing Clark Kent's future "legacy" as Superman—often seemed close to its natural conclusion, there are other avenues creators could have taken the concept, including a spin-off or "expanded universe" premise: in the second half of its final season, *Smallville*'s producers chose to introduce the relatively recently popularized DC Comics character "Conner Kent," a teenage hybrid clone drawn from the DNA of both Clark Kent and Lex Luthor, who was also being simultaneously featured in Warner Bros.' animated *Young Justice* television half hour, which debuted in the spring of 2011. In its later years, *Smallville* countered its lower network ratings with consistently strong showings in Internet downloads and international syndication viewership. Though the top U.S. networks, ABC, CBS, NBC, and Fox, continue to compete for ratings in a time of changing viewership habits, very few shows during the 2001–2011 decade had the consistent success in creative approach, audience demographics, and marketplace share of *Smallville*. In its ten years on the air, the show outlasted familiar genre stalwarts such as *Buffy the Vampire Slayer* (1997–2003) and all the individual runs of the *Star Trek* television series, becoming the longest-consecutively-running science fiction/fantasy show ever,[2] and in monetary terms, one of the most successful productions ever made for television.[3]

While *Smallville* endured consistent criticism throughout its series run from both genre/comic book fans and observers of so-called "quality television,"[4] the show was redeemed through a growing critical and cultural reappraisal and shifting viewership habits during its later seasons; perhaps most importantly for its investors, DVD box sets of all nine seasons to date were consistently found among the top sellers on Amazon.com and in physical stores even into the final year. The show was regularly one of the top ten programs in data surveys of in-home digital video recorders and gained a significant international following through DVD sales and download activity.[5] *Smallville*'s distinct mix of heroic mythology, romantic melodrama, and playful comedy retained many original fans of the show and constantly attracted new followers.[6] Indeed, the global success of *Smallville* and its mythology seems to work as a relevant contemporary example of how classic comic book storytelling can have an influence not only on television drama, but on intellectual properties and multimedia relationships between the show's creators, fans, and critics. The cinematic explosion of feature film adaptations of comic book superheroes throughout the 2000s (due in part to the increasingly diverse availability of digital visual effects technologies, which can bring to life all manner of spectacular characters and scenarios) cannot be discounted as also having influenced *Smallville*'s continual survival. But in televisual terms, Angela Ndalianis has argued how comic book serial narratives have actually been influencing television programming since the 1960s, providing a framework for narrative (re)organization, recapitulation, and extended anticipation.[7] While it has surely had more than a few plots that stretch the premise of its universe, *Smallville* continued to showcase impressive production values, including consistently strong direction and editing and high-quality visual effects, all of which helped create a unique aesthetic style and attitude that strongly appealed to a worldwide audience of many ages and cultural backgrounds.

What inspired me to write about the show was the premiere episode of its eighth season, broadcast in the United States in September 2008. Titled "Odyssey," the episode resituates and in certain ways "reboots" the *Smallville* universe surrounding young Clark Kent, an alien sent to Earth from the doomed planet Krypton and raised in the fictional town of Smallville (essentially Kansas), and who is destined to become the "world's greatest protector," Superman. DC Comics' Superman story, conceived as a proper comic book by Jerry Siegel and Joe Shuster in 1938, has inspired numerous television shows, animated productions, radio serials, and film series, all placing their unique stamp on the culture of their respective generations, but *Smallville*'s survival and cultural impact is a compelling story all its own. Given that the show is still passionately discussed and consumed by fans, critics, and scholars worldwide, it is safe to argue that *Smallville*'s impact on genre television and popular culture is continually worth analyzing.

The show's first three seasons concentrated heavily on the small-town genesis of Clark Kent, as raised by his adoptive parents, Jonathan and Martha, who discovered his ship during a meteor shower.[8] While Clark struggled with his newfound abilities during his all-too-human teenage years, he also helped solve the ever-growing mysteries of a town physically and psychologically impacted by the meteor shower that brought his ship to Earth. Throughout the fifth, sixth, and seventh seasons of the series, the world around Clark matured and darkened—Clark lost his Earth father, Jonathan, to a heart attack, and his mother to Congress, but interestingly the show began to introduce well-known characters who would play a big part in the *future* of the Man of Steel: Lois Lane and Jimmy Olsen. However, at the end of the eighth season of the show, *Smallville*'s version of Jimmy Olsen (which arguably had been pretty "faithful" to his comic book origins up to that point) was killed off and was revealed to in fact be "Henry James Olsen," older brother of the character who would eventually grow up to become the famous Jimmy Olsen of Superman lore. This approach of "ret-conning" a major character and his history with the show raised complicated feelings for many fans of the show. The show's producers later implied that the decision was at parent company Warner Bros. behest, in order to "line-up the mythology" correctly with the general Superman time line, as the Jimmy portrayed in the show was of a similar age as Clark, who was still at least a couple of years off from fully adopting the Superman moniker; in traditional Superman lore, Jimmy is seemingly many years younger than Clark and Lois Lane. The decision remains contentious and confusing for fans of the show, but Ndalianis has argued that the entire Superman mythology has been a consistently strong example of "the slippery possibilities of serial and cross-media storytelling."[9] *Smallville* also exhibits signature cult television tropes in the ways it relies, in its later seasons, on nonlinear narratives that "encompass multiple timeframes and settings," creating "an infinitely large metatext and sometimes the seemingly infinite delay of the resolution."[10] In complicating the adventures and mythology of past, present, and future, *Smallville* became something entirely different, significantly veering off from what seemed its natural trajectory, morphing into, as certain fans (and now DC Comics personnel) asserted, an "Elseworlds" show.[11]

Interestingly, Sara Gwenllian-Jones and Roberta Pearson have argued that, broadly defined, "cult" television shows usually have audiences in the millions, so despite being emphasized as "cult" television, these shows operate largely within a much more mainstream marketplace and atmosphere than "cult" feature films. Indeed, *Smallville*'s central focus on one of the most iconic superheroes in history itself largely forced producers to remain relatively accessible in content, style, and technique, with only rare variations in aesthetic approach. More frequently in its later years,

Smallville pursued an equally strong emphasis on pop cultural and political commentary that gradually began to call attention to its own seemingly paratextual presence. *Smallville* gradually perfected a kind of "narrative elasticity"[12] between seriality and self-contained storylines—and braved the difficulty of having to regularly slow down, extend, or modify the show's base premise (the character evolution of Clark Kent into Superman)—as the program aged through the decade. Additionally, its consistent weaving in of "iconic moments" identifiable to fans of the character and franchise seemed to come at regular intervals, despite the show's ever-expanding narrative trajectory, encouraging ever more complex "intensive and interpretive audience practices."[13]

Having explored all manner of twists and turns in the relationships of its central characters throughout its first seven seasons, and having slowed Clark's journey to adulthood as far as meaningfully possible, *Smallville*'s journey seemed as if it was moving toward a natural—perhaps even belated—conclusion during its seventh year. Indeed, though it is the nature of American-produced episodic/seasonal television to be in a constant state of renewal, for the second five years of the show, *Smallville*'s producers were never quite sure if each successive season would be its last; thus, there was a familiar pattern of building up certain narrative elements during the first half of a normally twenty-two-episode season and gradually stretching things out at a slower pace once word came down that the show was once again renewed for another year. With the introduction of Clark's cousin Kara (who in Superman mythology later becomes Supergirl), as what looked to many like a potential spin-off property, and the departure of original cast members Michael Rosenbaum (Lex Luthor), John Glover (Lex's father, Lionel Luthor, created for the show), and Kristin Kreuk (Lana Lang), as well as—according to industry buzz—the *near* departure of Allison Mack (Clark's trusted friend Chloe Sullivan, also created specifically for the show), coupled with rumors of cast frustration with storylines, and network-mandated budget cuts, *Smallville* was seemingly ready to fly up, up, and away into franchise history. But some surprising developments *off*screen—a writers' strike resulting in a shortened season; the out-of-left-field departure of the show's creators, Al Gough and Miles Millar; and again, importantly, continually strong ratings and DVD sales for previous seasons—prompted the small fourth-place network the CW (formerly the WB) to renew *Smallville* for an eighth year (star Tom

Welling had already committed the previous year to a contract with an option for season eight and later signed on for the ninth and tenth seasons together; Rosenbaum, Kreuk, and Glover departed when their seven-season contracts ended).[14]

Many of the show's fans had found the last couple of seasons difficult to swallow due to stagnating character development (particularly Clark's) and questionable relationship pairings (Lex Luthor romancing Lana). Clark's noticeably unchanging blue shirt–red jacket–blue jeans wardrobe, while meant to reflect the primary colors of the Superman costume, became more of a metaphorical straitjacket, a signature of the restrictions the show's producers were forced to adhere to, both because the characters were a victim of the show's extended success, and because the studio, network, and creators had never planned on turning *Smallville* into a full-blown Superman narrative. Season seven ended with a narrative whimper, its last few episodes spent tying up loose ends from seasons past in an attempt to wrap some sort of conclusion around a saga that was at its natural creative end, but forced to continue because of the demands of the marketplace. The season finale was a strange downer: Lex, having finally discovered the full nature of Clark's abilities, confronts him at the Fortress of Solitude in the Arctic, activating a device that triggers the destruction of the fortress and buries both under the icy rubble. Chloe is arrested by the "Department of Domestic Security" for her hacking activities (which had often helped Clark save lives), and Lana, Clark's first love, abruptly awakes from a coma and leaves Clark a video good-bye message. Rather than any compelling desperate situation or significant tactical or social conundrum, this season finale left audiences (including myself) feeling quite depressed and pessimistic about what the show had become, and where it could possibly go next.

Frames from the first television teaser for season eight of *Smallville* included the intertitles "A Hero Is Lost" and "The Search Begins" among numerous quick clips of the season premiere episode, already clearly framing this season as a new beginning of sorts. The premiere's title, "Odyssey," also conjured images of a mythological quest following great tragedy. Though many were skeptical about what *Smallville* could offer as it jumped into its eighth year, from its opening moments, the first episode of the season shows and tells us that this interpretation of Clark's journey is different from anything that has come before, in a very satisfying way. Gough and Millar's departure seemed to open up a creative freedom for the writers that had not existed before. Through scripting, cinematography, dialogue, and editing, new show runners Todd Slavkin, Darren Swimmer, Kelly Souders, and Brian Peterson (all previous writers on the show) used "Odyssey" to playfully and quite brilliantly free themselves from the last few seasons' disappointing creative turns and plot constraints.

The familiar "Previously on *Smallville*" clip montage (comprised mostly of moments from the previous season) opens the episode, and its signature quotes from the show's central characters place Clark at the beginning of his great journey into adulthood. "I sent you to Earth for a purpose, Kal-El," his Kryptonian father Jor-El instructs. Martian J'onn J'onzz tells Clark, "You've learned a lot from your time in Smallville; your father would be proud." Lana via videotape: "I need you—but the world needs you more." Martha Kent: "Just because I'm leaving [the Kent farm], doesn't mean you have to stay." Oliver Queen: "This isn't the end of the story, Clark—this is just the beginning." The show then properly begins in the Arctic, at an outpost where agents are searching the spot of the demolished Fortress of Solitude for clues to Lex's disappearance. Tess Mercer, a cold but very attractive redhead with killer eyes and instincts, walks into the tent and aggressively assumes command, claiming that her "access is unrestricted." Straightaway, there's a sharp exchange of dialogue that distinctly brings to mind a certain Alaskan vice presidential candidate from 2008's U.S. presidential election campaign. The camp's leader scoffs at her: "You're nothing but an obscure regional VP [Vice President]; do you actually believe you're qualified?" Tess replies, "Lex believes it, and that's all that matters." When the same executive again later raises his suspicions about her motives, Tess cuts back, "Nobody questions my loyalty [to Lex]." (And in a future episode, Tess proves her mettle by personally offing the questioning exec, on screen and in graphic bloody detail.)

The similarities in look and dialogue may have surprisingly been by chance, as "Odyssey" was written and filmed at least six weeks before then governor of Alaska Sarah Palin was announced as the Republican vice presidential candidate on August 29, 2008. Nonetheless, the evolution of the character throughout season eight retains an attitude and demeanor that is undoubtedly Palinesque. In fact, "Odyssey" makes numerous comments on recent political and cultural divides in the United States, themes that the show had never before been brave enough to tackle (and the political subtext interestingly became much more noticeable during the series' ninth and tenth seasons). As "Odyssey" begins, Clark has been missing for over a month, and his friend Oliver Queen (who is already masquerading as underground hero/vigilante Green Arrow) has organized a search party to find him, which includes *Smallville*'s versions of Aquaman[15] and Black Canary (who can release deafening sonic screams). For their covert actions as the yet-to-be-named Justice League, they are referred to by Lexcorp employees as "terrorists," and when a couple of them are captured in a Guantanamo Bay–like facility where Chloe is also being held, they are hung by chains and interrogated, the implication clearly alluding to torturous tactics.

However, the most telling and compelling moments in *Smallville*'s eighth-season premiere are those that comment on the show's own recent history, both on screen and behind the scenes. While forging a new creative direction, "Odyssey" also features many revealing, almost snarky lines of dialogue that seem to be directly referencing the show's troubled past few years—and perhaps the program's former show runners. Upon discovering *Daily Planet* reporter Lois Lane spying in her office, Tess Mercer (knowing something's up) comes on like a critical audience member, chastising producers for failing to deliver significant character evolution: "and the floors, they've lost their sheen—you're not getting lazy, are you?" Smartly preempting possible criticisms of the Tess character as a replacement for Rosenbaum's highly regarded performance as Lex Luthor, Chloe calls Tess a "Luthor wannabe." Tess even utters to Lois at one point, "I have to admit it's difficult to imagine a mini-Lois running around," a comment that seems to be a subtle dig at one of the central plotlines of *Superman Returns*, Warner Bros.' 2006 failed big-screen franchise starter.[16] Additionally, it is revealed that Oliver Queen has a "history" with Tess and calls her by a nickname: "Mercy." The name "Tess Mercer" was created by the show's new producers in reference to both 1978's *Superman* antagonist "Miss Tessmacher" and "Mercy Graves," Luthor's chauffeur-with-stilettos created for the 1990s Bruce Timm–produced *Superman: The Animated Series* (1996–2000). Tess also immediately joins the show's tradition of playfully verbalizing Superman's many famous associated phrases: "Mr. Luthor is a firm believer in Truth and Justice, Ms. Lane," she notes in "Odyssey."

As the episode progresses, Oliver locates a powerless Clark in Russia (!), and we discover that he has been slaving away with a crew of caviar peddlers (!), but it is when Oliver and Clark relax on the plane ride home that they have their most interesting exchange, commenting on the inherent ridiculousness of Clark's seventh-season finale scenario:

> *Clark:* "How does an ice fortress just disappear into thin air?"
>
> *Oliver:* "I feel like there's a punch line in that question."
>
> *Clark:* "It all must be part of my father's plan—it turns out that his idea of 'controlling' me was taking away my powers."

And with a wink and smile, we have a very simple twist and throwaway explanation of season seven's dead-end plotline. But Clark remains "mortal" throughout the rest of this episode, and after running into Lois and saving Chloe, he encounters his own mortality in a scene that prefigures the events of season eight's finale. After Clark and Oliver arrive at the "Gitmo"-like complex in an attempt to rescue their friends, Oliver is briefly overtaken by a mind-altering injected serum from a Lexcorp employee, and in demanding to know where Lex Luthor is, he begins to shoot arrows (his signature weapon) directly at Clark. Here the show begins to play with viewers' expectations and to plant interesting twists within its narrative and its signature visual effects moments and iconography. Oliver's first arrow hits Clark in the chest, right near his heart. He is stunned, bleeding and in pain, and as he struggles to pull the arrow out of his body, Oliver shoots a second arrow. A slow-motion digitally enhanced effect shot (an aesthetic style familiar to viewers of *Smallville*) closes in on the arrow and follows it toward Clark's chest. The visual effects style displayed here is normally instituted to create the expectation that Clark will superspeed (conveyed in slow motion to us) out of danger or somehow stop the offending object. In this case, Clark, still sans powers, is not able to use his superhuman abilities to either catch the arrows or speed out of the way. The second arrow impales him and runs straight through, blowing out the window behind him. A reverse shot from outside the building shows the arrow crashing through the stained-glass window after it runs through Clark's chest.

As Clark falls to the floor, Chloe and Oliver, whose mind-controlling serum has (conveniently) just worn off, come to his side. Seemingly near a "mortal" death, significant people in Clark's life are visualized in the form of a brief flashback montage that relates moments from throughout the show's history, accompanied by a melancholic music cue and the sound of Clark's slowing heartbeat. The sequence includes Clark's first love, Lana, in a shot from *Smallville*'s very first episode in 2001; Clark's Earth parents, Jonathan and Martha Kent; and Martha Kent at Jonathan's funeral, a shot from season five's "Reckoning" (2006), the show's momentous one-hundredth episode. This very brief montage has two functions: narratively, it is of course meant as a visualization of Clark's inner thoughts as he believes he is close to death; but seen in the context of the episode (and perhaps season eight) as a whole, the moment is a key component in the new show runners' attempt to subtly resituate and creatively reboot the *Smallville* universe. This montage serves as a brief introduction, or reintroduction, to Clark's Earth parents and his first love, all central characters who had a significant impact on Clark within the *Smallville* universe but who are no longer regularly involved with/cast in the show. Clark's flashbacks fade into a godlike image of J'onn J'onzz (a shape-shifting alien known in the comics as the Martian Manhunter), who, in *Smallville*'s incarnation, has been "watching over" Clark for many years, as a promise to his Kryptonian parents (J'onn began appearing in *Smallville* during the show's sixth season). In a moment that visually and emotionally brings to life the extraordinary nature of what it might be like to witness the display of superheroic abilities, a dramatic score builds, and J'onn lifts Clark over his shoulders and immediately bursts through the window into the sky in a red blur as Oliver and Chloe watch in wonder and worry. The final shot before an editing pause for an advertising break is a frontal close-up of J'onn flying Clark toward the sun, where Clark's life force and powers will be restored, as he draws his superhuman abilities on Earth from our sun.

A commercial break holds the tension, and we arrive back at the Kent farm, introduced by a signature establishing shot of the barn that still appears in one form or another in every single episode, even though the majority of events on the show now take place in the city of Metropolis. Clark awakes in the barn that has been the scene of so many iconic moments in the show's history, and he and J'onn have a sincere and serious discussion about superhuman abilities and destiny, during which Clark begins to ponder a dual identity, and J'onn reveals the tragic consequences of his own heroism.

> *J'onn:* "I promised Jor-El that I would only be a watchful guardian—but I could not stand by and let you die. Jor-El knew he was sending you on an impossible odyssey—to be given the power of a god, yet exist among humans."
>
> *Clark:* "Sometimes I feel like I need to be two separate people. Either way, I can't keep expecting you to save me."
>
> *J'onn:* "That was the last time—the burning sun may strengthen you, but it had the opposite effect on me. It stripped me of my powers. . . . We both know that yours is a greater destiny. With the fortress destroyed, you have to do it without Jor-El's guidance."
>
> *Clark:* ". . . Or anyone else's."

During its last two seasons, *Smallville* had gradually begun to dramatize the idea that exposure to the Earth's sun can restore Clark's extraordinary abilities in moments of weakness. The basic notion that Superman's powers are gained from our yellow sun has existed in his comics for many decades, but it became a primary factor in the character's reemergence following the 1992 "Death of Superman" storyline. It was explained that Superman's body stored solar energy, and though appearing "dead" after an epic struggle with the monster Doomsday, he was in fact only in a comalike state, recharging his body's resources. That *Smallville* here directly incorporated the sun's importance in Clark's life energy on Earth, coupled with the planned introduction of the Doomsday character throughout the season, hinted at where the show was headed for season eight's finale.

Continuing their conversation, Clark describes his life flashing back before his eyes while he was dying, seeing his father, mother, and Lana: "I've written eulogies. I've seen people walk away from me. But I've never really said good-bye—I've been holding on to a life on this farm that hasn't existed for years"—again here echoing what many longtime viewers of the show were feeling for the past few seasons. J'onn asks Clark what he is going to do. Clark turns around with conviction and replies, "Let it go." J'onn smiles and picks up Clark's signature red jacket. He throws it to Clark, who, accompanied by familiar *Smallville* musical themes, puts it on dramatically, as if he were donning the iconic red cape of his future heroic persona. Clark nods confidently.

Clark's new proactive nature affects the way he acts, both with the yet-to-be-named Justice League, and with Lois Lane herself. At the conclusion of the episode, Clark meets up with Oliver, A. C. (Aquaman), and Dinah (Black Canary), and Clark's attitude prompts Oliver to tell him, "Pretty soon, you'll be sporting a homemade costume and leading a double identity, just like the rest of us." When Clark then goes to meet up with Lois at the *Daily Planet*, he surprises her with news that not only has he secured a job at the revered metropolitan newspaper, but also that he will be sitting right across from her. Clark, who had previously been reluctant to begin working at the *Planet*, astounds Lois with his decision. "I guess I wanted to be in the middle of the action," he proudly proclaims as he places his nameplate opposite Lois. Clark's beaming smile as he walks toward camera and out of the office, satisfied that he has suitably outwitted the intrepid reporter, displays a kind of boyish, optimistic expressiveness that actor Tom Welling had not shown in the role in years. One of the few dramatic faults of Clark's storyline here is that, despite making a life-changing decision to pursue a "day job" so that he can be "closer to the action" in the city, it is never actually explained precisely how he scored a plum spot working right across from, and seemingly at equal rank with, the already-employed Lois Lane. Viewers are also left to wonder just how the producers might decide to develop and make plausible Clark's "disguise," as in *Smallville*'s continuity, Lois has now known Clark for nearly five years and there are no eyeglasses in sight (though the show has displayed Clark flirting with a pair or two before).[17]

As season eight progresses, Clark starts dressing in business attire for work at the *Planet*, and he (secretly) begins taking a more direct, active role in the emergencies in Metropolis. On his first day at work, Clark comes in ill-attired in flannel, and in a lighthearted moment Lois borrows a coworker's extra dress shirt and forces Clark into an indoor phone booth to man up, where he puts on a new, but strangely familiar, shade of blue. In the second episode of the season, "Plastique" (2008), the sobering real-world realities of terrorism begin to be reflected in the show more regularly, as the episode opens with a bus explosion affecting many bystanders and forcing Clark to intervene and save Tess Mercer. While *Smallville*'s narrative choices here clearly don't constitute an embrace of the deep complications of, and meditations on, the "war on terror" that were prevalent in the acclaimed revival of *Battlestar Galactica* (2003–2009), there is still a noticeable shift in dramatic tension in Clark's world that subtly reflects everyday problems with a more astute and pointed sensibility than in the show's previous seasons. As time progresses, it becomes much harder for Clark to keep his "Good Samaritan" deeds under wraps, even with the powerless J'onn J'onzz covering for him (as local detective "John Jones") and Oliver Queen donning a second costume (with red and blue themes) in order to keep Jimmy Olsen from linking the mysterious "Red-Blue Blur" to Clark's use of the red jacket and blue jeans.

Also telling of the new show runners' attitude toward storytelling is the treatment of Kara, Clark's cousin, who was introduced in the beginning of season seven (with the reported intention of spawning a spin-off show). When that didn't happen, Kara landed in limbo, both narratively and figuratively. Her character arc topped off midway through the season; she disappeared, showed up with amnesia, and then was sent to the Phantom Zone (a virtual wasteland created by Jor-El to house intergalactic criminals). Kara is interestingly not mentioned *once* throughout the first seven episodes of the show's eighth season and is brought back only for a one-off return appearance in the eighth episode, wherein Clark and Lois get trapped in the Phantom Zone. The show's ability to have fun with its own mythology knows no bounds: Oliver, upon learning of the existence of the intergalactic prison from Chloe, chides, "Phantom Zone, huh? Seriously, who names these things?" But Clark clearly takes his mythology seriously, as he tells a distraught Lois in the zone that "no one's going to mess with Lois and Clark." A couple of iconic shots appear in the episode, including a climactic moment where Kara lends a hand (literally, on the familiar "House of El" crest, i.e., the Superman *S* shield) to help Lois and Clark escape from the Phantom Zone. But despite a few powerful scenes between Clark and Kara, one gets the painfully obvious feeling that this episode is merely meant as "closure" for a character that perhaps never should have been written into *Smallville* in the first place—and it is knowingly related in the show's dialogue itself. In a touching conversation at the Kent farm at the conclusion of the show, Kara tells Clark, "I don't fit in here—my journey is somewhere else." Even in essentially admitting that the introduction of Kara into *Smallville*'s universe was a mistake, the final scenes between Clark and Kara evoke a bittersweet sadness that is more affecting than any of Kara's prior appearances in season seven.[18]

Season eight's creative direction was also greatly enhanced by the introduction and development of a character named Davis Bloome, a paramedic who spends his days saving lives, but who is secretly developing destructive tendencies in his unconscious. Gradually, he begins to discover that he perhaps may not be who he thinks he is—and indeed something much more disturbing. This is the producers' new vision of Doomsday, the supremely powerful Kryptonian monster (in)famous in the DC Comics universe for being the only character to essentially "kill" Superman. Producers tapped *Battlestar Galactica* veteran Sam Witwer to play Bloome, and the actor's previous attachment to the critically acclaimed sci-fi show helped bring additional critical and cultural credibility to *Smallville*. The show's take on Doomsday smartly ties multiple Superman mythologies together: in the eighth episode, it is revealed that General Zod[19] and his wife Faora genetically engineered Doomsday because they could not have a child of their own, and they attached his DNA matter onto Clark's ship so that Doomsday would arrive on Earth to later destroy the "Last Son of Krypton" (one of the later episodes of season eight features flashbacks to Davis Bloome's early years on Earth—and a short-lived acquaintance with a young Lex Luthor).

Bloome's tragic evolution into the creature that will eventually "kill" Superman (a new narrative created almost entirely by the show's writers and producers) is dark and disturbing, and added another interesting thread to an already rich tapestry of contemporary superheroic mythology that kept *Smallville* alive—season eight's finale is, not surprisingly, entitled "Doomsday" (2009) and featured a brief showdown between Clark and the monster. At the beginning of the season, producers hinted that recreating the iconic comic book death scene would be "quite an exciting cinematic moment," but though fan buzz anticipated that such an event might be the focus of the finale, another "death" for Clark, to mirror the season opener, was applied only metaphorically, as Clark, distraught over the death of Jimmy by Doomsday's hand, decides to give up his Clark Kent identity and focus solely on being a silent avenger. This is where we can see that "Odyssey" was indeed roughly framed as an introduction and preparation for such an event: Clark's near death in the season opener mirrored his "death" in the finale—except this time, no one else (including J'onn J'onzz) could save him. In the comics version of the story, Superman is memorialized, buried, and disappears for a year, while four potential replacements show up, all claiming to be him; while *Smallville* doesn't replicate that storyline for its ninth season, it does set up a bit of a dark "double" storyline by way of bringing cloned versions of nemesis Zod and Clark's Kryptonian father Jor-El to *Smallville*.

Smallville's ninth season revolves around Clark's adoption of new heroic duties, but also his attempt to stay in the shadows. He begins to wear the famous *S* on his chest, but his choice of outfit, a black shirt and pants covered with a dark trench coat, reflects the nature of his character, his regret over the death of "Jimmy," and his delay in deciding how to handle Davis Bloome/Doomsday. Clark's trench coat does give him a dramatic capelike feeling during arrivals and departures, not equaled by the more colorful interim outfit that Clark begins to wear in the show's tenth season. In the first episode of season nine, "Savior" (2009), Clark begins his long-planned-for "training" under the tutelage of Jor-El in the Fortress of Solitude, and we interestingly see him testing out his as-yet-undemonstrated flying ability from New York's Statue of Liberty (though it's a fabrication of a city created in Clark's head through Jor-El's advanced Kryptonian/Fortress technology). "My old life seems very far away," Clark says to Chloe early in the ninth season. Throughout this year of the show, Clark deals with a younger, cloned version of Zod, who, it is revealed, was an ally of Jor-El's back on Krypton, and who tried to prevent a war but differed in philosophy from Jor-El (somewhat echoing the philosophical struggle between Charles Xavier and Magneto in the long-running series of *X-Men* feature films begun in 2000). Clark even gets some public-persona education from the show's creative new interpretation of classic Superman nemesis Metallo, whose tragic origin actually gives the character both sympathy and purpose and allows him to school Clark on the proper way to be a hero by not remaining in the shadows: "You stand apart from the world, while the rest of us live in it . . . even when it breaks your heart." *Smallville*'s ninth season arguably improves on what was established during its eighth, and again sets the show up nicely for not only its own season finale (entitled "Salvation" [2010]), but Clark's superheroic destiny, which is finally concluded in season ten.

In discussing the evolution of contemporary television forms, Jason Mittell argues that "a new paradigm of television storytelling has emerged over the past two decades, with a reconceptualization of the boundary between episodic and serial forms, a heightened degree of self-consciousness in storytelling mechanics, and demands for intensified viewer engagement focused on both diegetic pleasures and formal awareness."[20] *Smallville* is very much part of this new paradigm, and it survived for a decade on television, through home video, and with the support of an avid and highly enthusiastic online fan base that, while at many times divided, valued the long-running show for not only its characters and mythology, but its consistent ability to deliver weekly entertainment that communicates in both genre terms and in cultural symbolism and meaning. In observing and studying *Smallville*'s last few seasons, one gets the sense that the overall creative direction behind the show is more cool, calculated, and logically plotted than seasons past; in fact there is an overriding feeling that a much clearer plan surrounded all of the major production decisions, arguably giving *Smallville* a new life—a rebirth in a television market that is increasingly fragmented by changing viewing habits and cable and Internet television's continuously strong competition in ratings. As the show's characters have "grown up" throughout the past eight years, so also has the global television market matured into something very different, and much more complicated, than it was in 2001. In this sense, *Smallville*, Clark, and the hero he eventually becomes (but in most ways, truly already is in these last seasons of the show) become interesting metaphors for the transforming television industry, just as the show continued to convey Superman's core values and longevity, strength, and lasting sense of purpose throughout history. As the world changes, it seems Superman will always be there for us in one incarnation or another, but *Smallville* has successfully endured trials equal to those of its central hero, and like him, the show continued to surprise its observers with its consistently creative combination of classic mythology and contemporary narrative approach.

Notes

1. Early in the tenth season, the character is revealed to be a part of the Luthor family: half-sister of Lex and daughter of Lionel. (After being killed off during the seventh season, Lionel reappears in season ten in the form of an "alternate universe" version of himself who crosses into "our" world.)

2. *Smallville* is expected to be cited in the *Guinness Book of World Records* in 2011 for "Longest Running Consecutive Sci-Fi TV Show." Though some critics argue that the BBC's *Doctor Who* (1963–Present) has an impressive decades-

long run, its various series were apparently not considered "consecutive" in their broadcast nature (though the show was indeed honored by *Guinness* in 2009 for being the "Most Successful Sci-Fi Series" in television history in terms of overall impact). In "consecutive" episode count, *Smallville* reached 216 episodes in total, beating previous record holder *Stargate: SG-1* (1997–2007), which ran for ten years and on two networks but only reached 214 episodes. See "*Smallville* Will Break *SG-1*'s World Record," *Gateworld*, 9 March 2010, http://www.gateworld.net/news/2010/03/smallville-will-break-stargate-sg-1s-world-record (accessed 10 February 2011) and "*Doctor Who* Honored by Guinness," *Variety*, 26 July 2009, http://www.variety.com/article/VR1118006512?refCatId=2159 (accessed 10 February 2011).

3. Though determining exact numbers is nearly impossible with studios' often "creative accounting," it is widely thought by industry observers that *Smallville* generated revenue in the tens or possibly even hundreds of millions of U.S. dollars each year it was on the air, through DVD sales, international syndication sales, ancillary marketing, and advertising. Alfred Gough and Miles Millar, the show's creators, filed a lawsuit against Warner Bros. Television and the CW Network in early 2010 claiming that the studios "improperly reported production costs that resulted in $4 million in withheld revenue," among other accusations. See Nellie Andreeva and Matt Belloni, "*Smallville* Producers Sue Warner Bros., CW," *The Hollywood Reporter*, 26 March 2010, http://www.hollywoodreporter.com/news/smallville-producers-sue-warner-bros-22063 (accessed 10 February 2011); Matthew Belloni, "Warner Bros. Fights Back in *Smallville* Profits Lawsuit," *THR, Esq.* (*The Hollywood Reporter*'s legal blog), 1 June 2010, http://hollywoodreporter.blogs.com/thresq/2010/06/warner-bros-fights-back-in-smallville-profits-lawsuit.html (accessed 10 February 2011); Matthew Belloni, "Exclusive: Setback for *Smallville* Creators in Warner Bros. Profits Lawsuit," *THR, Esq.*, 14 December 2010, http://www.hollywoodreporter.com/blogs/thr-esq/setback-smallville-creators-warner-bros-59815 (accessed 10 February 2011).

4. For more on this concept, see Mark Jancovich and James Lyons, eds., *Quality Popular Television: Cult TV, the Industry and Fans* (London: BFI Publishing, 2003).

5. Press announcement, "The CW Continues to Score Big in Live+7," *The CW Network*, 2 December 2009, http://www.thefutoncritic.com/ratings/2009/12/02/the-cw-continues-to-score-big-in-live-plus-7-33691/20091202cw01/#ixzz1E1Du4dH2 (accessed 10 February 2011).

6. Indeed, one of the arguments coming from *Smallville*'s fan base and certain other industry observers as to why Warner Bros.' feature division should cast Tom Welling as the big-screen Superman, and/or transfer the show's mythology to a feature film, was that it would instantly provide a completely new stream of

revenue for the studio through members of the public anticipating a new blockbuster adaptation of the familiar comic book hero; the argument was that, ideally, a feature film based on *Smallville*'s mythology would have encouraged additional consumers to purchase past seasons of the show on DVD in order to "catch up" to prepare for the feature film. "It seems like a no-brainer," fans would often say when discussing the franchise potential on Internet message boards.

7. See Angela Ndalianis, "Television and the Neo-Baroque," in *The Contemporary Television Series*, ed. Michael Hammond and Lucy Mazdon (Edinburgh: Edinburgh University Press, 2005), 83–101.

8. The meteor shower that brings Clark's Kryptonian ship and many fragments of kryptonite (meteor rock fragments of the planet Krypton) to Earth is just one of the many new twists that Alfred Gough and Miles Millar brought to their reinvigoration of the Superman legend.

9. Angela Ndalianis, "Enter the Aleph: Superhero Worlds and Hypertime Realities," in *The Contemporary Comic Book Superhero*, ed. Angela Ndalianis (New York: Routledge, 2009), 270.

10. Sara Gwenllian-Jones and Roberta E. Pearson, "Introduction," in *Cult Television*, ed. Sara Gwenllian-Jones and Roberta E. Pearson (Minneapolis: University of Minnesota Press, 2004), xii. See also Terrence R. Wandtke, ed., *The Amazing, Transforming Superhero! Essays on the Revision of Characters in Comic Books, Film and Television* (Jefferson, NC: McFarland, 2007).

11. "Elseworlds" is a long-running official sublabel for storylines from DC Comics that take place outside its current narrative universe. See http://dc.wikia.com/wiki/Elseworlds (accessed 10 February 2011).

12. Gwenllian-Jones et al., "Introduction," xi.

13. Gwenllian-Jones et al., "Introduction," xvi. In *Smallville*'s case, fans composed YouTube montage videos set to contemporary pop and rock songs, as well as wishful-thinking "ship" reconfigurations of the show's main characters' relationships with each other, and well-edited "pitches" for a possible—but not likely—feature film spin-off.

14. Though Kreuk would return for five episodes in the eighth year, reportedly to complete her contract agreement, *Smallville*'s seventh season had been cut short by the writers' strike, and Kreuk was also committed to filming *Street Fighter: The Legend of Chun-Li* (2009) during the spring of 2008. Glover, whose character had been killed off during the latter half of the seventh season, returned for four episodes during the show's tenth and final season as an "alternate universe" version of himself; Rosenbaum also agreed to return for *Smallville*'s May 2011 series finale.

15. *Not* played here by "Vincent Chase," the fictional actor of HBO series *Entourage* (2004–Present), a contemporary comedic document on Hollywood actors.

During one of its early seasons, its lead personality Vincent Chase gets recruited by director James Cameron to star in a big-budget *Aquaman* feature film. *Smallville* had also earlier attempted to spin off its Aquaman character in an original series called *Mercy Reef*, though with a different actor, Justin Hartley, in the lead role. A pilot was filmed but was not picked up for a series, whereupon Gough and Millar hired Hartley to play Oliver Queen/Green Arrow for *Smallville* instead.

16. The film was hurt by its enormous production cost (rumored to be near 260 million U.S. dollars) and relatively disappointing worldwide gross, its problematic narrative (which featured Superman discovering that he and Lois have a five-year-old child born while he was off Earth searching for remains of his home planet), and its "vague history" of cultural remembrance that mostly tied it to Richard Donner's *Superman* (1978). Warner Bros. later asked Christopher Nolan (who had successfully revived the studio's Batman film franchise in the 2000s) to develop and produce a new cinematic take on Superman for 2012, which was to be directed by Zack Snyder and was rushed into development partially to prevent the studio from losing certain fundamental character rights to the estates of Jerry Siegel and Joe Schuster in a long-running court battle.

17. As it turns out that *Smallville* lasts another two years beyond season eight, Clark (and presumably Welling) chooses not to adopt the signature Clark Kent "disguise" glasses until late in the tenth season, disappointing many fans, but ultimately grasping on to the final vestiges of its premise of being a show about the journey to *becoming* Superman.

18. Kara would return, however, for a few more appearances during seasons nine and ten.

19. Zod, albeit a younger version of himself, appears throughout season nine in the form of a "clone."

20. Jason Mittell, "Narrative Complexity in Contemporary American Television," *The Velvet Light Trap* 58, no. 1 (2006): 29–40.

INDEX

9/11, vii, xiv, 25, 29, 34

ABC, 110, 117, 154
Ackles, Jensen, 24, 148n17
acting, xii, 3–4, 12–13, 16, 24n17, 38, 69, 76–78, 80, 91, 112, 116, 118, 121, 134–135, 142, 144–145, 164, 166, 170n15
Action Comics, 94–95, 97, 101–102
adaptation, viii, x, xv, xxiv–xxv, 4–7, 10, 17, 21–22, 49, 53, 58, 66, 74, 93–94, 109–110, 112, 155, 170n6
Aden, Roger C., 135–136, 145
Adobe After Effects, 78
adolescence. *See* teenagers
Adventures of Superman, x, *xi*, 90, 109
Allen, Bart, 78
Alyn, Kirk, x
American Cinematographer, 70
American football, 8, 29–30, 51, 92
American Monomyth, viii–ix, 28
Animation World Network, 70
anorexia, 39
Apple, 124
Aquaman, 78, 92, 160, 164, 171
Aristotle, 44n29
audiences, xviii, xxi, xxvi, xxvii, 5, 8, 13–14, 30, 50, 59, 62n9, 65, 66, 76, 79, 111–113, 140–141, 153, 156, 158; demographics, 4, 71, 114, 120, 123, 154
Australia, 133–134

Banks, Miranda J., xvii, 8
Barlow, Aaron, 102
Bascom, William, 27
Batman, xiv, 30, 99, 171
Batman Begins, 43n20
Battis, Jes, xvii, xxiii, 43n23
Battlestar Galactica, xxvi, 129, 135, 141, 164, 166
Baym, Nancy, 110, 117–118
Baywatch, 51
BBC, 151n57
Beck, Mat, 67–70, 74, 78, 83
Berger, Richard, 10
bildungsroman, xxi, 3, 21–22
Bird, S. Elizabeth, 140
Black Canary, 160, 164

blogging, viii, xxi, xxv–xxvi, 109, 114–116, 120–125, 130–132, 134, 136–146, 150n49, 150n52
Bloome, Davis, xxvii, 166–167
Blue, Callum, 80
Booker, M. Keith, xv
Booth, Paul, 141–142
Bourdieu, Pierre, 117
Brainiac, 81
British Columbia, xxvi, 129, 138, 140–141, 143
Brooker, Will, 130, 133, 135, 136
Buffy the Vampire Slayer, xiv, xvii, xx, 21, 26, 38, 39, 41, 42n5, 48–49, 62n6, 62n9, 89, 112, 131, 154; "Hush," 21; "Once More, With Feeling," xx
bulimia, 39

Cain, Dean, 67, 92
Cameron, James, 171n15
Campbell, Joseph, 31, 35, 36, 131
Canada, xx, xxi, 133, 142–143, 150n49
Carrie, 49
CBS, 114, 154
CGI, xxiv, 67–70, 72, 79–83, 112
Channel 4, vii
Charmed, 49
Children of the Corn, 26, 41
"Children of the Corn," 41
Christianity, ix, 29
cinema, 27, 30, 41, 66, 68, 70–71, 83, 136, 143, 155, 159, 166, 171n16; in the 1940s, x; in the 1980s, 92
cloning, 10, 35, 99, 154, 167, 171n19
Cloverdale, BC, xxvi, 46, 129–130, 134, 136–137, 147, 150n49, 150n52; Business Improvement Association, 138, 145; website, 140–144, 146
comic books, vii–ix, xiv, xx–xxi, xxiii, xxv, xxvii, 3–7, 10–13, 26–27, 30, 41–42, 46–48, 58, 61n3, 63n19, 81, 89–90, 92–102, 104, 109, 112–113, 119, 154–156, 162–163, 166, 170n6, 170n11
communism, x–xi
convergence culture, xviii, xx, 111, 132, 141, 147
Coogan, Peter, xiv
Coppa, Francesca, 122
Copyright. *See* intellectual property rights
Corben, John, 39–40
Coyle, Jake, 121
Creek, Jeremy, 30–31, 33
Crossroads, 24n22
Curry, Arthur, 78
Curtain, Tyler, 140
CW Network, 9, 71, 117, 125, 157
CWTV.com, 112, 114, 120

The Daily Planet, 6, 160, 164
Darth Vader, xii
Davis, Glyn, 9
Davis, Marc, 121
Dawson's Creek, vii, xvii, 46–47, 89–90, 112
DC Comics, 92–93, 96, 101–104, 119, 154–156, 166
Denison, Rayna, xxiii–xxiv, 102, 132
The Depression, x
Detective Comics, 99
disability, xxii, 55
Disney, 62n4
Doctor Who, 141, 168n2
Donner, Richard, 171n16

Doomsday, 70–73, 76–77, 163, 166–167
Douglas, Tom, 29
DNA, 10, 25, 154, 166
drugs, 38, 40, 46
Ducovny, Allen, 95
Duffy, Michael S., xxvii, 74
The Dukes of Hazzard, 16
Dundes, Alan, 27
Durance, Erica, 116
DVD, 14, 30, 41, 43n16, 71, 82, 91, 101–104, 134, 136, 154, 157, 169n3, 170n6; commentaries, 67; extras, xx, 42, 70, 76, 131–132
DVR, 103, 112, 154

Earth, 6, 28–29, 36, 54, 95, 136, 155–156, 159, 162–163, 166, 170n8, 171n16
Eco, Umberto, 11, 27, 40
Entertainment Weekly, 65
Entity FX, 67, 70, 73–74, 77–78
Entourage, 170n15
ER, 51
Everwood, 47

fandom, xxvi–xxvii, 131, 138, 143, 146; communities, 57, 110–111, 113–115, 117–121, 123–125, 126n23, 135–136, 142, 147; cult, viii, xix, xxv, 7, 9, 15–17, 22, 135; digital, xxv, 109–113, 115–116, 120–125; fan art, 111, 115, 121, 123–125; fan fiction, viii, 15, 56, 124, 126n18, 127n45, 131–132, 139; fan pilgrimage, xxvi, 129–130, 135–136, 145; and fundraising, 144; subcultures, 110–111, 118, 125, 141; video, xxv, 114–115, 120–125, 126n18
Farscape, 133–134
Fawcett Publications, 100
feminism, 19
Feuer, Jane, xxi, 11, 23n10
Fingeroth, Danny, ix
The Flash, 92
Fordman, Whitney, 29
Fortress of Solitude, 61, 158–159, 161, 163, 167
Foucault, Michel, 146
Fox Network, 103, 117, 154
Fraser Valley, BC, 135
Freedman, Eric, 131

Gelder, Ken, 141, 146
gender, viii, x–xi, xvii, xxi, 8, 10, 56, 114–115, 120, 124, 139
geography, xxvi, 129–138, 145–147
Geraghty, Lincoln, 28
Gilmore Girls, 89
Glover, John, 7, 69, 144, 157–158, 170n14
Gough, Alfred, xiv–xv, xxiii, xxvii, 38, 65, 70–72, 79, 153, 157–159, 169n3, 170n8, 171n15
Gray, Jonathan, 130–132, 141
Green Arrow, 20, 34, 92, 160, 171n15
Guantanamo Bay, 160
Guy-Bray, Stephen, 53–54, 56
Gwenllian-Jones, Sara, 16, 156

Hall, Carter, 71
Haraway, Donna, 39
Harries Dan, 111
Hartley, Justin, 171n15
Hawkman, 71
Hercules, viii–ix
Heroes, xiv, xxviiin7, 117
heterosexuality, 22, 23n8, 46–47, 54, 57–58, 139

heterotopia, 145–147
Hills, Matt, xx, 116, 130, 135, 145–146
history, viii, xv, xix, xxiii, xxvii, 5, 11, 17, 20, 26–27, 75, 95, 97, 119, 133, 138–139, 143–144, 156–157, 160, 162, 168, 169n2, 171n16
Hollywood, xiv, xxvi, 101, 129, 145, 170n15; runaway production, 133, 148n10
homoeroticism, xvii, 9, 53–54, 57, 61n3, 139
homosexuality, 46, 54, 59
horror, xix, 26, 30, 41, 46, 59, 106n34, 131
Human Target, 117
Hunt, William Holman, 30
Hutcheon, Linda, 5, 7

identity, viii, ix, xv, xxiii–xxiv, 28–29, 32, 36, 38–39, 42n6, 57–58, 66, 70, 94, 110, 114, 117, 125, 133, 137–138, 140, 162, 164, 166; national, 143, 151n57
iMovies, 124
Impulse, 78
individualism, ix–x, 63n19
intellectual property rights, 89, 93, 96, 98, 101, 104, 124, 155
Internet, xviii, xx, 15, 24n20, 56, 102, 110, 116, 125, 126n18, 137, 139, 141, 154, 168, 170n6; forums, xxv, 113–115, 117–118, 121–123, 132; streaming, 103, 112, 124; videos on, xxv, 120–121, 130
iTunes, 103

J'onn J'onzz, 159, 162, 165–166
Jancovich, Mark, 110, 115, 118, 119
Jaws, 72
Jenkins, Henry, 110, 111, 113, 115, 116, 120, 123, 130, 132, 141
Jesus Christ, ix, 28, 29
Jewett, Robert, viii–ix
Johnson, Catherine, xix, 26, 39, 42n5
Johnson-Smith, Jan, 67
Jones, Cary M., 112–113, 132
Jones, Sam, III, 79
Jor-El, xvii, 19, 21, 53, 91, 159, 163, 165, 167
Judaism, ix
Jung, Carl, 30, 35
Justice League of America, xx, 71, 160, 164

Kal-El, 26, 33, 35, 53, 61, 81, 159
Kara Zor-El, 33, 81, 157, 165, 171n18
Kansas, MO, xxi, xxvi, 14, 41, 46, 62n9, 89, 129, 133, 134, 140, 143, 147, 155
Kent, Clark, x, xiv–xv, *xvi*, xvii–xviii, xx–xxiv, xxvii, 3–4, 7, 10–11, 13, 16–19, 22, 28, 43n16, 45, 47–48, 61, 65–67, 74–79, 81–82, 89, 101, 112–113, 116, 119–120, 139, 142, 144, 147, 154–155, 157, 166, 171n17; as a reporter, viii, xii, 6, 94, 95, 164; as a student, vii, 8, 29–30, 91
Kent, Conner, 10, 25, 27–28, 154
Kent Farm, 36, 47, 50, 52, 55, 135, 159, 162, 165
Kent, Jonathan, xii, xv, 15–16, 34–36, 55, 60, 81, 89, 155–156, 162
Kent, Martha, xv, 28, 89, 155, 159, 162
Kidder, Margot, 91
King, Stephen, 41
Kirk, James T., 57, 139

Kohnen, Melanie, 139–140
Kompare, Derek, xviii–xix
Kreuk, Kristin, 79, 116, 157–158, 170n14
Krypto, 92
Krypton, viii, xv, 19, 29, 33, 45, 54, 81, 83, 89, 101, 155, 159, 162, 166–167, 170n8
kryptonite, 6, 10, 19, 32–33, 37–40, 46, 49, 59, 62n6, 79, 119, 170n8; blue, 34; red, 24n23, 40, 62n5, 83
Kryptonsite, 14, 117–118, 121–122, 125, 126n23
Kustritz, Anna, 57

Landman, Jane, 133–134
Lane, Lois, xii, 6, 10, 20–21, 34–35, 39, 41, 47, 91–92, 94, 105n8, 116, 127n45, 156, 160–161, 164–165, 171n16
Lang, Lana, xii, xv, xvii, xxiii, 6, 10, 18–19, 21, 24n24, 29, 32–33, 36–39, 48, 51, 55, 60–62, 78–79, 89, 91, 116, 123, 127n45, 143, 148n17, 157–159, 162–163
language, 26, 53, 58, 63n19, 110, 118, 123, 127n45, 134–135
Lawrence, John Shelton, viii
The Ledger, 113, 131–132
legality, xxi, xxiv–xxv, 54, 93–104, 107n37, 111, 121
LeVine, Deborah Joy, 90
Levy, Pierre, 114
Lexcorp, 160–161
Lois & Clark: The New Adventures of Superman, 5, 7, 35, 47, 50, 67, 90, 92, 109
Lord of the Rings, 123
Los Angeles, 133, 134
Lost, 110
Lury, Karen, 68, 70, 83
Luthor, Lex, 25, 27, 30–31, 33, 35, 45–48, 50–51, *52*, 53–61, 63n19, 82, 89, 91, 113, 116, 123, 127n45, 139–140, 143, 154, 157–161, 166, 168n1; comparisons to Alexander the Great, 52–53
Luthor, Lionel, xii, xvii, 7, 19, 34, 52–55, 60, 69, 113, 157, 168n1
Luthorcorp, xviii, 51, 55, 62n10, 113

Mack, Allison, xviii, 7, 77, 116, 132, 157
Magneto, 167
The Man in the Gray Flannel Suit, xii
Man of Steel. *See* Superman
Manovich, Lev, 109
Marsters, James, 81
Martian Manhunter, 81–81, 162
masculinity, x–xii
The Matrix, 70, 123
Maxwell, Robert Joffe, 95
McManus, Robert, xv
MegaUpload.com, 122
Mercer, Tess, xxvii, 153, 159–160, 164
Metallo, 39, 80, 167
Metamorphoses, 28, 44n28
Metropolis, vii, 6, 14, 47, 54, 62n10, 78, 80, 83, 162, 164
Meyer, Turi, 72
Microsoft, 124
Millar, Miles, xiv–xv, xxiii, xxvii, 36, 38, 65, 72–73, 83, 153, 157, 159, 169n3, 170n8, 171n15
Mills, Brett, 151n57
Mittell, Jason, xix, 133, 141, 167
mobile phones, 137
Moddelmog, Debra, 27
Montreal, 34

Moonlighting, 90
Moores, Shaun, 137–138
Moses, 28
The Muppets' Wizard of Oz, 138
music, xx, 13–16, 91, 103, 121, 162, 163; videos, 114–115, 121–124, 126n18
Mystery Men Comics, 99
myth, viii–x, xiv, xxii–xxiii, xxviii, 3–13, 22, 25–31, 33–42, 44n28, 63n19, 92, 131; Greek, 36, 53; hero, ix, 48, 154

narrative, vii–ix, xiv–xvii, xix–xxiii, xxvii–xxviii, 3–5, 7, 10–15, 17–22, 23n10, 24n18, 25, 28, 30, 32, 37, 39, 41, 42n5, 45, 47, 50, 59, 62n9, 73–75, 93, 97, 102, 112, 119, 123, 130–134, 139, 141–145, 151n57, 154–158, 161–168, 171n16
NBC, 117, 154
Ndalianis, Angela, xx, 12, 20, 92, 155–156
The New Deal, x
Nielsen Ratings, 15, 24n20, 103, 114
Nietzsche, Fredrich, 91, 97
Nixon, Richard, xiv, 98
Nolan, Christopher, 171n16
Norton, Rictor, 46

Odysseus, viii–ix, 34–35, 44n29
The Odyssey, 38
Olsen, Jimmy, 20, 28, 92, 156, 165
One Tree Hill, 47
The Organization Man, xii
Ostroff, Dawn, 9
O'Toole, Annette, 91
Ovid, 28, 37, 44n28

Palin, Sarah, 159
paratextuality, xxvi, 130–132, 134, 147, 157
parenting, 6–7, 18, 21, 28, 31–32, 38, 47, 89, 155, 162
Parker, Peter, xv
Pearson, Roberta, 156
Peirse, Alison, 134
Penley, Constance, 57
Peterson, Brian, 71, 159
Phantom Zone, 165
phenomenology, 130, 132, 137–138
Pierson, Michele, 68
Potter, Harry, 35
Prowse, Dave, xii

Queen, Oliver, 20, 159–160, 165, 171n15
Queer as Folk, 23n8, 57
queerness, xxiii, 9, 43n23, 45–46, 49, 53–54, 56–59, 139, 140

RabidShare.com, 122
Rabkin, Eric, 26, 28, 37
Red Jacket Defenders, 119–120
Reeve, Christopher, xii, *xiii*, 91
Reeves, George, x, *xi*, xii
religion, ix, 12
Republic Pictures, 104
Ricoeur, Paul, 92–93
Rosenbaum, Michael, xxvii, 14, 116, 139, 157–158, 160, 170n14
romance, xxii, 12, 18, 22, 90
Ross, Pete, 32–34, 44n28, 51, 62n9, 79
Roswell, xvii, 89

San Diego Comic-Con, xxv, 109
Sandvoss, Cornel, 117, 135
Sayour, Chris, 67, 69, 76–77, 82, 84n7

Scarecrow, 43n20
Schneider, John, xii, 16, 81
science fiction, vii, xv, xviii–xix, xxiii–xxvi, 8, 10, 18, 21, 26, 50, 59, 62n6, 67–68, 73, 129, 154
Scivally, Bruce, x
Seamon, David, 137–138
Second World War, x
Sedgwick, Eve, 53, 59
September 11, 2001. *See* 9/11
sexuality, viii, 21, 46, 57–59, 140
Shepherd, Matthew, 43n23, 49
Shuster, Joe, ix–x, xxiv, 4, 10, 94–99, 155, 171n16
Siegel, Jerry, ix–x, xxiv, 4, 10, 93–95, 97–99, 104, 155, 171n16
Siegel, Joanne, 93–97, 101–102, 105n8, 107n37
Siegel Larson, Laura, 93–97, 101–102, 105n8, 107n37
Simpson, Paul, 73, 83
Slash fiction, 56–57, 124, 126n18, 127n45, 139
Slavkin, Todd, 159
Smallville: as pastoral idyll, xviii, 46–47, 52–54, 57–58, 62n5, 63n11; High School, vii, xii, xv, xxiii, 8, 13, 18, 20, 28–33, 79, 113, 131; meteor shower, xviii, 6, 20, 30–34, 36–39, 49, 54, 62n6, 155, 170n8
Smallville: and merchandising, xxv, 104, 109; success of, 169n2; "Wall of Weird," 113; websites, viii, xxi, xxvi, 15, 113–116, 118, 124, 131–132
Smallville episodes: "Accelerate," 80, 82; "Asylum," 60; "Bound," 56; "Bride," 72, 77; "Checkmate," 81; "Collateral," 34; "Conspiracy," 27; "Craving," 38–39, 73; "Crusade," 81, 105n3; "Crimson," 105n3; "Devoted," 50–51; "Doomsday," 166; "Drone," xvii, 91; "Escape," 20; "Extinction," 59; "Fanatic," 19; "Fortune," 20; "Gone," 105n4; "Harvest," 41; "Heat," 20, 36, 81; "Hero," 33; "Hothead," 52; "Hug," 55; "Lazarus," 33–34; "Legacy," xiv; "Lineage," 55; "Mercy," 105n3; "Metallo," 80; "Metamorphosis," 28, 37, 39, 78; "Mortal," 19; "Nicodemus," 15; "Nocturne," 91; "Noir," xx; "Odyssey," 81–82, 159–160, 166; "Onyx," 105n3; "Persuasion," 83; "Phoenix," 50; "Pilot," 14, 29–31, 33, 35, 41, 43n20, 48, 51, 54, 59, 82–83, 91; "Plastique," 164; "Promise," 19; "Prototype," 68, 69; "Quest," 34; "Reaper," 91; "Reckoning," 19, 105n4, 162; "Relic," 62n5; "Requiem," 10, 19; "Rogue," 77, 80; "Rosetta," 53; "Run," 105n3; "Salvation," 80, 167; "Savior," 39, 167; "Scion," 10, 25, 27; "Slumber," 62n5; "Spell," 105n3; "Talisman," 45; "Tempest," 74; "Thirst," 105n3; "Truth," 61; "Upgrade," 26, 39–40; "Velocity," 55; "Whisper," 55, 79; "Wrath," 19, 36; "X-Ray," 79; "Zero," 14; "Zod," 105n4
Smallville.net, 113
Snyder, Zack, 171n16
soap opera, 17, 22, 24n18
Sony, 124
Souders, Kelly, 72, 159
special effects, xix, xxi, xxii, xxiv, 7, 27, 33, 37, 65–75, 77, 81–83,

86n44, 148n10; bullet time, 76, 80–82, 92, 95
Spelling, Aaron, 49
Spider-Man 2, xv
Spielberg, Steven, 72
Spock, Mr., 57, 139
Staiger, Janet, 116, 118
Stamp, Terence, 19, 91
Star Trek, 24n17, 26, 28, 57, 74, 122, 130, 139, 144, 154
Star Wars, viii, 128n46, 131
Star Wars Episode I: The Phantom Menace, 123
Stargate SG-1, 129, 138, 169n2
Street Fighter: The Legend of Chun-Li, 170n14
stunts, xxiv, 66–70, 73, 76–77, 82–83, 84n7, 86n41, 86n44
suburbia, xii
Sullivan, Chloe, xviii, 7, 48, 77, 78, 80, 113, 116, 131, 157
Superboy (comics), 89, 92–93, 97–99
Superboy (TV series), xiv–xxv, 7, 109
Superboy, xxiv, 93
Supergirl (film), 81
Supergirl, 7, 81, 157
superheroes, viii–x, xii, xiv–xv, xvii, xxi, 11, 28, 34, 48, 57, 155–156
Superman (comics), xxiii, xxvii, 13, 46, 48, 93, 109, 113
Superman (film), 92, 171n16
Superman II, 91, 92
Superman III, xiii
Superman and the Mole Men, x
Superman: The Animated Series, 160
Superman: as American icon, viii–x, xviii, xxi, 29, 35, 47, 65–66, 90, 93, 112, 144, 156, 163; catchphrases, 65, 86n44, 91–92, 95; costume, vii, x, xx, xxiii, 6–7, 65, 74, 76, 91, 94, 97, 101, 142, 158, 164–165; in the courts, xxv, 93–104, 107n37, 171n16; on film, xii, xiv, 5, 26, 35, 41, 77, 81; logo, 6, 29, 31, 35, 90–91, 100–104, 167; as "Man of Steel," xii, 5, 21, 91, 156; and marketing, xviii, xx, xxv, 66, 101, 103, 110–113, 169n3; as messianic figure, ix, 29–31, 33, 41, 49; mythos, viii, xiv, xxi, xxv, 4–10, 21, 42, 89–95, 101–103, 104n2, 131, 133; as the "Red-Blue-Blur," 7, 28, 34–35, 77–78, 81, 162, 165; on radio, viii, 5, 91, 95–96, 104, 155; secret identity, 7, 19, 32, 45–46, 57, 164; on television, 110, 125; trademarks, 93, 95–97, 100–104
Supernatural, 134, 148n17
superpowers, xv, xxiii, 19–20, 27, 31–33, 44n28, 77, 90, 92, 99; flight, xxiv, 8, 65–66, 76, 78, 81–83; hearing, 78–80; heat vision, 20, 36, 74–76, 80–83; speed, 7, 35, 41, 47, 67, 70, 74, 76–83, 89, 161; strength, 36, 74, 89, 163; x-ray vision, 74, 78–79
Superman Returns, 40, 160
Suvin, Darko, 50
Swann, Dr., xiv
Swimmer, Darren, 159

Taken, 138
The Talon, 14, 62n10, 113, 136, 143, 144
technology, xviii, xxi, 34, 39, 57, 67, 102, 103, 112, 121, 167
Teague, Jason, 24n24, 148n17
teenagers: and alienation, xv, 29, 36, 37, 40, 45, 46, 62n6, 155; and difference, 12, 25–26, 28–29, 36,

42; and growing up, xxi, xxvii, 3, 6, 10–11, 13, 17–22, 29, 156, 168; and heroism, 31, 33–35, 61, 162; as meteor freaks, xviii, 31, 34, 36, 37, 119; and monstrosity, xxii, 25, 27–28, 31, 36–40; telefantasy, xxii–xxiii, 25–26, 28, 38–39, 41, 42n5, 134

television: in the 1980s, xxii, 11; in the 1990s, 92; advertising, xviii, xxvi, 8–9, 17, 131–132, 162, 169n3; broadcasting, 17, 22, 42, 73, 102–104, 136, 153, 169n2; cult, xviii, xix–xx, xxvi, 17, 129–130, 134, 141–142, 156; drama, vii, xv, xvii, xix, xxii, 10–15, 22, 26, 32, 35, 50, 90, 155, 162–165, 167; and genre, viii, xix, xxvi, xxvii, 21, 26, 30, 41, 47, 93, 99, 111, 129, 131–133, 153–155, 168; gothic, 48–49; hybridity in, xix, 67; industry, vii, xxvii, 12, 73, 103, 133, 157, 168, 169n3, 169n6; intertextuality in, xviii–xix, xxi–xxii, 40–42, 86n44, 134, 142; marketing, xviii, xx, xxv, 66, 101, 103, 110–113, 169n3; melodrama, vii–viii, xvii, 8, 20, 132, 154; network, xiv, xviii, xix, xx, xxvii, 5, 8–9, 17, 22, 57, 89, 109–114, 117, 119–125, 131, 153–154, 157–158, 169n2, 169n3; prime-time, 10, 47, 153; quality, xviii, xix, xxix, 154; teen, vii, viii, xvii, xxi; serial, vii, xix, xxii, 4, 10–13, 21–22, 23n10, 26, 32, 42, 42n5, 96–97, 131–132, 156–157, 167; spinoffs, xiv, xx, 117, 131, 154, 157, 165, 170n13, 171n15

televisionwithoutpity.com, 119, 139

Telotte, J.P., 70, 73, 74

Terezakis, Bill, 67–68, 70–71, 73, 77

Terminator: The Sarah Connor Chronicles, 71

terrorism, 29, 160, 164

Time Warner Corporation, xxiv, 89, 93, 101

TiVo, xxv, 103, 112

The Torch, 113, 131–132

Torchwood, 151n57

tourism, xxvi, 129, 137

transmediality, 131, 141–142

True Blood, 122

Twilight, 122

Twister, 74

Tyler May, Elaine, x

United Paramount Network (UPN), xiv

United States of America, xxi, 30, 62n10, 96, 103, 112, 125, 133, 142, 154, 155, 159; Bicentennial, xiv

Universal Pictures, 106n34

utopia, ix, 54, 146

V, 117

Vampire Diaries, 117

vampires, xxii, 22n1, 38

van Dijck, José, 141, 145

Vancouver, BC, xx–xxi, xxvi, 46, 73, 76, 132–134, 145–146; filming locations, 63n10, 129–130, 135–136

VCR, 57, 111

Victoria, BC, 143

video games, xiv, xviii, 121, 131

video recording, 72, 77, 103, 114, 121, 154, 159, 168

Vietnam, xiv

villains, ix, xxiii, xxvii, 27, 30, 35, 40, 43n20, 46, 49–50, 57, 60–61, 61n3, 71, 76, 119
visual effects, xxiv, xxvii, 66–70, 73, 75–78, 81–83, 155, 161
vlogging, xxv, 114–115, 120–121, 123, 125

Waitman, Grace, xv
Waller, Amanda, 81
Warner Bros., xiii, xvi, xviii, 52, 94–97, 101–104, 107n35, 107n37, 110, 119, 154, 156, 160, 169n3, 169n6, 171n16; The WB, vii, xiv, xvii–xix, 42n6, 49, 71, 89–90, 102, 110–114, 116, 119, 125, 131–132, 157; TheWB.com, 112, 113
Watergate, xiv
Wayne, Bruce, 92
Wee, Valerie, xviii,
Welling, Tom, xii, xv, *xvi*, xxi, 7–8, 11, 13, 16, 67, 76–78, 82–83, 91, 101, 112, 116, 136, 139, 142–144, 158, 164, 169n6, 171n17
White, Perry, 91–92
White Queen, 81
Whyte, William, xii
Williams, John, 91
Wilson, Sloan, xii
Winchester, Dean, 148n17
Witwer, Sam, 76–77, 166
The Wizard of Oz, 26, 30, 41, 133
Wonder Woman, 117

Xavier, Charles, 167
The X-Files, xxvi, 48, 49, 62, 122, 129, 136
X-Men, 167

Yockey, Matt, 40
Young Justice, 154
YouSendIt.com, 122
YouTube, 114, 120, 122–125, 127n43, 130, 170n13

Zod, General, 20, 26–27, 41, 80–81, 91–92, 166–167, 171n12

ABOUT THE CONTRIBUTORS

Jes Battis is an assistant professor of English at the University of Regina, Canada, and teaches in the areas of speculative fiction, creative writing, and literature of the Restoration and Enlightenment, as well as the history of sexual dissidence. He has written on authors such as J. R. R. Tolkien, Samuel Delany, and Anne Carson. He also delivers workshops on genre fiction. Recent publications include *Investigating Farscape: Uncharted Territories of Sex and Science Fiction* (2007), *Blood Relations: Chosen Families in Buffy the Vampire Slayer and Angel* (2005), and the edited collection *Homofiles: Theory, Sexuality, and Graduate Studies* (2010). He is also a novelist.

Karin Beeler is professor and chair of the Department of English at the University of Northern British Columbia in Prince George, Canada. She has published in the areas of film and television studies and in the field of Canadian literature. Her books include *Tattoos, Desire and Violence: Marks of Resistance in Literature Film and Television* (2005) and the coedited volume *Investigating Charmed: The Magic Power of TV* (2007). Her fascination with visual media, myth, and the fantastic is also evident in her most recent book, *Seers, Witches and Psychics on Screen: An Analysis of Women Visionary Characters in Recent Television and Film* (2008).

Stan Beeler is professor of English at the University of Northern British Columbia, Canada. His areas of interest include film and television studies, popular culture, and comparative literature. His publications include *Reading Stargate SG-1* with Lisa Dickson (2006), *Investigating Charmed:*

The Magic Power of TV with Karin Beeler (2007), and *Dance Drugs and Escape: the Club Scene in Literature Film and Television since the Late 1980s* (2007).

Rayna Denison is a lecturer in film and television studies at the University of East Anglia in the UK. She is a specialist in Asian and American film and television, with published research on Japanese anime, comic book movies, children's television, and transnational Asian cinema. Her other comic book movie publications include "It's a Bird! It's a Plane! No, It's DVD! *Superman*, *Smallville*, and the Production (of) Melodrama," in *Film and Comic Books*, ed. Ian Gordon, Mark Jancovich and Matthew P. McAllister (2007) and "(Trans)national X-Factor: Patrick Stewart, Britishness and the Promotion of *X-Men*," in *Critical Survey* (2006). She is currently writing a book titled *Film Genres: Anime.*

Michael S. Duffy completed an MA in cinema studies from New York University and a PhD in film studies from the University of Nottingham and is currently an adjunct professor in film and media studies at Towson University in Maryland. His work has largely focused on how industry and technology impact the aesthetic nature of what we see on screen, as well as filmmakers, feature films, and television produced during the period of transition from practical to digital technology in media industries. He has presented at numerous international conferences and chaired panels relating to special/visual effects and science fiction. He has articles in preparation on the digital posthumous nature of Brandon Lee (*The Crow*, 1994) and his father, Bruce Lee, director Guillermo del Toro's organic and aesthetic approaches to filmmaking, and New Zealand's regional digital appropriation during the 1990s. He is researching and preparing two books, one an edited collection exploring histories and theories of special/visual effects, and another looking at the industry's treatment of actors' posthumous performances.

Ian Gordon is an associate professor of history at the National University of Singapore. He has published widely on the comic arts and American television. His recent publications include *Comic Strips and Consumer Culture, 1890–1945* (1998) and coedited collections *Comics and Ideology* (2001) and *Film and Comic Books* (2007).

Juli Stone Pitzer is a doctoral candidate in film and media studies at the University of Kansas with interests in television, media, and film history. She is also a filmmaker and received her MA in communication: film and video production at the University of Memphis. Her research in movie theater development and historic preservation led to the documentary film *Preserving the Past: Topeka's Jayhawk Theatre* (2011).

ABOUT THE EDITOR

Lincoln Geraghty is reader in popular media cultures in the School of Creative Arts, Film, and Media and director of the Centre for Cultural and Creative Research at the University of Portsmouth. He is author of *Living with Star Trek: American Culture and the Star Trek Universe* (2007) and *American Science Fiction Film and Television* (2009) and the editor of *The Influence of Star Trek on Television, Film and Culture* (2008); with Mark Jancovich, *The Shifting Definitions of Genre: Essays on Labeling Film, Television Shows and Media* (2008); and *Channeling the Future: Essays on Science Fiction and Fantasy Television* (2009). He is currently serving as editor of the *Directory of World Cinema: American Hollywood*, an online and print publication (2011), and his next book, entitled *Cult Collectors: Nostalgia, Fandom and Collecting Popular Culture*, is forthcoming.

www.ingramcontent.com/pod-product-compliance
Lightning Source LLC
LaVergne TN
LVHW090749161225
827852LV00001B/12
* 9 7 8 0 8 1 0 8 8 1 3 0 3 *